W9-AIB-558

AMONG THE VALIANT

Mexican-Americans in WW II and Korea

AMONG THE VALIANT

Mexican-Americans in WW II and Korea

By RAUL MORIN

1966
BORDEN PUBLISHING COMPANY
ALHAMBRA, CALIFORNIA

3rd Printing

PRINTED IN THE UNITED STATES OF AMERICA

CONTENTS

THE VICE PRESIDENT

WASHINGTON

Dear Raul:

As a Navy officer and as a Member of Congress during World War Two, I had occasion to become familiar on numerous occasions with the contributions made during that conflict by American soldiers of Mexican origin.

Every such experience renewed my pride in the fact that Texas was the native State of so many of these soldiers.

The American soldiers of Mexican origin served with distinction. They fought courageously. They gave their lives, when need be, valiantly.

Evidence of their valor and their patriotic devotion to duty is contained in the official records of many combat units and in the distinguished roll of winners of the Congressional Medal of Honor.

It is a privilege to pay tribute to these, my fellow-Americans. I salute them as brave men who did credit to the flag they followed into battle.

Sincerely,

Lyndon B. Johnson

Mr. Raul Morin
4226 Brooklyn
Los Angeles, California

Dedicated to

My Wife and Children

Photographs courtesy of U. S. Office of War Information

PREFACE

This story is dedicated to the American heroes of Mexican descent who fought with the United States forces in World War II and in Korea. In writing solely of Mexican and Spanish-Americans, it is not to slight other Americans nor to imply that the Mexican-American won the war. We want to pay tribute to all American fighting men, be they white, red, black, yellow, or brown. We feel just as proud of the Colin Kellys, the Dobbie Millers, and the Sadio Munemoris[1] as we are of the Martinez', Garcias and Rodriguez'.

My idea of writing a story about the combat infantryman was born during the lengthy convalescent period I spent in several United States Army hospitals during the years of 1945, '46 and '47, recovering from war wounds.

During those thirty long months of inactive duty I read more than my share of narrative war tales of the "I was there" variety, which filled the pages of so many magazines, books and newspapers. Authentic as they were and written by name writers and semi-professionals, I could not fully be convinced that the authors had actually experienced, first-hand, the stirring dramatic and explosive action they so vividly wrote about.

Possibly my negative reaction was accounted for by the fact that during my comparatively short time at the front I had never actually seen any soldier-journalist or writer on the scene of combat action. Many war correspondents and young "literary embryos" remained close behind the front but did not engage in actual combat. I wanted to hear what "GI Joe" had

---

[1]Irish, Negro, and Nisei-American Congressional Medal of Honor winners in World War II.

to say about his real experiences . . . to hear him describe the *Hell* he went through, what he felt and how he would relate it.

Could it be done? I wondered . . . how would it sound if I wrote something myself? Would the information I had on hand be enough to depict the true picture? I had plenty of time on my hand; why not give it a try?

Having a passing ability to draw, the original plan was to explain—in comic book form—the role of the infantryman from notes and sketches taken during the time I spent in the service and at the front lines.

During those days I began to hear stories of the many Mexican-American soldiers who distinguished themselves in battle. Many of them had been awarded the Congressional Medal of Honor and other decorations for courage in action. I felt that a story about the Mexican-American GI's would be easier for me to attempt than that of the original idea of making a comic-type book about the infantry alone.

The task of putting words in effective phrases was difficult and for a time the whole project was discarded, until such time as I had somewhat mastered the fundamentals of journalism.

The years slipped by, and due to many home activities the project never made any headway. Meanwhile, two significant developments affecting those of us of Mexican descent had much to do with bringing back the old yearning to record the facts and exploits of the Spanish-speaking GI related to the war.

One was the better war novels that became best-sellers and the great war pictures which became big hits; most of these concerned the combat infantrymen. I could not help noticing the glaring omissions of the Spanish-named soldiers of the United States Army. They were either left out altogether or given an insignificant role. This was the inspiring motive for the book. The other development was that in many parts of this country our veterans who returned from the wars were being treated with second-class citizenship. All America should know of the great contributions made by the Mexican-American soldiers in both WW II and the Korean Conflict. In this way they can better understand today's brother American and lessen the few remaining stigmas harbored against the Spanish-speaking people to help promote a better democracy for all who live in America.

Many ex-combatmen who read this story may quit reading in disgust, or question the right to bring out only the Spanish names, leaving out many outfits and individuals who participated in many of the battles related herein, and I apologize for omitting names of significance that would find a place elsewhere. The story of the Mexican-Americans is a great war story. To relate the complete story would require a much longer book. There were many not mentioned who went through so much!

Originally, this story was meant to be dedicated to the foot soldiers who experienced actual frontline combat and campaigned in the European and Pacific War Theaters during World War Two with the Army, Marines and Airborne. However, in my quest for information on frontline GI Joes, so much useful information was volunteered on the other services, that I could not resist mentioning a few of the most outstanding fighters in the Navy and Air Force who also added glory to the service record of the Mexican-American.

Besides the 17 Infantrymen Medal of Honor winners, there were many who were awarded other medals such as the Distinguished Service Cross, awarded for bravery under fire and which ranks next to the Congressional Medal of Honor, the Silver Star, and the Bronze Star, awarded to hundreds for valor and courage in battle. There were also many other rugged individuals who stood out among combatmen and were greatly admired by their companies, but who did not get any kind of award. These were the real heroes because they did not think so much of their accomplishments, never boasted about them, and did not want to talk about their exploits because they feared it would sound too much like "bragging."

The following chapters are not fictional. They are true facts gathered over many years. From the first notes made during army training days, I began to accumulate some of the material. Most of the notes and sketches made at the frontlines were lost during my evacuation from the war zone. Later, I was able to piece together more information from scattered notes found in personal property when my overseas bag finally caught up with me. Also, news releases and Army publications supplied me with some very good leads.

Upon my return to the homefront, the quest for still more information on the combat infantryman was continued. Thousands of wounded veterans had ended their Army career in one of the many Army hospitals and everyone of them had a story—if you could pry it out of them. In such general hospitals as Stark, De Witt, Crook, Hammond, Dibble, Birmingham, Brooks, and Letterman, I met and talked to and at times sketched many ex-combatmen. From them I gathered valuable information. Only the fact that so many were being discharged daily prevented me from acquiring much more material data.

Later, I was able to secure more data from veterans' organizations, among them: Veterans of Foreign Wars, American Legion, Disabled American Veterans, Catholic War Veterans, Amvets, American GI Forum, and others. The Office of War Information and news clippings from hometown papers also were very helpful. Then there were frequent trips throughout the Southwest where I met and talked to many of the persons mentioned in the book in Arizona, New Mexico, Texas, Colorado, and throughout California.

Additional material and aid was provided by Dionicio Morales, Congressman Chet Holifield, Vicente Ximenez, Johnny Flores; Frank and Consuelo Paz; Dr. Hector Garcia, founder of the American GI Forum; Ralph Guzman; Delfino Varela; Jacobo Duran; Manuel Armijo; John Flores; Gabriel Navarette; Filberto Muñoz; Col. E.D. McCall, 36th Div. 141st Inf. Regt.; Los Angeles Councilman Edward Roybal; Eliseo Carrillo; Juan Acevedo; Pete Despart; Senator Lyndon Johnson,[1] California Assemblyman Edward E. Elliott; Juan Falcon; Bob Gonzales; Tony Vicente; Senator Dennis Chavez; Ignacio Martinez; Manuel Martinez; Dr. Francisco Bravo; Los Angeles Superior Court Judge Carlos Teran; Joseph Alvarado; Joseph Juarez; Olivia Morin Flores; Col. Thomas S. Bishop, 36th Div. 141st Inf. Regt.; George Sotelo; Medardo Rangel, and many many others.

Special credit must be given to the American GI Forum of the United States who made possible the publication of this book by adopting it as a national project at their National convention held in Las Vegas, Nevada in 1961. Through fund-raising drives, advance sales, subscriptions and donations the GI Forum was able to subsidize the first edition of "Among the Valiant".

---

[1] Former President of the United States.

I

THE DAY OF PEARL HARBOR

Sunday, December 7, 1941. Every American was equally jolted by news flashes of the sneak attack on our fleet at Pearl Harbor. The news of the Japanese raid was just as alarming, but sounded more exciting to the almost-four-million persons of Spanish and Mexican descent living in the southwestern part of the United States because it was being discussed in an exciting half-English, half-Spanish language that sounded twice as alarming to the stranger.

The whole world watched the latest developments with great interest. Experts on world affairs had been waiting for the day to come when America too would join what was shaping up as a second world war. On the morning of December 8th, history was repeated, the Congress of the United States of America declared war against aggressive axis nations just as had happened some twenty-odd years before when we entered World War I.

It was this nation that attracted the major attention. With the United States now involved, the war was sure to take on a different aspect. True, America as a nation was expected to undertake a big part with the other allied nations, but we, as individuals, were at this moment more directly concerned with our own little world—our own selves. We began to worry more about the part each of us would play rather than what America's big part would be.

As I recall, it was in one of the small shops in picturesque Olvera Street—the tourist mecca of Los Angeles—where we gathered to discuss the exciting news of Pearl Harbor with friends and passers-by. The conversation ranged from sober to comical, with lots of joking on the many possible effects the war would have on us who were of Mexican extraction.

"*Ya estuvo* (This is it)," said one, "Now we can look for the authorities to round up all the Mexicans and deport them to Mexico—bad security risks."

Another excited character came up with, "They don't have to deport me! I'm going on my own; you're not going to catch me fighting a war for somebody else. I belong to Mexico. *Soy puro mexicano!*"[1]

The person that made the first remark was, of course, referring to the many rumors that were started during World War I about having the Mexicans in the United States considered security risks when it was feared that Germany was wooing Mexico—insisting that Mexico declare war against the United States and align itself with the Axis powers — with the promise that if the Axis were victorious, Mexico would then be given back all the territory that formerly belonged to the southern republic.

The real down-to-earth fact was that the two who had made the remarks, Emilio Luna and Jose Mendoza, were first and second-generation Americans of Mexican descent, never having had ties with any other country. (Both Luna and Mendoza later went into the service, serving with honor in the Marine Corps and Army, as revealed in the following chapters). This was just their way of enjoying a little *vacilada,* a form of humor that serves as a morale builder. The idea being that by belittling your fellowman or your ethnic group, once you grasp the intent, it serves to bring those being kidded closer to one another.

At the time of Pearl Harbor, approximately 250,000 Americans of Mexican descent lived in and around the Los Angeles

---

[1]"I am 100% Mexican!" Spoken as a patriotic citizen of Mexico.

area. This is not to be confused with statistics released through the Mexican Consulate office which lists all persons of Mexican descent. We are concerned only with Mexican-Americans, those born here and those who have become American citizens since immigrating from Mexico and establishing residency here.

Other large Mexican-populated areas in California were Orange and San Bernardino Counties, and the sprawling San Joaquin and Imperial Valleys. This gave California a population close to 750,000 citizens and aliens of Mexican descent.

In other parts of the U.S.A., the state of Texas led with close to a million Spanish-speaking residents. The majority of them lived in the lower Rio Grande Valley and in the Counties of Webb, Bexar, Nueces, El Paso, Hidalgo, Cameron, and Willacy. New Mexico's 248,000 were along the upper and middle Rio Grande Valley in the Santa Fe, Bernalillo, Socorro, Sierra, and Donna Anna Counties. Arizona's total of Spanish extraction was 128,000. They were located mostly in the Maricopa, Greenlea, Pinal, Pima, and Santa Cruz Counties, with the Salt River Valley having the largest concentration of the Spanish-speaking population. Colorado numbered 118,000, the majority being in San Luis Valley in the south and the biggest concentration in Pueblo and Denver in the north.[1]

Thus, approximately 85% of the Mexican-American population was located in the five southwestern states. Most of the other 15% lived in Kansas, Nebraska, Utah, Michigan, Pennsylvania, Wisconsin, Minnesota, Ohio, Missouri, Wyoming, Nevada, Indiana and Oklahoma, with the largest number in Illinois, mostly in Chicago. This totalled approximately 2,690,000 Americans of Mexican descent living in the United States. One-third were within the draft age limit. Most were second and third generation Americans by birth. A small number had been born

---

[1]Statistics supplied by Vicente T. Ximines, Bureau of Business Research, University of New Mexico.

in Mexico, largely in the frontier states of northern Mexico along the U.S. border, but had since become American citizens.

Along with other Americans, we all answered the call to arms.

II

OUR MEXICAN-AMERICAN BACKGROUND

The history of the Mexican-Americans in the southwest begins with the Spanish conquest in Mexico and the gradual colonization that extended into what was then the northern regions of Mexico. This territory included widely distributed settlements such as Texas, New Mexico, Colorado, Arizona, Utah, Nevada, and California.

As these areas were acquired by the United States after the Mexican War of 1846, the Mexican population remained and grew slowly through the process of immigration and by normal population growth. However, the extensive immigration of people from Mexico goes back to the early part of the 20th century.

In the latter part of 1910, the oppressed people of Mexico revolted against the tyranny of Porfirio Diaz who had been ruling them with an iron hand for 30 years. This bitter struggle that was to change the life of all Mexican citizens lasted for more than four years. It disrupted all family life and spread poverty, disease, and starvation.

To escape the hard rigors of *La Revolucion,* the people began to flee across the border, into the United States. Thousands of Mexican families abandoned their mother country and sought sanctuary in the neighboring country. With no restrictions or immigration quotas to stop them, crossing over was an easy matter. Registration and the right answer to a few questions was about all that was required.

The war-torn families that crossed the *Rio Bravo* added to the existing large numbers of Spanish-speaking inhabitants of the southwest. They found much in common with the people who had been living in Texas, New Mexico, Arizona, Colorado, and California since the days that Spain had ruled. Many of them were descendants of the *Conquistadores* who had conquered the wild territories. Many others still held large land grants given to them by the king of Spain.

Throughout the years—under Spain, under Mexico, and lastly under the United States—these people had retained their language, their customs, and their religion. Integration between refugees of the revolution and the original settlers of the southwest occurred without any interruptions in the society of the two groups, due to the fact that both spoke the same language and otherwise lived much alike.

The type of employment for the new arrivals was not the most desirable nor the highest paid, but it was better living than that of the old country. In fact, it was more than they had expected in a new and strange land. They were offered jobs —which they hastily accepted—in lowly-paid, temporary, migratory work. Most of it was of the stoop-labor variety, such as agricultural field work, and common labor in railroad and construction gangs.

The border states were soon crowded with field laborers. Work became scarce and the pay lower. It was rumored that work was plentiful further north, and better in the middlewest and northern states. Newcomers and old residents then started migrating to Kansas, Missouri, Michigan, Minnesota, Ohio, Illinois, and Indiana.

During World War I, as early as 1916, the northern march was well underway, as recorded in a report made in Chicago to the Council of Social Agencies:

> "Starting out from San Antonio, Texas, which was a distributing center for Mexican labor, they made their way north through Kansas City and St. Louis.
>
> "The early Mexican immigrants came mainly as 'engan-

chados' (hooked ones), contract laborers, to work in agriculture, and the sugar-beet fields of Michigan, Wisconsin, Minnesota and Indiana. Another large and important group came north (Middlewest) as railroad section hands. Both groups came to perform seasonal work and at the termination of their respective labor contracts found themselves near such large centers as Detroit, Milwaukee, Gary, Indiana and Chicago."[1]

BORN IN THE U.S.A.

It was the US-born descendant of the immigrants and early settlers who began to fill the role and assume more traits of Americanism. In the early days this was not an easy matter. I well remember that those first years were filled with surprises, pity, frustration and disappointments.

By virtue of having been born in the United States, we began on equal footing with other Americans. After a normal happy childhood, we ran into our first little surprise. We learned, first from our parents, then from our scrupulous Anglo neighbors, that we were of a different breed . . . we were *Mexicans.* We calmly accepted this fact, then went along with the teachers and instructors in school to learn Americanism: the English language, American History, laws and customs of this country. Surprise and puzzlement came at home when we tried to put into practice the things we had learned at school. We were often reprimanded, scolded and laughed at for such things as, speaking the English language, refusing to take the food we ate at home for school lunches, and for changing our name from Jose to Joe.

Our resentment came in our early teens from being shunned

---

[1]*The Mexican-American in Chicago.* A survey by Frank X. Paz, Council of Social Agencies, Chicago, Illinois, 1948.

and teased by the *Gringos,* as we learned to call our non-Latin friends.

Pity came from the understanding souls around us and from the people of Mexico, who kept reminding us that we were neither Mexican nor American. As we grew up, we experienced frustration in trying to live the American way when we discovered all of our shortcomings. We had no special talents, no opportunities were offered, nor any high paying jobs. It was all an uphill struggle.

Living in our segregated neighborhoods did not help any. The custom we had of staying together, the plain discouragement that we received from moving to other sections of the town—all forced most of us to live "on the other side of the tracks."

By the time we had matured, determination had grown in many of us; a determination that comes from awakening and realizing that we too were meant to be just as free as any other citizen. We too, were entitled to work, play, and to live as we pleased. Weren't *all* Americans entitled to the same opportunitites?

Had it not been for the giant depression in the late twenties, our first move toward social and economic improvement would already have been felt. We were determined to break away from the second-class citizenship status that many of us had been relegated to; however, the depression cut short the small gains we had made. Our progress came to a temporary halt.

The lean, long days hit us a little harder because very few of us came from wealthy families or had parents who owned successful business enterprises. The employment opportunities that had opened in factories, plants, in business and in commerce no longer existed as unemployment rose higher and higher.

In the late Twenties and early Thirties, the average United States Mexican laborer was classified in the unskilled or semiskilled category. Many who held good paying jobs in cities and towns had no other choice but to turn back to farm work and stoop labor in the field—to work in the much-hated jobs that for years, since the early border-crossing days, had been classified as '*suitable for cheap Mexican labor only.*'

Our educational progress was retarded everywhere when youngsters of high school age were forced to drop out of school to seek work and help the family earn a living. Many of us joined the CCC forestry camps, others worked in NYA and many took to the road roaming up and down the country, seeking work or just leaving to lessen the burden at home.

THE PRE-WAR YEARS

After 1932, the country began a recovery period, and so did we. We launched a new drive to improve our standard of living. Some good paying jobs were available again. We began to make good progress in economic improvement. Here and there young men were offered bigger and better employment opportunities, not only better paying jobs but also positions with a future.

More of our youth were finishing high school and going into college. Barriers were opened and many white collar workers began to appear. Stabs were made at civic organizations and in politics with small successes. Progress was made notably in the states of Texas and New Mexico, in sections where there had never been any Spanish-named candidates for office before.

Among the organizations that began to gather strength were the old established "*Alianza Hispano-Americana,*" a fraternal and beneficial society, and the "*League of United Latin-American Citizens.*" Organized in 1929 for the purpose of giving voice to all American citizens of Latin extraction, the LULAC's were the first large Mexican-American organization in the

United States to make English its official language. Its main objectives were:

> "To remove stigma and prejudice and racial, religious and social discrimination; to foster education, culture and tolerance, and to fight peonage, child labor and general mistreatment; to oppose radicalism and violence, but to seek equal representation, on juries, in public office, in business and in education, and to secure equal rights and opportunities for Latin-Americans."[1]

This would clearly indicate that by now we were coming into our own. We could now be classified as the average citizen with a desire for self-improvement, equal and just as qualified as any other citizen.

But this situation did not prevail throughout the southwest where the bulk of the Mexican-Americans were concentrated. Only in the large cities of Los Angeles, San Antonio, Albuquerque, Denver, El Paso, and Chicago were signs of improvement visible. Unfortunately, the larger part of the Spanish-speaking lived in the smaller villages and towns where much prejudice still existed.

In spite of the rapid strides we were making, and our over-all improvement, in small communities we still faced the constant struggle to gain full recognition as American citizens, to make our Anglo neighbors see and realize that we were no longer the stereotype Mexican they always had pictured us to be. In some towns of the great southwest, we were still referred to as "Mexicans with an inferiority complex." We were placed in the categories of: cheap laborers, thriftless, lazy, unorganized, lacking in leadership, unkempt, and uneducated. This naturally made for many discriminatory practices against us, no matter where we hailed from. Yet, despite all of this, we never adopted a defeatist attitude.

---

[1]Burma, John H., *Spanish Speaking Groups in the United States,* Durham, North Carolina, Drake University Press, 1954, P. 101.

Even with the constant discrimination and continued denial of equal opportunities, when war came to the United States, no one could accuse us of draft dodging or fleeing to Mexico to avoid military service as charged in World War I.

Just prior to Pearl Harbor, many developments had occurred among the Spanish-speaking living in the USA. We felt that a great change was being made in our lives since the dark days of the depression. A change that was to transform us from the lackadaisical timid person to an alert, progressive, up-to-date citizen. The feeling was that little by little we had been forsaking the old way of doing things, we had learned more of the American way of life; and we could forsee the day when we Americans of Mexican descent would be fully integrated with the vast number of other ethnic groups that make up America.

Most of us were more than glad to be given the opportunity to serve in the war. We knew there was something great about this country that was worth fighting for. We felt that this was an opportunity to show the rest of the nation that we *too* were also ready, willing, and able to fight for our nation. It did not matter whether we were looked upon as Mexicans, Mexican-American, or belonging to a minority group; the war soon made us all *genuine* Americans, eligible and available immediately to fight and to defend our country, the United States of America.

III

DRAFTEES AND VOLUNTEERS

The first volunteers were those who joined the regular army before World War II. They enlisted during peace time at military centers such as: Fort Sam Houston, Fort Bliss, Fort McArthur, and the Presidio at San Francisco, headquarters for the 4th and 5th Army Corps areas.

On October 29, 1941, Pedro Aguilar Despart of Los Angeles was the holder of number 158 in the national draft lottery, the same number pulled out by President Roosevelt; and thus became the first Angeleno to be drafted for selective service in World War II.

On December 8th of the same year, the National Guard was federalized on President Roosevelt's proclamation. Many civilian members who had signed up in the guard 'just to keep in shape,' or to play soldier once in a while, suddenly found themselves in the role of real soldiers in many National Guard Divisions.

After the bombing of Pearl Harbor, the draft boards set up the machinery to send a steady stream of selectees into the Armed Forces as the nation stepped up mobilization for all-out war. Even alien non-citizens living in the United States were immediately classified 1-A and drafted into the service.

Many of the Spanish-speaking aliens that Uncle Sam drafted were later given the opportunity to become naturalized American citizens by taking the oath while a member of the United States Armed Forces.

In June, 1942, Mexico also joined other Latin-America countries in declaring war on the Axis. Soon many young Mexican na-

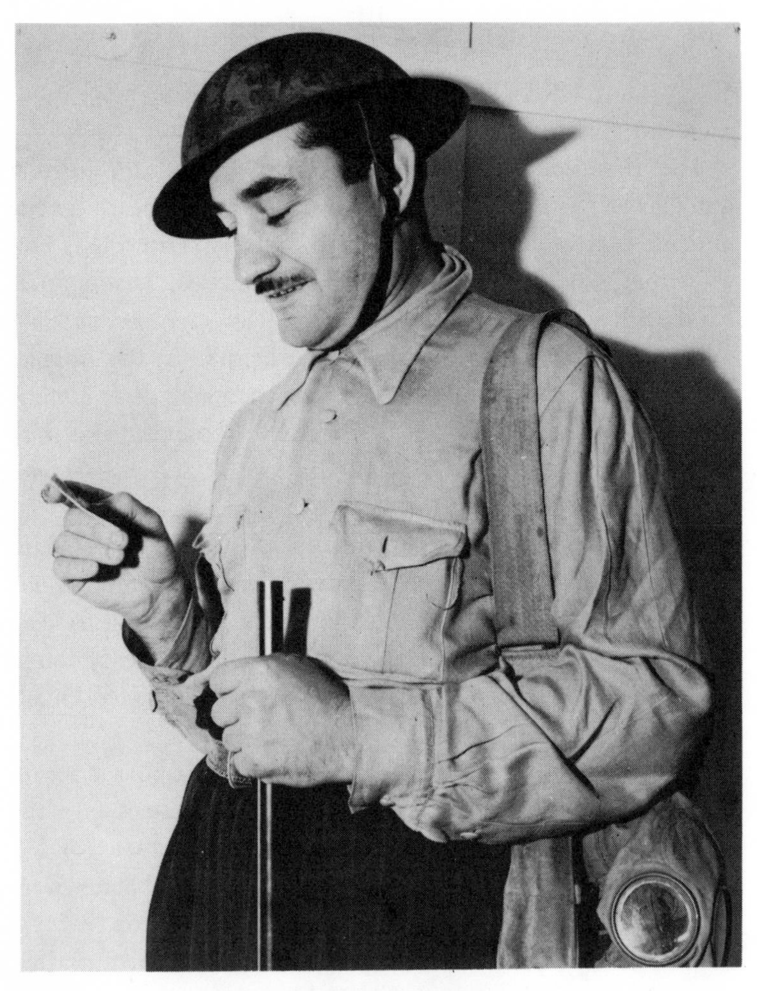

PETE AGUILAR DESPART
Los Angeles, California
draws No. 158 in national lottery to become first draftee
of U.S. Army on October 29, 1941

ationals crossed the border at such points as Monterrey, Nuevo Leon; Matamoros and Nuevo Laredo, Tamaulipas; Piedras Negras and Villa Acuña in Coahuila; Ciudad Juarez, Chihuahua; Naco and Nogales in Sonora; and Mexicali and Tijuana in Baja California to volunteer for service with the United States.

Other volunteers here in the States were the many young high school students who, upon reaching the age of 18 (or 17 with their parents' permission,) immediately signed up before being drafted, so that they could get into the branch of their choice. Many others also volunteered in time to beat the draft call and go into the Navy, Marines or Air Force, to keep from getting stuck in the 'unglamorous Army.'

The draft boards in Los Angeles, Nogales, Albuquerque, San Antonio, El Paso, Corpus Christi, and the Lower Rio Grande Valley of Texas were never caught short-handed when they had a large quota to fill. These boards were loaded with Spanish names on their files; and very few were ever exempted, reclassified, or found too essential to be drafted. Local rural youths were being drafted so fast in comparison with others, that land owners of large farms and ranches, faced with manpower shortage, voiced stern protests with the local draft boards.

WHERE THEY CAME FROM

The Army received the larger portion of the draftees. Navy quotas were easily filled by the large number of volunteers. From the draft boards, the selectees were sent to the nearest induction center. Here were all types of raw recruits. They came from farms, from large cities, from small villages, from the backwoods, and from the hills—from all parts of the United States and from some parts of Mexico.

They had been laborers, small businessmen, farmers, truck drivers, craftsmen, students, and just plain *vàgos* (vagrants). While the majority of the Spanish-speaking recruits in the local camps were from the large cities of the great Southwest, the names most often-repeated, when they would get together, were those of the many small *barrios* (neighborhoods) and suburbs which many called 'home' and constantly mentioned in their conversations. Such places as *Maravilla, Chiques* (Oxnard), Simons, Jimtown, *Limonera, Sespe,* San Antonio's "Westside," *Calle Ancha* in Austin, "Magnolia" in Houston, Bessemer in Pueblo, "Larrimer" in Denver, *El Pachuco, Juariles, La Smelter,* Hollywood, *La Daisy, El Dorado, El Ranchito,* Chinatown, and *El Hoyo* were well represented. They usually had endearing nicknames for their hometowns (or gang groups) with which they identified themselves. They bragged about "Sanjo," "Fernando," "Corpos," "Verdugo," "Fresno," "Recles," "El Globo," "Jerome," "Tucson," "Santa Rita," "Las Cruces," "Tucumcari," "Conejos," "Trinidad," "La Junta," *"Foré Wes,"* "Del Rio," "San Marcos," "San Benito," "Los Dos Laredos," "Varelas", and such.

Besides being from the well-known neighborhoods of towns in the Southwest, many of the Mexican-Americans in the induction centers hailed from such rarely-mentioned places as North Platte, Nebraska; Garden City, Kansas; Cheyenne, Wyoming; Missoula, Montana; Ogden, Utah; Chester, Pennsylvania, and other far away places like Gary, Indiana; Detroit, Michigan; Lorain, Ohio; St. Louis, Missouri; and Oklahoma City, Oklahoma.

One could always tell where they came from by their manner of speech (when they expressed themselves.) It was quite easy to distinguish the fast-English-speaking Angelenos from the slow-Spanish-speaking Texan or New Mexican. The *Caló* talk (slang words) of the border habitant from El Paso and Juarez was in contrast to the home-spun Spanish of the Coloradoan or Arizonan. Those that originated from far away localities where very few of our people live stood out because their knowledge of Spanish was limited and they much preferred the English language.

The gathering of so many from different sections afforded the Spanish-speaking people living in the United States a valuable and much-needed opportunity to study and improve their social life. Here for the first time they had an opportunity to observe, compare, and personally get to know many others of our ethnic group and what they were like.

There were, of course, many Latins who were part of the large Spanish-speaking segments in the United States not closely identified with those living in the great Southwest. Many were native-born or descendents of Puerto Ricans, Cubans, Central and South Americans, and Españoles from Spain. The largest group, by far, were those living in the Southwest, mostly identified as "Mexicans" or Mexican-Americans.

A study of this particular group will give an idea of what a "crazy, mixed-up" group they were—the different kinds of "Mexicans" that were to be found in the Army.

First, we had the American-born of Mexican parents. Although born, raised, and educated in the United States, this type still clung to many of the Mexican customs and traditions. Well acquainted with American folklore, nevertheless, they enjoyed the music and songs that came from across the border. Their speech was more Spanish than English, sometimes a mixture of both. They had a marked preference for the companionship of other Mexican-Americans.

Quite different were those born and raised in Mexico. Some had left there since early childhood, others more recently, although all had become naturalized citizens. The latter were still very "Mexicanized." Most of them had a good education, were very well versed in Mexico's history, and possessed much of the rich culture that abounds in the land of the Aztecs.

They were good orators, they could quote from Amado Nervo,[1] and with the same ease recognize a Diego Rivera.[2]

They acknowledged all of Mexico's national holidays and were devoted to their religion. Their favorite entertainers and idols were most likely to be stars of the screen, radio, and sports-world from Latin-American countries. They felt ill at ease in the presence of others when the conversation ran mostly in English, even when they understood the language.

Undoubtedly, the largest group were those born in the United States whose parental lineage ran back to the original settlers and the early immigrants of the Southwest. In this group were the Spanish-Americans from New Mexico and Colorado, the *Tejanos* from Texas, and the *Pochos* from California. Those belonging to this group were definitely more "American." They spoke and read less Spanish. They mingled very well with either the Anglos or Latins. For companions they preferred their school chums or townfolk, regardless of their racial background. They enjoyed Spanish songs, Latin rhythms, and Mexican *mariachis,* but also were very "hep" to the latest American songs, dances, and the latest "craze" or sayings of our modern-day youths. They enjoyed eating both Mexican and American food as well as other dishes of foreign make. They engaged in sports and social activities of both ethnic groups, but would not get too excited over Mexico's history or holiday festivals that were regularly celebrated all over the Southwest.

Among them were many *encartados,* or half-breeds; and to be found were Mexican-Italians, Mexican-Filipinos, Mexican-Negroes, Spanish-Mexicans, French-Mexicans, Irish-Mexicans, Mexican-Germans, and English-Mexicans. Then came the Mexican-raised Anglo's who had spent most of their lives among the Mexicans. These spoke good Spanish and always associated with

---

[1]Immortal Mexican poet.
[2]Famous Mexican mural artist.

Mexican-Americans. They loved everything Mexican, and had become so accustomed to being around the Mexicans that when they were asked, "*Que eres tu?*" (What are you?), they would answer—sometimes smiling, sometimes serious—"*Yo soy tan mejicano como tu.*" (I am as Mexican as you are.) Many of these came from Texas and from towns along the border; even a few below the border.

From the standpoint of idiom or mannerisms, the GI's of Mexican descent were not too different. The only difference, if any, was in what they called themselves, or rather, what they were accustomed to being called by the people back home.

The so-called "Spanish" were in many instances accused of being ashamed of the term "Mexican." Being native-born and raised Americans, they never felt any sentiment for Mexico or its people; they had never lived there. Their Anglo friends, out of politeness or in ignorance, called them 'Spanish.' Not being Anglo or Mexican, the term which referred to them was pleasing, and they long since became accustomed to it.

Then came the "Spanish-Americans" or Hispanos. Most of these were from New Mexico or Southern Colorado. They had been told long ago that only the people from south of the border were Mexican. They were all native-born Hispanos and expounded the fact that history revealed the Spaniards had been the founders and settlers of Santa Fe and other points from where they had originated.

Next came the so-called "Latin-Americans." Most of these lived in Texas; a few came from the northern or middle-western states. They had struggled for many years to prove to everyone that they were from this country and not Mexicans from Mexico. Then, as stated by writer and research worker Pauline Kibbe, in a move to off-set discrimination and to differentiate themselves from the immigrants of Mexico, they had popularized the hybrid term "Latin-American."

> (Because of) . . . "A growing self-consciousness on the part of the Spanish speaking and the desire on their part to escape from a subordinate status."[1]

Last, were the *mejicanos* (Mexicans), the proudest of all our groups, those boasting of being *"chicano,"* or *mejicano.* They had nothing but scorn for those who denied their racial ties or pretended not to understand Spanish; although these were not necessarily from Mexico, some were. Most had been raised in predominantly "Mexican" surroundings along the border towns and in southern Texas or southern Arizona. It was hard to tell whether they were native or foreign-born.

Strangely, the so-called "Spanish" did not speak Spanish. The Spanish-Americans and Latin-Americans spoke more Spanish than English, or with a mixture of "Americanized-Spanish" and English, which no true American or Mexican could very well manage to interpret. The *mejicanos* would feel insulted if you spoke English only when Anglos were not present.

Native Californians were known as *Pochos;* New Mexicans as *Manitos.* Others were called just plain *Chicanos* or Tejanos; *del Terré or del otro lado,* for those from south of the border.

All the different terms to describe the Spanish-speaking people of the Southwest have stemmed from the attempts by these groups to be set apart from the aliens. The futility of it all is noted by the small impression made on the other Americans. Whenever they would bring up our group in their conversation, we would always be referred to as "those Mexicans." They have failed to notice the difference of any group.

---

[1]Kibbe, Pauline, *Latin-Americans in Texas,* New Mexico University Press, Albuquerque, 1946.

Many of us, too, have shared that feeling with a slight dissent. We do not notice any big characteristic difference in our people, only that they cannot be called Spanish, Mexican, or Latin-American, since we are not in Spain, Mexico, or in Latin-America; and to be called Americans would not suffice because of our different cultures, language, and complexion.

For this reason we have made the term "Mexican-American" our choice. We then imply that we are proud to be Americans, and at the same time are not trying to deny our Mexican ancestry. Another widely used identification term for our group, perhaps the more proper of the two, is the long-worded term, "Americans of Mexican descent."

IV

BEGINNING WITH BATAAN

It was at Bataan that the first pages of the glorious chapter of the Mexican-American war-record during World War II were begun.

Except for a few who were stationed in Hawaii on December 7th, our first men to fight in World War II were those stationed in the Philippines on the morning of December 8th, 1941.

Only a few were with the Marines who manned the garrisons at Wake, Guam, and Midway when those islands also were attacked on December 7th. Most of the early inductees and volunteers were still in the States going through their initial training period. The fighting men who defended those undermanned island bases during the early Pacific-war-days were old Army regulars and a few of the first (pre-war) volunteers with the Navy and Marines.

Many American soldiers of Mexican descent figured in the first battles of the Philippines with the 200th and 515th Coast Artillery (AA), the two outstanding units stationed at Clark Field, 65 miles from Manila, when the Japanese struck on December 8th. The ranks of the two groups were filled with men from New Mexico, Texas, and Arizona. These were part of the New Mexico National Guard stationed in the Philippines long before war between the United States and Japan broke out, having arrived there in August, 1941, after some hard training at Fort Bliss, Texas.

Sgt. Felipe N. Trejo, a member of the 200th, was the first

Santa Fe, New Mexico, soldier of WW II to give his life defending his country. Epimenio Rubi, the first local boy from Winslow, Arizona, to lose his life in WW II, was also among the heroic defenders of Bataan.

A glance at the partial list of names on the last payroll of members of the 200th and 515th C.A.C. for March, 1942, signed just prior to the fall of Bataan, reveals the large number of Spanish names and indicates the prominent part those of Mexican blood played at Bataan.

PAYROLL OF BATTERY "C" - 200TH CA (AA)

For Month of March, 1942

FIRST SERGEANT

Armijo, Manuel A., 20843120

STAFF SERGEANTS

Baker, Marvin L., 20843133

Roessler, Paul A., 20843157

SERGEANTS

Duke, Lewis E., 20843957

Garcia, Cruz, 20843139

Kiesov, Walter C., 20843144

Phillips, Connie D., 20843144

Sanchez, Pete, 20843176

CORPORALS

Apodaca, Ramon, 20843123

Gonzales, Rubel, 20843180

Lopez, Genaro B., 20843145

Love, Johnny E., 20842576

Pyetzki, Merrill H., 20842594

Rivera, Gavino, 20843156

PRIVATES FIRST CLASS

Boyles, John T., 20843583

Gutierrez, Jesus B., 20842477

Gutierrez, John F., 20843125

Lucero, Alphonso M., 20842748
Trujillo, Manuel, 20843177
Van Buskirk, Francis H., 20843168

PRIVATES

Duran, Barney A., 20842503
Duran, Robert, 20843138
Gannon, Charles F., 20842712
Gateley, William E., 20842706
Leyba, Macedonio B., 20842519
Leyba, Ramon B., 20842518
Turrieta, Carlos T., 20842534
Urioste, John, 20843167
Sanchez, Frank, 20843160
Tafoya, Eddie A., 20843164

STAFF SERGEANT

Robinson, James A. Jr., 38011650

SERGEANTS

Coleman, William R., 38011613
Teague, Rufus D., 38012372

CORPORALS

Armijo, Ernesto J., 38012513
Chacon, Amadeo, 38012609
Jackson, Robert C. Jr., 38011529
Nunn, David M., 38011619
Van Beuning, John G., 36050857
Veal, Richard A., 38011817
Williams, Robert L., 38012053
Yates, Otis A., 38012092

PRIVATES FIRST CLASS

Allred, William M., 38011941
Bright, William L., 38011237
Celusniak, Louis B., 38030820
Contreras, Juan, 38029675
Cree, George W., 38012548

Garcia, Tomas, 38012216
Gater, Hubert B., 38011863
Gebhard, Roy B., 38030873
Hagedorn, William J., 38011996
Hamblin, Orland K., 38011226
Hatton, Everette C., 38012052
Herrera, George S., 38012299
Howard, George W., 38012065
Iskra, Charles, 38011961
James, Vernie L., 38012675
McAndrew, Harold J., 36034175
McCants, Herbert W., 38012077
McGee, William D., 38012114
Owen, Roy E., 38012567
Reyna, Antonio, 38011836
Roberts, James S., 38012342
Romero, Eugenio M., 38012604
Sanchez, Teofilo M., 38012397
Smith, Albert D., 38012100
Simoni, Tony P., 38011839
Stephens, Edgar J., 38012668
Tovar, Alex E., 38011264
West, Robert L., 38029829
Woolworth, Jesse, 38011987

PRIVATES

Alderete, Ramon S., 38011944
Blazevich, John, 38011916
Chavez, Adolfo Jr., 38012370
Contreras, Francisco, 38012631
Copeland, Sid, 38012108
Gloria, Andres E., 38011840
Greenberg, Hyman, 36106751
Hill, Alfred C., 38031324
Hoskins, Earl C., 20842513

Hubbell, Harold, 38011834
Jim, Glenn, 38012463
Lawrence, Wayne O., 38031518
Lopez, Nicolas, 38031294
McCombs, Leonard R., 36050786
Merritt, Thomas A., 38031075
Milligan, Chesley, 38011820
Morgan, Jacob C., 38011974
Muñoz, Manuel M., 38011937
Ojinaga, Vicente R., 38011953
Oliver, Enoch C., 38011912
Reyes, Eusebio, 38030569
Riley, Glendon S., 38012373
Rodriguez, Basilio L., 38030628
Sanchez, Cristobal D., 38011242
Sanchez, Alfonso M., 38011272
Savedra, Elias, 38012606
Slaughter, Lonnie T., 38031345
Sweat, Albert F., 38029072
Tafoya, Gradiel, 38012217
Thomson, Francis R., 35160081
Unger, Robert S., 35206363
Vigil, Vicente P., 380112221
Villalobos, Macario, 38011930
Vivian, Sam, 38011862
Waldman, Arthur, 36106797
White, William B., 36106548
Wiest, John H., 36106691[1]

These and many other Spanish-speaking soldiers fought with other American and Filipino defenders of Manila when the Philippine Capital was bombed and ravished. Out-numbered

---

[1]Payroll file, 200th CAC (AA), New Mexico National Guard, March 1942, Armijo, Manuel A., New Mexico Veterans' Service Commission. (Partial list)

by superior forces, they were forced to evacuate the Cavite sector in favor of Bataan. There, alongside Manila's 31st Infantry Regiment, the 4th Marines, and the Philippine Scouts, they made a heroic stand, demonstrating sheer courage and fortitude against a large and well-equipped invading Japanese force. Their plight and that of the other embattled defenders at Bataan served to rally patriotic Americans all over the nation. Long lines of volunteers formed at recruiting stations. Brothers, friends, relatives of the Philippine defenders and many other eager young men sought quick entry into our fighting forces.

During January, February, and March the stubborn defenders of Bataan kept the Japanese at bay. The heavy artillery fired by the men of the 200th and the 515th, aided by other gunnery sectors, drove back the attacking Japanese forces. In one instance, after a twenty-four hour duel between the big guns, the cannoneers silenced eleven enemy batteries and shattered several tanks and armored units.

The brave defenders held on to their stronghold, refusing to give up hope that help from the United States would arrive in time. Days grew into weeks, weeks into months and help never arrived. Rations and medical supplies diminished, ammunition became scarce. It was evident to commanding officers that it would be impossible to hold out much longer.

With most of the troops at near-starvation point, many badly wounded, and no relief in sight, it became necessary for Commanding Officer, Major General Edward P. King, to negotiate a surrender with the Japanese General Yamashita.

On April 9th, what was left of a brave fighting force, surrendered. Of the original 78,000 troops on Bataan, 36,000 surrendered with Major General King. The remainder, who refused to give themselves up, braved shark-infested waters to swim to Corregidor where General Jonathan Wainwright still battled the enemy and gained time in the war in the Pacific.

The 200th and 515th Coast Artillery battalions continued to give battle even after the order to cease fire was given. The brave men, adamant to the end, proudly proclaimed they preferred to die fighting. Only at the insistence and by personal appeal of General Wainwright, who pointed out to them that other American lives were being jeopardized, did the men of the 200th and the 515th lay down their arms.

The gallant Americans and the Filipinos who surrendered at Bataan soon discovered what a cruel and brutal enemy the Japanese could be. In the infamous "March of Death" that followed, they were subjected to the most inhuman treatment ever known in a war between civilized countries.

> "The "March of Death" began at daylight on April 10th, when thousands of prisoners, after their surrender, were herded together at Mariveles Airfield on Bataan, stripped of all belongings and whatever food they possessed. Those found with Japanese tokens or money were bayoneted or beheaded. Grouped in numbers of 500 to 1000 they were marched along the National road toward San Fernando. The Japanese slapped and beat them as they marched along without food and water on a scorching hot day."[1]

Marcos Real, Santa Fe, New Mexico, and Julian Guajardo of Fort Worth, Texas, were among the many ill-fated captives who suffered the barbaric acts dealt to those who made the Bataan Death March. Denied rest, food or water, they were forced to march the 85-mile distance, continously abused and prodded by merciless guards who paced them on bicycles. The ordeal lasted 12 days and many who were exhausted fell out and were left behind at the mercy of the cruel tormentors. Meanwhile, at Corregidor, Americans still continued to resist.

---

[1]Miller, Francis Trevelyan, *History of World War II,* Readers Service Bureau, Chicago, Illinois, 1945, p. 459. Based on reports made by three American officers, survivors of the "Death March", who managed to escape from the Japanese after a year of captivity.

They were under heavy bombardment by Japanese guns from inland, ships on shore, and from the air. But the defenders held on. Henry Duran, of Los Angeles, with the 59th Coast Artillery at Corregidor, told of the terrific bombardment by Japanese heavy guns and how, in spite of the terrific odds, our fighters were never down-hearted. He wrote: "We took a lot of punishment from the continuous shelling, but our morale was never low. Everyone in our batallion was prepared to fight on till the very end."

Americans and Filipinos, continued to resist at Corregidor until they too, like the victims at Bataan, were virtually starved and practically defenseless without ammunition, food and medical supplies. On May 5th, the Japanese forced their way into the besieged island fortress and the last organized resistance gave way in the Far East when General Wainwright surrendered Corregidor.

After their capture, Duran, Richard Gonzales and Otilon Medina, also of Los Angeles, joined with members of the 200th and 515th and many other survivors of the "Death March" at Japanese prison camps where they were subjected to further indignities. Scores were killed or died daily from lack of medical attention inside the prison barricades at Camp O'Donnel, Cabanatuan, and Bilibid. These prison camps left vivid memories in the lives of those lucky enough to survive.

One of the most colorful characters among the survivors at Bataan, according to his prison buddies, was Joseph Sanchez of Los Angeles. Known as 'Pickle' to his friends and the guards at Bilibid, Sanchez' civilian life occupation was what has been described as a 'crystal ball gazer.' In prison circles he was called "the Robin Hood of Bilibid."

Caught in Bataan when the Japanese stormed the island, Sanchez, a machine gunner in the 194th Tank Battalion, was in the thick of battle with the brave defenders who resisted the invaders for more than three months. On January 6th he received severe leg wounds in one of the heavy artillery battles between American and Japanese forces. His leg had to be amputated because of the embedded shrapnel.

While at Bilibid prison, Sanchez fashioned a home-made wooden leg out of Philippine mahogany. This same leg is today on exhibit at the Armed Forces Medical Museum in Washington, D.C. It was presented to the museum by William F. Silliphant, Captain U.S.N.

Silliphant was a prison mate of Sanchez and the two cultivated a close friendship. "Sanchez" says Silliphant, "was a happy-go-lucky character who was well-liked by everybody and his antics were a morale-builder for all the prisoners. Every Sunday, on his way to church services, he would put on all his best clothes, consisting of shorts, tie and cap, and go down the prison lane with his hand-made wooden leg, greeting and shouting to everyone.

"He was a gambler and he knew how to win, he would help out the less fortunate with his winnings. He took from the 'rich' and gave to the 'poor', which earned him the name of "Robin Hood".

"With his guitar he would play and sing and with other entertainers he would go around camp to cheer up the other POW's. He was also a 'professor in Spanish' at the camp school for prisoners."

Later, after Sanchez and Silliphant had both been liberated and sent back to the States, they were again together at Bushnell General Hospital. There Sanchez was fitted with an artificial leg and he presented Silliphant with the wooden crutch as a war and prison memento.

Finding himself with no futher use for the hand-made stump, Silliphant decided to donate it to the Armed Forces Museum where it was put on exhibit as a sample of selftreatment by wounded men of World War II. Inscribed on the leg are the words *Mona, Pickle,* and *Bilibid.*

V

NORTH AFRICA

The next big campaign of World War II in which our fighting men participated was in French North Africa where Allied Forces initiated the first offensive move in the Mediterranean Theater of War. Most of the men in the African campaign were 'regular' Army. Many were in the National Guard units that now comprised part of such Divisions as the 1st Infantry, 2nd Armored and the 3rd Infantry Divisions. With the 2nd Armored and the 3rd Infantry were many men from southwestern United States, and these included many Mexican-Americans from along the border States.

Among the participants with the American landing forces in operation "Torch" at Oran, French Africa on November 8th, 1942, were Leopoldo V. Gonzales of Santa Fe, New Mexico, Cleofas Ramirez, Harlingen, Texas and Bill Pedigo of Alamosa, Colorado. They landed with the 2nd Armored Division alongside the 1st, 3rd, and 9th Infantry, and other unattached units who were the first from the United States to engage the enemy.

Gonzales, a tall blue-eyed New Mexican, descendant of a prominent old Spanish family of Santa Fe, undoubtedly qualified for one of the most-traveled soldiers of World War II. He started his Army career in 1940 as a member of the 104th Infantry Anti-Tank Unit of the New Mexico National Guard, after it was mobilized at the Santa Fe CCC camp. From Santa Fe, Bob traveled along with the 104th to Fort Sam Houston. From there he went to Camp Bowie, followed by maneuvers in

Louisiana at Camp Claiborne, then on to Camp Alexandria and to Fort Bragg, South Carolina.

He returned to Fort Sam Houston in December, 1941. When the Japanese attacked Pearl Harbor, Bob was at the San Antonio Army Camp. From Fort Sam he was sent to Camp San Luis Obispo and then to March Field in California. Camp Haan came next and then Borrego Springs for some hard training in the hot California desert. Back to Texas at Camp Hood, he was transferred into a Tank-Destroyer Battery which formed part of the Second Armored.

Soon after that he was back at Fort Sam, where new supplies and all-new-equipment was issued to his unit, and preparations were made for overseas duty. They trained-out at Indian Town Gap, Pennsylvania. From there, they traveled to Staten Island where they shipped-out overseas with the First Division.

As part of a large convoy they crossed the perilous Atlantic, arriving at Belfast, Ireland, on May 17th, 1942. After some 'bag' training in the Irish Sea, came two more months of the same in New Castle, England. From there, the Division moved to Greenock, Scotland, which was their last stopping place prior to hitting the African shore in the European theater of operations.

"All of us Spanish-speaking G.I.'s got a kick out of listening to the Spanish news that came over the ship's radio as we crossed the Gibraltar Strait," reported Bob Gonzales. "The excited Spanish newscasters called the invasion the biggest naval force they had ever seen; bigger than the sea forces of the once-mighty Spanish Armada."

After the landing in Oran, Gonzales' unit, the 704th Tank Destroyer, went through many fierce tank battles along with the 706th, 804th, and 807th TD units, all part of the 2nd Armored. They battled back and forth in the hot desert country against German Panzer units, along with French and Italian Forces.

As Bob put it, "We got our baptism of fire in French Africa where we faced the French Foreign Legion, the Italian Army and the German Wermacht. We fought against rifle and cavalry troops, German paratroopers, and learned to respect the famous 88mm anti-tank gun, the most feared German weapon which we were to face many more times."

With the 2nd Armored, Gonzales got to see action in many torrid tank battles as American armored forces and Rommel's 10th Armored Division battled back and forth in the hot desert country. On February 14-15, 1943, in the Sidi bou Zid area in Tunisia, during one of the many engagements, Gonzales' unit was assaulted by 50 of the new German monster Mark VI "Tiger" tanks, screened by German Stuka airfighters and dive-bombers. Driven back 18 miles, they pulled back, regrouped and next morning they counterattacked. American tanks and T.D.'s drove ahead braving fire from the super 10th German armor and slowly gained the upper hand as they pushed the Germans back, making it possible for American Infantry to come in and occupy the newly-won ground.

Gonzales' Army travelogue continued: From Tunisia with the 2nd Armored they regrouped at Clemenceau, near Morrocco, then went on to the invasion of Sicily, July, 1943. From Sicily, Gonzales left the front to return as guard of German and Italian prisoners of war. Returning to the United States via Liverpool, England, the prisoners were taken to Fort Hamilton, New York. He was then given a thirty-day furlough to visit his hometown in New Mexico. Reporting back to Camp Patrick Henry in Virginia, Bob then went to New York, where he paraded with other G.I.'ş in America's Third War-Loan Drive.

After passing through Virginia, he sailed overseas again, landing once more in Oran, Africa, now-occupied by Allied Forces. Issued equipment and sent back to the front, he landed at Paestra, south of Salerno, where he caught up with the

Second Armored Division. Once again he went into the front lines.

He continued on until the Division was stopped at Cassino. He fought in the Anzio beachhead at Mt. Cassino on the Gustav Line up to April, 1944. His unit reached Rome on the 3rd of June at 4:00 p.m. He fought again at Castel Gandolfo, where his outfit joined the 34th Division to take Leghorn. He was then sent to the rear and the Division attacked the Gothic Line through Florence. Fighting bogged down near Florence due to severe winter weather.

Returning to action on the Gothic Line, Gonzales was wounded at La Posta on September 20th, 1944, suffering third degree burns and loss of teeth when the tank he was riding in was hit by enemy shell fire. Evacuated to Florence, he was sent to the 15th Evac., 94th Evac., 12th General and 428th convalescent hospitals.

He was assigned R.T.U. (return to unit). His unit had moved to Seneiccio Valley, staying in the rear echelon behind the lines where Bob caught up with them.

Back to action at La Bologna, his unit reached Milan on April, 1945. He was stationed there during final negotiations for peace. Bob stayed in Italy for a month after the end of hostilities, then sailed for home. His circuitous route took him from Pizzaria to Fort Layenth, Africa, from Dakar to Natal, Brazil, from there to the south of the Amazon, Georgetown, British Guiana, then to Borrenquin Field in Puerto Rico. He arrived back in the States at Miami, Florida, then to Camp Blanding at Jacksonville, and from there to Fort Sam Houston. Processed at Fort Bliss, he finally was given a medical discharge on August 9th, 1945.

Among the others who initiated their battle experiences in Northern Africa were: Juan Falcon, a line sergeant, Florencio Rodriguez and Frank Carrillo, riflemen, from Los Angeles, who on November 16th landed in Fedala with C Company of the 15th Infantry Regiment of the Third Division. This trio, along with others who were part of the large invasion forces in Africa, went right into the thick of the fighting against German, French, and Italian defenders.

The three Angelenos with the 15th Infantry participated in the battle of Fedala, and three days later they figured in the capitulation of Casablanca. They faced the mighty 88's and battled the Germans in hand-to-hand combat with rifles, bayonets, pistols and knives.

From Africa, Falcon, Carrillo, and Rodriguez continued with the 3rd Division fighting in Sicily, Salerno and all the way through into the Anzio beachhead.

VI

AT ATTU

May, 1943. Much had taken place in both the Pacific and the European Theaters of war. The Marines had captured Guadalcanal and now were driving through the Solomons and New Guinea. The battle of North Africa had ended with the capture of the once mighty Africa Korps.

In the Aleutians, the United States initiated a move to drive off the Japanese that were in Attu and Kiska, and the ensuing events uncovered another 'first' for Mexican-American soldiers of W.W. II. For it was here that Private Jose P. Martinez made history, graphically told in the following documentary:

PVT. JOSE P. MARTINEZ

Awarded the Congressional Medal of Honor. (posthumously).

Private, Company K, 32d Infantry, 7th Infantry Division. On Attu, Aleutians, 26 May 1943. For conspicious gallantry and intrepidity above and beyond the call of duty in action with the enemy. Over a period of several days, repeated efforts to drive the enemy from a key defensive position high in the snow-covered precipitous mountains between East Arm Holtz Bay and Chichagof Harbor had failed. On 26 May, 1943, troop dispositions were readjusted and a trial coordinate attack on this position by a reinforced battalion was launched. Initially successful, the attack bogged down. In the face of severe hostile machinegun, rifle, and mortar fire, Private Martinez, an automatic rifleman, rose to his feet and resumed his advance. Occassionally he stopped to urge his comrades on. His example inspired others to follow. After a most difficult climb, Private Martinez eliminated resistance from part of the enemy position by BAR fire and hand grenades, thus assisting the advance of other attacking elements. This success only partially completed the action. The main Holtz-Chichagof Pass rose about 150 feet higher, flanked by steep rocky ridges and reached by a snow-filled defile. Passage was barred by enemy fire from either flank and from tiers of snow trenches in front. Despite these obstacles, and knowing of their existence, Private Martinez again led the troops on and up, personally silencing several trenches with BAR fire and ultimately reaching the pass itself. Here, just below the knifelike rim of the pass, Private Martinez encountered a final enemy-occupied trench and as he was engaged in firing into it he was mortally wounded. The pass, however, was taken, and its capture was an important preliminary to the end of organized hostile resistance on the island.[1]

The career of Jose P. Martinez in Attu assumed great importance, not only as United States History but to all Americans of Mexican descent because he was the first draftee enlisted man in the Pacific Theatre to distinguish himself in battle by winning the Congressional Medal of Honor in World War II.

The name of Martinez was first found in a news-communique out of Attu, an official War Department news release dated May 27, 1943.

> "May 27, 1943. Jose P. Martinez, Ault, Colorado, 23 year old Private with an infantry regiment of the 7th (Hourglass) Division died from Japanese bullets after he had led his fellow doughboys in a successful attack on

---

[1]War Department Citation G.O. No. 71, October 27, 1943. *The Medal of Honor,* official publication, Department of the Army, U.S. Government Printing Office, Washington, D.C., 1949, p. 281.

PVT. JOSE P. MARTINEZ
Ault, Colorado
Congressional Medal of Honor
Attu, Alaska, World War II

a vital pass in Attu, between East Arms Holtz Bay and Chichagof Harbor. His name has been recommended for the Congressional Medal of Honor by his officers."

Jose Martinez, one of nine children, was born in Taos, New Mexico, on July 20, 1920. Although he has been known as the first 'Mexican-American' soldier of W.W. II to receive the Medal of Honor, his family originates from a long line of American born Spanish-speaking ancestors from the state of New Mexico who have always been regarded as 'Spanish-Americans,' just like other Spanish-speaking citizens from the 'Land of Enchantment.'

In 1927 his father packed and moved the family north into the state of Colorado, where he hoped to make a better living working in the fields. He had heard that good money could be made by a large family such as his.

The family worked up and down the Northern Colorado farm belt, as did many other Mexican and Spanish-American families in those days. Finally, he decided to settle in Ault, a small town near the Rockies. In Ault, Joe attended school with his brothers and sisters, helped the family in farm work, and assisted in managing the trucking business in which the elder Martinez boy was engaged.

Joe loved the rich country where he grew up. The clean fresh air that would sweep from the high Sierras, the cold brisk winters, the high snow-covered peaks and the picturesque rock formations along the countryside roads. He dreamed of how he would someday own a farm where he would harvest his own crops, raise his own cattle and hoge, here in "God's Country."

When the Army began drafting men, Delfino, Joe's older brother, was one of the first to go from Ault. Joe yearned for the day when he too would be called. He wanted to be alongside Delfino.

The call finally came. Joe left his farm country and his

dreams behind on August 17th, 1942. Jose P. Martinez felt proud to be a member of the United States Army. From the induction center at Denver, he was sent to Camp Roberts, California, where he took his basic training. Upon completion of basic, he was sent to Camp Butner for some additional infantry training. He eventually found himself in the 7th (Hourglass) Division. He shipped out April 13th, 1943, with the 7th to Alaska via Seattle, Washington.

Within two weeks Joe's regiment boarded ship and sailed north, straight to Cold Bay on the northern tip of the Alaskan Peninsula. On May 1st, their convoy was joined by transports, cruisers, destroyers, and aircraft carriers—all headed for the Aleutian Islands then occupied by the Japanese.

The presence of an enemy force on the North American continent alarmed all of America. Army Chiefs of Staff made preparations to rid the Aleutians of Japanese and wipe out the threat to American soil.

After a heavy bombing attack, the Japanese had occupied the two small islands since early June of 1942, when they had landed a small force in Attu and Kiska. Joe's battalion was part of the task force that was sent to drive the Japanese out of the Aleutians. Headed by Major General Eugene M. Landrum, the force included elements of the 7th Infantry Division, a battalion of the 4th Infantry and the Alaskan Scouts.

Early morning on May 11th, the task force neared the shore of Holtz Bay on Attu. Joe's mind was preoccupied with the day's task. He ate a light breakfast. After that, he wandered out on deck, scanning the high rocky mountain peaks of Attu. The snow-covered pinnacles reminded him of the high rockies back home in Colorado.

Now he wondered how he would behave in battle. Would he be afraid? He didn't feel he would be; he had trained well for this. He would be ready. H-Hour had been designated as 0700.

On deck, the troops checked out their gear and equipment, and listened to their last-minute instructions.[1]

The ships of the task forces pounded Holtz Bay and the hill on the island with such a tremendous barrage that it rocked the landing barges and deafened the roar of the engines. Joe's battalion, under Colonel Frank L. Cullen, stormed ashore on Holtz Bay, expecting to take the Japanese by surprise. Another force landed at Massacre Bay with orders to drive back the enemy, and then together, the two forces were to concentrate in a drive to push back the enemy into Chichagof Harbor where the Japanese had established their headquarters.

The enemy quickly rallied and put up a stubborn defense. They poured heavy artillery from the high knoll, harassing the landing troops below on Red Beach. Americans brought in howitzers, and an artillery battle was waged. The American artillery failed to dislodge the Japanese from their well entrenched positions. It became necessary to send out ground troops to engage them in close combat.

Private Jose P. Martinez was in the platoon that was given the order to attack on that cold foggy day of May 26, 1943.

The battalion was reinforced with troops that had landed on Massacre Bay. The attacking force made slow progress. They moved in closer to the enemy. The G.I.'s moved cautiously from rock to rock while intense machine gun, rifle, and mortar fire stymied their drive. They were pinned down and no one dared to move out into the hail of fire the Japanese poured down. The men sought protection from the exploding mortar shells that were falling all around. Seeking to break out of the desperate situation, the C.O. then asked for a rifle platoon to move up at all costs.

Before the word reached the Sergeant down the line, a lone

---

[1] Rech, Franklin M., *Beyond The Call of Duty,* Thomas Crowell Company, 1944, p. 112.

figure rose from the ground and started up. It was Pvt. Jose P. Martinez.

Having been chosen to handle the BAR, (Browning Automatic Rifle) for the platoon, Martinez decided to take matters into his own hands. He felt it was his duty to do something about their situation. In the face of hostile fire, he rose to his feet and took off alone. Now and then he would wave an arm to the others to follow him. "Come on, lets go!", he would yell.

The pinned-down G.I.'s couldn't believe their eyes. Here was Marty, the quiet Mexican kid from Colorado, *who wasn't even in charge of the rifle squad,* setting the example and urging the others to follow. Inspired by his actions, they started to follow. Martinez climbed steadily up with the battalion following him. Incredible, the whole battalion was moving forward, led by a Private! On reaching the bench-like plateau, he engaged the Japanese in two foxholes. Their rifle fire was no match for Martinez' blazing BAR. He cleaned out the two nests and hurled hand grenades at the other enemy soldiers above him. The Japanese increased their machine gun and rifle fire.

Once more the attack bogged down. Withering fire from the front and from above kept the infantrymen hugging the earth. There was no movement, then a lone figure once more arose and started up the snow slope that led to the pass. Once more it was Pvt. Martinez. Now he was within closer enemy range and the bullets struck all around him. The brave Martinez was thinking of the others behind him and had no time to think of himself. Of one thing he was sure: it was either the enemy or him. . . . He was not afraid!

He was forced to move across open ground. Now he faced heavy crossfire from above and frontal fire from the foxholes. He came upon two enemy trenches. Jumping in, he quickly opened up with his Browning automatic and killed five more of the enemy. Without hesitation, the fearless G.I. from Colorado then moved up to the second trench and accounted for two more Japanese. He reached the pass, still under heavy fire from the surrounding ridges. Standing on the ridge, overlooking the pass leading into the Chichagof Harbor, Martinez emptied his rifle into the positions just below and beyond the pass.

The last part of his citation reads, "... he was mortally wounded with his rifle still at his shoulder, absorbing all enemy fire and permitting all units to move up behind him and successfully take the pass."

Thus, the twenty-three year old Martinez died a glorious death and the Alaskan hills were covered with American blood. Many others fought, bled and died in the Aleutian campaign but it was a Private, a former farm laborer, Jose P. Martinez' heroic action that enabled the American forces to clear the pass of Japanese by May 30th. He earned praise, admiration and recommendation for the Congressional Medal of Honor from his fellow soldiers, commanding officers and Battalion Commander.

The glory of Joe Martinez will never be forgotten because historians and educators have seen fit to have his story told and retold in American college classrooms, and written in the junior high and high school history books all over America. Annual scholarships bear his name and a local Chapter of the Disabled American Veterans has been named in his honor in Colorado. A local Post of the American Legion now exists in Los Angeles, California, named after the Mexican-American hero.

All were proud of Joe, but Mexican-Americans were just a little more proud of him. His widely heralded achievement occurred at a time when attitudes toward Mexicans in the United States were at a low ebb because of unfortunate happenings in Los Angeles.

The Zoot-Suit riots[1] in the Angel city had left a very bad impression of Mexican-Americans throughout America. Frank Lares of Los Angeles, who was then stationed in Fort Greely with Battery D, 250th Coast Artillery, in Kodiak Island, Alaska, recalls that the Pachuco Riots of June, '43, were in all the headlines, even in Alaska. He remembers how uncomfortable he felt when his own fellow comrades stationed at the same camp would give him dirty looks and ask embarrassing questions, such as, "What kind of citizens are those Mexican Zoot-Zooters that would beat up on our own Navy men?"

After the news got around about Jose P. Martinez' one-man heroic drive in the Aleutians, no questions were asked about pachuco gangs. Lares felt very proud of Martinez and very proud that he was a Mexican-American.

---

[1]On June 3, 1943, the "Zoot-suit" riots flared up in the streets of Los Angeles. For weeks, a reign of terror existed. Groups of servicemen hunted down and beat up boys of Mexican descent-so called "Pachucos" who wore the then-popular Zoot-suits. They ripped off their pants or clipped their hair, in many cases while policemen stood by. The incident which started the rioting was never acknowledged by the men in uniform or the newspapers. Several sailors in a bar in the Mexican section had attempted to entice two *senoritas* from their escorts and a fight started.

From *"My L.A."* by Matt Weinstock, Current Books Inc., A. A. Wyn, New York, N.Y. p. 125.

The so-called "Zoot-Suit" riots made front line news in newspapers all over the nation.

VII

THE MEDITERRANEAN

SICILY

The next battlefront where many Mexican-American combatmen took part was the invasion of Sicily on July 10th, 1943.

Hundreds of our young men made the landing with the 1st, 3rd, 9th, 42nd and 45th Infantry Divisions; the 2nd Armored and with the 82nd "All American" Airborne division, who landed five hours before all others.
Henry P. Kirker of Garden Grove, California, Commander of Ex-POWs, W.W. II of America, 1957, recalls the many Mexican-Americans who parachuted down with the 504 Regt. of the 82nd in the initial thrust. Kirker, a member of Co. G of Battalion "X", who was shot down and later taken prisoner by the Germans says, "We were lucky to be a part of Battalion "X", the unit that made the famous 'fortunate blunder.' We landed far off our assigned area, and were missed by our own planes who mistakenly started firing on our own troops. The others were not so fortunate."

The invasion of Sicily was the first action for the "Thunderbird" [45th] Division. The 45th was a former National Guard outfit made up of men from the Southwest. Among them were many of our boys from Arizona, New Mexico, and Texas.

The late Ernie Pyle, in his war masterpiece "Brave Men," mentions the many Spanish speaking G.I.'s who were with the 45th in Sicily. Among them, two frontline sergeants, Sgt.

Martin Quintana of Albuquerque and Sgt. John Trujillo of Socorro, New Mexico.

> "A large percentage of the battalion spoke Spanish and occasionally I heard some of the officers talking Spanish among themselves, just to keep in practice, I suppose. That New Mexico bunch missed more than anything, I believe the Spanish dishes they were accustomed to back home. Their folks occasionally sent them cans of chile and peppers, and then they had a minor feast.
>
> "They were part of the old New Mexico outfit, most of which were lost in Bataan. It was good to get back to those slow-talking, wise and easy people of the desert, and good to speak of places like Las Cruces, Socorro, and Santa Rosa[1] . . ."

Other Spanish names Pyle mentions in the Italian campaign are: Cpl. Max Hernandez, a tankman from Del Mar, California; Sgt. Guadalupe Tanguma, a line sergeant of San Antonio, Texas; and Pfc. Manuel Gomez, jeep-driver of Laredo, Texas, who drove Pyle all over the Italian front.

The Sicilian campaign lasted slighly over a month. It may have been termed easy by some of the writers, but the fellows who fought in the high ridges of Troina, Rendazzo and on the Bloody Ridge of San Stefano, spent some of their most gruelling days and nights of their combat career there. Most of the fighting in those mountains called for the use of mules and 'mule skinners' to take supplies up and bring down the many battle casualties.

By the end of the 38-day campaign our casualties were estimated as 7,500. Many names, such as Garcia, Martinez, and Sanchez, are stamped on the white crosses and are adorned by the insignias of the 3rd, 9th, 34th, and 45th Divisions in the

---

[1]"Brave Men", Pyle, Ernie, N.Y. Grosset, Dunlap, 1943—p. 43.

military cemetary at San Stefano, where lie scores of American bodies of the G.I.'s who lost their lives in Sicily.

COMPANY E
THE *ALL-CHICANO* INFANTRY COMPANY

One of the most colorful infantry companies that fought in the Mediterranean during W.W. II was Company E, 141st Regiment of the 36th (Texas) Division. They started their front-line action when American troops landed at Salerno.

Company E, Texas 36th Division was peculiarly different from all other infantry units that landed in the European campaign. The entire company was made up of Spanish-speaking soldiers. They included Mexicans, Mexican-Americans and the so-called Latin-Americans. Many of the enlisted men spoke limited English. All of the non-coms and platoon officers were Americans of Mexican descent.

Most of its members were former citizens of El Paso and nearby points who were in the original E company of the Texas National Guard. These were supplemented by other Spanish-speaking G.I.'s who later were drafted or volunteered into wartime service.

It was in the early days of 1941 when the 36th trained under the hot Texas sun and in the marshy swamps of Louisiana that Co. E, on orders of Division Commander Burkhart, became an all-Mexican unit. All officers and non-coms of Mexican extraction in other companies of the 141st regiment were transferred to E Company of the Second Battalion to carry out the training programs.

The move, unprecedented in United States Army history, worked out for the betterment of the Division and for the moment, better for the Mexican-American G.I.'s, because of the promotions and commissions given to the old veterans of the Division.

The transfers from other companies into E Company made

the unit one of the strongest and certainly an outstanding company in the 36th. While the other companies filled their ranks with raw recruits sent in by the draft boards, E Company was up to full strength with seasoned and well-conditioned G.I.'s who had been in the Division since pre-war days. They stood out in drills, field problems, weapon firing and infantry tactics. They built quite a reputation for themselves in the regiment during their early training days.

The assembling together of a large Mexican-American element in one infantry company resulted in a tight-woven camaraderie that was unequaled among Mexican-American G.I.'s during W.W. II. While it is true that there were many other Divisions who had a large number of Spanish-speaking G.I.'s in their ranks and there were many Mexican-American soldiers in the training camps of the Southwest, no group ever developed the pride and comradeship that E Company did. This was not just a group of newcomers thrown in together to begin service training at the same time. Most of the G.I.'s in E Company had known each other since early boyhood. They had been together since the early 'Guard' days.

From Camp Bowie they started out eating together, training together . . . sleeping together . . . speaking Spanish when serious and English for military discipline. Together they enjoyed not only the regular Army chow, but also their preferred Mexican dishes which many times were prepared by the company cooks who also were of Mexican descent.

In early 1943, the 36th Division was shipped out of Staten Island, New York, Europe bound. Everyone agreed that 'Easy' company *"Era la mas alegre."* They were a fun-loving group with many laugh-provoking individuals who were always springing crazy antics among the company.

Enrique Fuentes, from Crystal City, and *"Güero"* Garza of San Antonio, were a couple whose specialty number was *"Las Comadres"* act. In this comedy-riot act, they would impersonate two back-yard gossiping old maids in manner of speech, gossipy wit, and even in style of dress with makeshift costumes of bedsheets and pillows. On the boat trip across the Atlantic, this couple kept the troops entertained with their fun-zest and comedy acts. Of all the companies on board, none had as many entertainers as E Company with its many instrumentalists and its semi-professional singers. There were; duets, trios and quartets who kept up a steady dancing and singing tempo with their Mexican and Spanish *boleros, rumbas, guarachas* and *ranchero* music and songs. Added to the 'Latino' atmosphere was the fact that the two ships that carried the 36th overseas were appropriately named the "Argentina" and the "Brazil."

MANUEL "EL FEO" GONZALES

Salerno, September 9, 1943. The 36th and 45th Infantry Divisions led the assault on the Salerno beachhead. The doughs in E Company of the 141st, in the 36th, were some of the first combat troops to land on Italian soil. Everyone in the Division was anxious to find out how the Mexican boys would react under fire. Would they perform as they had in the training camps where they had taken so many top honors?

It didn't take long to find out . . . Within one hour the 'boys' in E Company became *Men.* They waded right into the thick of things, battling back and forth with the Nazi defenders. It wasn't long before a Mexican-American became the first hero of the whole Division. This was a big, tall, bronze-faced *Chicano* Sergeant named Manuel S. Gonzales, better known to his friends as "El Feo" (Ugly).

The big sergeant spoke very little English, having been born and raised in the *barrio Chicano* of Fort Davis. Within minutes of hitting the beachhead at Salerno he set out to silence a machinegun nest that had stopped his squad, and in so doing, he earned the admiration of his men, his superior officers and the Distinguished Service Cross for himself. His exploits on the Salerno beachhead are recorded by Francis Trevelyan Miller in his World War II History book, as follows:

SGT. MANUEL GONZALES

> "His unit was pinned down almost from the start by artillery and machinegun fire. The nearest enemy post was armed with four machine guns and a mortar.
>
> "Gonzales a sergeant with the 36th, slung his Browning automatic rifle over his shoulders, loosened his pistol belt, and started to crawl towards the German lines. 'I had so many hand grenades with me,' he said later, 'that as I look back to it, I wonder how I could move at all.'
>
> "A German hand grenade burst beside him as he crawled; its shell gored his back and his left hand and arm, but he did not stop until he had reached the German position.
>
> "When Gonzales came crawling back to his outfit, the mortars and machine guns were all silenced."

Another infantryman with the 36th at Salerno was Arturo Rivera from Mission, Texas, who miraculously escaped death with shells blasting all around him when he hit the beachhead later that day.

While bringing in a group of German prisoners, Rivera was set upon by German infantrymen who manned a machinegun and sprayed lead all around him, killing many of their own men. Wounded in the head and shoulders, Rivera nevertheless manage to herd the remaining prisoners and delivered them intact to the battalion CP.

The 36th continued their front line action in Italy along with other Divisions in the 5th Army led by General Mark Clark. Gonzales continued to perform like a hero against the enemy, although he was very reluctant to accept any plaudits. A report that came out of the Italian front by a war correspondent of the International News Service bears this out.

Graham Hovey, who wrote the article, reveals the character of Gonzales in an interview with Gonzales and his C.O.:

> NAPLES, May 2.-(INS)-"What did you say his name was?"
>
> Lt. Evan J. Mac Ilraith of Evanston, Ill. said, "Gonzales, Manuel S. Gonzales, he's from somewhere in West Texas near the Mexican border some spot where they don't speak anything but Spanish. He's a Staff or Tech Sergeant now, I think, and he was a regular 'Commando Kelly' in combat.
>
> "This guy was such a terrific soldier all the way that I have trouble recalling his individual exploits, even though he was in my company. A wonderful squad leader, he'd volunteer for anything, any time, and at Salerno, when his squad was practically wiped out, he fought a one-man battle against the Germans for 24 hours.
>
> "All of what he did there will never come out—the number of Germans he killed, for instance—because nobody saw him do it and he won't talk about it. But we know he knocked out an 88 mm. gun nest with a hand grenade. That was really wrecked. I saw it. He must have hit an ammunition pile. Got some machinegun nests, too.
>
> "But he really got shot up on Mt. Castellone, and I guess he's all through with combat. They'll probably ship him home."
>
> We found Gonzales, a big, bronze man with a tremendous shock of black hair, dressed incongruously in combat boots and a blue bathrobe. He had been chatting with an army chaplain. As he saw Mac Ilraith, his thick lips parted in a huge smile and dimples which looked like miniature foxholes appeared on the big, copper-colored face. He said, pumping Mac's hand:

"I'm glad to see you, Lieutenant. I'm glad you came today because I go back to company tonight."

Said Mac Ilraith:

"Sergeant, you're amazing. Back to company! I thought they'd put you on limited service this time."

Said Gonzales:

"No sir. I don't want limited service. I want to go back to company. I've got too much friends there. I don't want to miss this. I want to get back to company."

A.W.O.L. DENIED

Mac Ilraith explained to me that Gonzales once ran away from an army hospital before being discharged to rejoin his company during a tough fight. Gonzales said: "No sir, sir. I never really went A.W.O.L. since I've been in the army.

"I had three operations this time and the second one kept me in bed 36 days and I lose too much weight. I'm weight 160 pounds now but I used to weigh 215 pounds."

Mac said:

"That's nothing to worry about. You used to be too fat. You could hardly move around."

WOUNDING TOLD

Gonzales grinned again, showing large, irregular white teeth, and as he rocked back on the cot, I could see an American flag tatooed on his left arm. He said:

"No sir, sir. I could always move."

How did you get hit?"

Mac Ilraith answered for Gonzales.

"Got three machine pistol slugs in his groin when he attacked on Castellone the last day of January. Went back under his own power after he got hit and reported at the aid station still on his feet. He wouldn't tell you that himself."

Mac told him:

"Tell him about getting the Distinguished Service cross from General Clark on Christmas Day. I think you're going to get some medals soon, too."

Said Gonzales, embarrassed:

"No sir, sir, I don't want no more. No sir, sir, no more medals. But I wish my mother would get that one. She hasn't gotten it yet."

Mac answered:

"She'll get it all right. If she doesn't I'll see that you get another one to send her."

LEARNS ENGLISH

Gonzales' mother, Mrs. Carmen Mendoza, and his wife both live in Fort Davis, Texas, where the 27 year old sergeant worked in a cement works prior to the war. His father, Angel Gonzales, lives in El Paso.

Gonzales said:

"Everybody speaks Spanish at Fort Davis. I just learned American language in the army. The boys in the company teach me at night. They're pretty good boys."

Said Mac Ilraith:

"Tell him what you did at Salerno. Knocked out some German tanks there, didn't you?"

"No sir. I threw some hand grenades at those tanks but it was no good. They just kept on coming."

Mac said:

"It's no use, He won't talk about himself.

"He won't tell you how he fought the Germans alone or how he volunteered for patrols or how he came right back into the line after being captured and having 'flu' and malaria and getting wounded."

I asked:

"What do you think of the Germans?"

Said Gonzales:

"I think they are good but I think we are better. We don't holler 'kamerad' but they do. They give up too easy but we don't."

I asked:

"Gonzales, you've seen a lot of combat. They say you're slated for rotation home. Why don't you take it?"

The grin vanished. He said:

"No sir, sir, I don't like rotation because they might send me to a new outfit. I want to stick with my company. When the war is over I want to rotate home for good, but I don't want to get far from my company until then."

Outside the hospital, I said to Mac Ilraith:

"You've never yet told me how you got the Silver Star."

Said Mac:

"Guys like Gonzales got it for me. It's a cinch to be a hero when you're commanding guys like Gonzales."

—by Graham Hovey.[1]

Having cleared the Salerno area of the enemy, General Mark Clark's 5th Army next drove towards Naples. On September 21st, the 36th once again spearheaded the drive with E Company one of the attacking units who entered the historical city. The German resistance was fierce but there was no stopping the Allied troops by then. The city was occupied by October 1st.

As they continued the drive up the Italian peninsula, heavy fall rains turned the roads into mud. Von Vietingoff, the 10th German Army General took advantage of every break in the

---

[1]GONZALES, TEXAS HERO—taken from "San Antonio Light," San Antonio, Texas, May 2, 1944, by Graham Hovey.

weather and strengthened the dug-in positions along the Volturno River, the first of many fortified strong blocks the Allies were to face.

The Allies were now at the gates of Cassino, but the German artillery and infantry outfits were fighting as strongly as ever. They commanded the high ground of the mountainous country. A chain of high ridges and deep rivers formed part of the natural obstacles that our fighting men had to overcome. Fighting was especially fierce at San Pietro where infantry companies of both sides lost many of their men and officers.

By early 1944, the Germans were forced back from the Winter Line to their Gustav Line, which extended along the Garaglino and Rapido Rivers where they established their strongest defensive positions. The Allies main objective was to capture the Cassino stronghold which protected the entrance to the Lire Valley and the gate to Rome. Some of the stronger fortified positions held by the Germans were along the Garaglino and the Rapido.

THE CROSSING OF THE RAPIDO

After being in the front lines all the way since the Salerno landing, E Company was finally given a rest and placed on reserve for a couple of weeks. After the brief respite they went back into action at the Gustav Line.

It was at the Gustav Line where E Company had the most dramatic moments of their whole campaign. The attempted crossing of the *Rio Rapido* was where the Mexican-Americans played the biggest role of the war in the Mediterranean.

The full story of the Rapido River crossing has never been told. This was, without a doubt, the most criticized of moves made by the United States Army in the European Theater in W.W. II and one of the principals was "E" Company, of the 141st Infantry Regiment.

The Rapido River was a natural barrier that held up the

Allied drive. After a quiet lull in the foul-weather fighting, the Allied forces began a drive to cross the Rapido. The French forces made a successful crossing at a point above where they encountered little opposition. General Clark mapped plans to have an American division make a crossing in the 5th Army sector, hoping to divert all German attention from the British 8th sector and then have both the English and Americans swing around to Cassino.

The 36th Division was picked to lead the crossing. Division Headquarters made plans to have one of their most effective Infantry Companies probe the position of the enemy and effect a crossing wherever feasable.

Picked for both of these dangerous jobs was E Company, the all-*Chicano* company.

When word came down from Division Headquarters to prepare for a crossing of the Rapido by assault boats on Jan. 17, Gabriel Navarrete from El Paso, then a Lieutenant, organized a patrol to probe the defensive positions of the Germans on the other side of the river. He chose some of the most capable men in his company. There was Master Sgt. Roque Lopez Segura of El Paso, who was an excellent swimmer, Benito Dominguez, a fearless and daring young stalwart from San Antonio, Manny Rivera of El Paso and a few others.

The patrol ran into one of the strongest fortifications they had ever encountered since the days of the landing at Salerno. Sgt. Segura swam out to the other side to tie a rope to the bank so the rubber boat could ford the swirling waters. In the darkness they could make out the heavy concentration of troops and fortifications. The bank on the German side was strewn with barbed wire entanglements. Rolls and rolls of wire were laid out up and down the river's edge. Large trees had been felled, and their trunks offered protection for the enemy and obstacles for the Americans. Gun emplacements that could rake the river with crossfire were revealed when the patrol ventured farther.

The patrol was discovered and trapped by the German guards who manned the other side of the river's edge. Heavy machine gun and rifle fire hit the small group. Manny Rivera, the machinegun Sergeant, and Navarrete were among the badly wounded. In this struggle, the brave Roque Segura sacrificed his life.[1] "It was a miracle to have been able to get out of their trap and make it back to our side," said Navarrete.

Struggling with those that were disabled, and badly wounded himself, the young Lieutenant managed to reach the American lines and report what his patrol had discovered. He specifically pointed out that Germans defending the other side of the river, at that point, had too many gun emplacements and were too large in numbers for one infantry company to effect a crossing at that sector. He knew that "E" Company had been chosen to lead the attack. The company had been too cut down in personnel, due to the men lost in the patrol. Himself hospitalized, he kept hoping that 'his boys' would be spared, that E Company be placed in Battalion support for that day.

The bond between Navarrete and the men in E Company was different from that of other infantry companies. Most of them had been together for a long time and knew each other since their early boyhood days in El Paso. "We came from the same *barrios* and attended the same school together," said Navarrete. "Even our parents had long been friends and neighbors. We all suffered the depression together. When I was given an Officer's commission, it was hard for me to get tough with the men in my company. We had been through so many

---

[1]Segura was given the Silver Star, posthumously. The Segura-McDonald V.F.W. Post of El Paso is named in honor of Roque Segura and S/Sgt. Felix McDonald, another Mexican-American who was KIA. (Killed in action).

"*vaviladas and parrandas*"[1] together, and every once in a while they would remind me of it."[2]

He was upset to think that "E" Company, his buddies and personal friends, were to be sent into a murderous trap, and because of his wounds he would not be able to be with them! Sentiment got the best of Gabriel Navarrete. Badly wounded as he was, and with orders to report to the battalion hospital, he instead took off to seek higher officers at the rear echelon quarters to warn them personally of the solid and impervious defense on the other side of the river.

He told Battalion Commander Major Landly that if an attempt to cross the Rapido with one company of infantry only were made, it would surely end in diaster. He insisted that they not use "E" Company for the assault.

Navarrete was told that the U.S. Army was not taking orders from an 'incompetent' Lieutenant who was badly wounded and talked incoherently. "You have tried to go over the head of your superiors, Navarrete. Do you know that you can be court-martialed for this?" he was told by Major Landly. "You are suffering from bad wounds and will be excused if you go back to the station hospital and forget about this," the Major added.

"The wounds hurt, it is true," answered Navarrete, "but I know what I am saying! I will stand court martial as I am not worried for myself. But remember this, Major, if the plans are not changed and you sacrifice my E Company, you are going to answer to me personally; I will be looking for you and I will be armed."

It was a reluctant young officer who unhappily went back to the battalion aid station for treatment. The idea that his disabled

---

[1]*vaciladas and parrandas*, sprees, good times.

[2]Navarrete was only being modest here. It has been revealed by the men who were with him that they had nothing but respect for him and he was greatly admired by all the men, not only in E Company but by all the other companies in the battalion as well.

company would still be called to lead the attack bothered him to the end. *It would be just plain suicide.*

So it was that on the early cold morning of January 21st, 1944, E Company spearheaded the crossing of the Rapido. The crossing is accounted by historian Francis T. Miller, as follows:

> The Germans had prepared for this onslaught. Flatlands were strewn with trunks of trees cut down in order to improve their field of fire. A low fog added to the Americans' woes. Hurriedly, the troops strove to dig foxholes in the cold, hard soil—and almost as fast, it seemed, they filled with water.
>
> Suddenly the fog dissolved and a clear sunlight left them almost naked to the defenders' fire. English-speaking Germans in a dozen parts of the line shouted to them, "Give up! Give up!" Rocket, mortar, and artillery shells drove home the exhortation.
>
> The men (in E Co.) had plunged through dense mine fields on their own side of the river, carrying on their backs heavy equipment, vital to the attack and assault boats in which they were to cross. Many boats were riddled with enemy fire and the little river ran red with blood.

The crossing attempt was a complete fiasco and the icy cold waters of the Rapido were filled with American (and Mexican) blood, not only from E Company but of the other gallant infantrymen who took part. Colonel Andrew Price, of Fort Worth, the Regimental Commander, gave praise to the brave men who never gave up in the face of difficult odds. "The boys fought until they did not have a bullet to shoot. They showed courage and fortitude."

In the absence of Lieutenant Navarrete, it had been Enrique "Sweet Pea" Ochotorena, of El Paso, a fearless squad leader famous for his many escapades against the Germans, who led the remaining 23 battered men back to safety.

At the hospital the following day, Navarrete's worst fears were confirmed. Asleep on a cot, he was awakened in the early morn by the moans of many badly wounded men who were being brought in. He instantly recognized the "T" patch of the 36th on their clothing.

"What about E Company? Does anyone know anything about E Company?" he pleaded.

"E Company? . . . They were wiped out," one of the casualties told him.

"It was Hell . . . we didn't have a chance," said another.

Navarrete immediately jumped out of his cot and got dressed. When he found out what had happened he armed himself and went gunning for the Major.

When he arrived at Battalion Headquarters, Navarrete was met by a Chaplain who pleaded with him to forget what he had in his mind, to think of his future, his family, and not to seek vengeance. Unheeding, Navarrete kept on. At Battalion they told him that the Major was now in Division Headquarters. To Division Headquarters he went, in a borrowed jeep.

By now, the whole regiment had gotten wind that Navarrete was gunning for the Major. Speculation arose as to whether he would be stopped and placed under arrest. They remembered that Navarrete had many times demonstrated his handiness with guns, his accurate marksmanship, and they knew he was an intrepid indivdual.

There had been the instance once when E Co. had captured a German prisoner which included a high-ranking Prussian officer who demanded an equal-ranking officer to surrender to. And when Navarrete, only a S/Sgt. then, had asked for his Luger, the German officer had spat on his face. The enraged Navarrete then had taken a few steps back, fired from the hip, and shot off the captured officer's gun, grazed his cheek with another bullet, then had made the German crawl to him and hand him the gun with a threat to put a bullet through his head. But to threaten a superior of his own Company was different; they saw nothing but trouble ahead for the young Lieutenant.

Navarrete would not listen to the advice and warning given to him by the Chaplain, his friends and other officers. He kept thinking of Lopez Segura, Capt. John Chapin and many others who had been led to their slaughter.

Upon arriving at Division Headquarters, Navarrete was met by a sentry who told him that General Walton Walker wanted him to report to his C.P. Navarrete went in, fully composed and erect, and saluted his Commanding General.

General Walker told the would-be avenger that as man-to-man, he understood Navarrete's feelings, and did not blame him for wanting to shoot it out with the Major. But this was the United States Army and he would not permit a junior officer to challenge a superior officer. He added that to avoid any further unpleasantries, he had transferred the Major out of the Division. And to straighten out the matter, he was ordering Navarrete back to the States for a well-deserved furlough and had elevated him to the rank of Captain.

The Rapido crossing was a complete failure. The Army brass tried to hush up the incident. No names or identification of the units who participated are mentioned in combat history publications of the 5th Army. There are no specific mentionings of any one company in the 36th Division's "5 Years—5 Countries—5 Campaigns," which has the historical accounts of the 141st Regiment in Italy during W.W. II.

Echoes of this costly military blunder were heard shortly after the end of the war when the 36th Division Association raised objections to the promotion of another star for General Mark Clark. The Association did not think the General merited the extra star, pointing to his bad military judgment at the Rapido.

Gabriel Navarrete, who had been under strict orders not to divulge information of the military operations in that campaign while in uniform, was set to 'tell all' when the Texas (36th) Association asked him to be ready to appear at the Pentagon for a hearing.

"Somehow, for some unexplained reason, the hearing never came off," said Navarrete, and General Mark Clark got his fifth star.

An almost deathly quiet followed the gallant failure at the Rapido. After the Rapido crossing, E Company regrouped and filled their depleted squads with replacements. They fought around the Cassino campaign, and then were taken out of the line for a brief rest. They went back into the lines at Anzio, and from there they fought their way into Rome.

In August, 1944, they participated in their second invasion with the 36th in the landing of Southern France at Toulon. They fought up the Rhine Valley into the Vosges, across the Moselle, and took the Colmar pocket. From Oberhoffen, they smashed across the Rhine into Germany at Wissenbourg, where they planted the Lone Star flag. From there, they went all the way into the heart of Germany. In Germany the 36th was credited with capturing two big Nazi chiefs as the war ended in the E.T.O., these being: the Number One German General, Field Marshal Von Runsted, leader of the Germans' biggest offensive; and Reichmaster Herman Goering, the biggest Nazi of all.

Thus ended the bloody battles for one of the best infantry companies in World War II, Company E of the 141st Regiment. These men were a fine example of the Mexican-American soldiers who made such a great contribution to America in the war. They had added a brilliant chapter to American war history.

CAPTAIN GABRIEL NAVARRETE
El Paso, Texas
Distinguished Service Cross, Bronze Star, 2 Silver Stars
Mediterreanean Theater World War II

GABRIEL NAVARRETE

Gabriel Navarrete joined Co. E as a private in the pre-war National Guard days as part of the 141st Regiment, 36th (Texas) Division.

He was born March 18, 1915. Education: Cathedral High of El Paso, and Texas Western College.

Received Lieutenant's commission on the battlefield for his outstanding leadership. Commanded E Company during the the Italian campaign as 2nd Lieutenant. He rose to 1st Lieutenant, Captain and promoted to rank of Major at the end of hostilities. This rank he now holds in the Army Reserve.

Medals awarded. Two Silver Stars, the Distinguished Service Cross, the Bronze Star and seven Purple Hearts.

Was recommended for a Congressional Medal, which was withdrawn when he challenged a superior officer.

Now holds position of Veterans' Service Officer of El Paso County, Administrates office in El Paso County Courthouse, Texas.

Married, has four children.

Has been honored by the Mexican Government, Veterans of Foreign Wars, American Legion, and Disabled American Veterans for outstanding war services.

LOS DIABLOS AZULES (The Blue Devils)

The 88th was another Infantry Division in the Italian front that included many of our men.

This was the first 'all-selectee' Division that was brought up to aid the battle-tested combat groups, who had been battling the Germans since back in Africa and Sicily, and now comprised part of the 5th Army in Italy.

Their men were called *"Los Soldados a Huevo"* (soldiers by compulsion) by ribbing infantrymen of the other divisions who had doubting suspicions of their fighting ability. They quickly dispelled all doubts by their sterling performance on the battle-field, by the impressive record of their infantryman and by the many decorations they earned. After a couple of months in the Italian campaign, they were calling them, *"Blau Teufels"* or the Blue Devils.

> March 15, 1944—While fighting near Cassino with the 349th Infantry Regiment of the newly arrived 88th Division, Johnny Flores,[1] rifleman from Los Angeles, went out on a daylight patrol and heard a funny noise in a house two miles behind the German lines. Investigating, Flores burst in upon a Kraut officer writing a letter. Mustering all the courage he possessed, he harshly ordered the officer outside. He was astonished to have fourteen other Germans rush in from an adjoining room, meekly surrender, and join the party to be marched back to the American lines. He felt worse after he goose-stepped the supermen to a POW cage and then discovered that his rifle had been jammed all during the performance.[2]

For this daring exploit, Flores was recommended for a Silver Star, but he never received it. Instead, he was court-martialled because of a run-in with one of the officers of his Company. The officer complained that Flores had laughed at him when he ordered him to put on his helmet while out on night patrol. Flores contended it wasn't customary to wear a helmet in a night patrol since he was the lead scout, and furthermore, the officer "wasn't even on the patrol." He (Flores) could not resist telling the officer he did not agree, in no uncertain terms.

Many months later, Flores was awarded the Bronze Star for his "heroic acheivement" in volunteering to occupy a tower

---

[1]A well-known youth leader with the Catholic Youth Organization, active in athletics and now assistant matchmaker for Joe Louis in Los Angeles.

[2]Delaney, John P., *The Blue Devils In Italy,* Infantry Journal Press, Washington, D.C., 1947, p. 51.

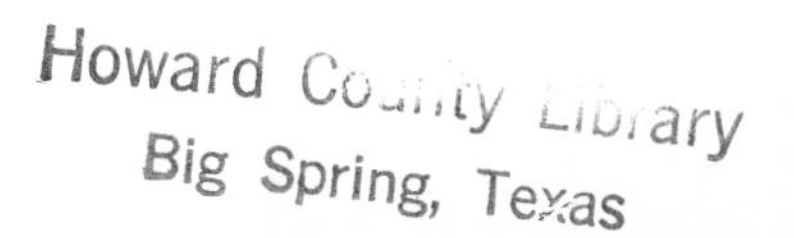

near the Arno River to observe German movements. The Germans spotted him, turned direct artillery on the observation post and reduced it to rubble. Flores received severe wounds on his back and neck. He was sent back to an Army hospital, then sent stateside and later honorably discharged.

There were many Mexican-Americans with the "Blue Devils." Being an all-selectee division and one of the first such divisions in Europe, they had many Mexican-born G.I.'s who were given a chance to become full American citizens while in the U.S. Army. There were also many officers of Mexican extraction who commanded infantry companies in the 88th. Among these were: Captain Carlos Teran,[1] Los Angeles, California; Lt. Mauricio Aragon, Avondale, Arizona; and Capt. Ernest Alonso, El Paso, Texas.

There were many other daring Mexican-Americans mentioned in the combat History book of the 88th "The Blue Devils in Italy," such as:

"Pfc. Felix B. Mestas, Laveta, Colorado, was awarded the Silver Star for bravery. Mestas manned a position on the forward slope for three days and with his BAR mowed the enemy down like grass as they vainly tried to get past him. On his last day in the most forward position, Mestas ordered his assistant gunner to leave, then killed 24 of the enemy before they overran his position. Mestas died giving his buddies time to regroup and beat off the attack. He received the Silver Star Medal posthumously."

"Sgt. Manuel Mendoza, "The Arizona Kid" from Tempe, Arizona, received the Distinguished Service Cross for his unselfish heroism when during a counterattack he opened up with a tommygun on 200 Jerries charging up the forward slope. Ten of them died where they fell, others lay wounded, but the rest

---

[1]Now Superior Court Judge in Los Angeles, the first American of Mexican extraction to be named to such a position since early California days.

came on. Mendoza, now using a carbine, emptied his entire ammo supply of five clips into their rushing ranks. A Flamethrower licked out at him but he felled the operator with a pistol shot. Jumping into a machine gun pit and pushing aside the dead gunner, Mendoza sprayed the surviving attackers until the gun jammed, then pitched hand grenades until the Germans withdrew. In spite of being severely wounded, he ran down the forward slope, retrieved enemy weapons lying there, captured a wounded Jerry and returned to consolidate his platoon's position."

"Hector M. Flores, Denver, Colorado, a Sergeant, en route to Belvedere at the head of his squad put three machine guns out of action took five prisoners after a hand-to-hand scuffle with one Kraut who succumbed to a blow on the head from his tommy gun.

"T/Sgt. Romeo Ramirez of Saticoy, California, another posthumous DSC winner, with a small band of 16 men clung through a bitter night to a half-wrecked and burning house. Ramirez and his group were cut off after the house had been surrounded. Ramirez posted his men at doors and windows and then gave battle. The Krauts finally set fire to the house with incendiaries. Although further resistance seemed useless, Ramirez induced his men to hold out. Through the night the fighting raged and when the dawn broke, the box score showed 22 Kraut dead, and 5 prisoners. On his side he lost 4 men, and 10 were wounded out of the 17 who had clung to the battered, half-burned building."

"Jose D. Sandoval of Santa Fe, New Mexico, fired his Browning automatic rifle until it heated and jammed. He then ran to a near-by machine gun whose crew was dead, unlocked the machine gun from its tripod and fired it from his hip, killing an unestimated number of the enemy.

"John S. Barron, Lane City, Texas, fighting near Mt. Grande with the 349th Infantry was one of the first to reach the ridge where he took a position near the corner of a house to cover his squad's approach. He was blazing away when a Kraut sniper wounded him in the leg. With only one round left, Barron 'butt-struck' a Kraut who rushed him then smashed his rifle over the head of a German officer who tried to get in the act.

"Rodolfo Sanchez of Boise, Idaho, head scout of E Company in the 351st, while marching along the road to Verona was suddenly surrounded by a group of Jerries which demanded that he surrender. Knowing that his squad would fall into ambush if he didn't warn them, Sanchez answered by firing his rifle grenade into the pavement at their feet. The shot killed three Germans and wounded seven as well as wounding Sanchez. Warned by his signal, the squad came up and captured the 30 survivors.

"Lt. Mauricio Aragon showed up one day at the 349 C.P. and told them he was very glad to have been awarded the Bronze Star, but that he would be much happier if the citation did not read "Posthumously Awarded." "When the shrapnel hit my wrist, on Hill 499, I told the platoon sergeant I was going back to the hospital," he related. Regimental Headquarters were a bit reluctant until field-commissioned Lieutenant Aragon appeared to convince one and all that the report of his death was erroneous.

These were *"Los Soldados A Huevo"* as the old regulars at first called them, *Los Diablos Azules.*

ANZIO AND CASSINO

The campaign in Italy continued on with many more Mexican-Americans covering themselves with glory on the battlefields. Two of them with the 34th Division, Pfc. David Gonzales of San Antonio, Texas, and Second Lieutenant Filberto Muñoz of Kansas City, Missouri, were among the troops who saw bitter fighting at Cassino.

On January 23, 1944, Lt. Muñoz, serving with Co. A, 135th Infantry of the 34th Division, led a patrol of 14 men, the first American troops to penetrate the town of Cassino which was the most bitterly contested German stronghold along the Gustav Line.

No sign of the enemy was found at the edge of the town, but as they advanced within 400 yards of the center of town, a German sentry gave the alarm. The well-hidden defenders, holed up among the buildings, opened up on the patrol with rifles, burp guns, and machine guns. Mortar crews in the nearby hills also opened up on them. Lt. Munoz was slightly wounded but managed to make it back to our lines with much valuable information. A few days later he was back in the line, and on February 5th, he was again wounded in Cassino, this time seriously enough to be shipped back to the States. Tech. Sgt. Raul Gonzales, Los Angeles, served with Co. 15th Regt., 3rd Division, at the Anzio Beachhead.

Gordon Moreno, Los Angeles, California, did some of his fighting in the high slopes against the German Ski troops with the U.S. 10th Mountain Division. Andrew S. Tamayo of Houston, Texas, with the 15th Infantry, 3rd Division, was in the drive to Naples and the crossing of the Volturno.

Pfc. John A. Lopez of Antonito, Colorado, who lost his life fighting with the 1st Armored in the 5th Army front was awarded the Silver Star, posthumously, for silencing a machine-gun nest singlehandedly. Although weak from loss of blood when hit by shrapnel, he held the German machinegunners at gunpoint until help arrived.

The 3rd, 36th and 45th Infantry divisions had the most battlefront casualties in WW II. All three fought in the Mediterranean, through Italy and in the invasion of France. All three numbered many Mexican-Americans in their ranks.

VIII

WAR TIME U.S.A.

March, 1944. The war was now at its peak after 2 years and 4 months. American combat troops were engaged in full scale against the enemy on both the Pacific and Italian war fronts. Russia was clamoring for a third front, and the opening of a new theatre by the Allies was expected at any moment.

The United States was going full blast in war production. Draft board quotas were being doubled. The Army was pouring more and more men into combat (Infantry) Divisions overseas. The big gaps caused by the high number of battle casualties at the front were being quickly filled by the gigantic Infantry-replacement training program set up by United States Army authorities.

Draft boards all over the country were now reaching into the older age bracket for their manpower. Married men were being reclassified and the draft age had been raised to include men over 26 years of age.

I too found myself among the many married men of the older age bracket who were reclassified and called to the colors during the war peak.

My 'greetings' came unexpectedly, but things happened fast those days. In the short space of a few weeks, we were reclassified, ordered to take the army physical, inducted and sent out to an Army base.

Three of us married men were called up at the same time: Gordon Moreno, a friend and neighbor of 31, Edward Perez, who was my age, 32, and I. Along with three teen-agers --Tommy Lovario, Manuel Sandoval, and Robert Nunez, all 19

—we were sent by bus from Los Angeles to Fort Mc Arthur at San Pedro, California, where we joined thousands of other draftees and took the I.Q. test to determine which branch of the service we were best fitted for.

Mc Arthur was a stopping place for all inductees from the Sixth Corp area. Here we were to be processed, issued clothing and to await shipment to a training camp. In the reception center were many other Mexican-Americans from different parts of Southern California and Arizona.

There were no lonely or depressed draftees among us. We developed quick friendships, and were not like the majority of the other inductees whose groups were usually larger than ours; these keeping to themselves and taking their new Army life very seriously. While the many other draftees were moody and quiet, our bunch actually were enjoying their first day in the Army, laughing and greeting each other happily.

"Ese!" (Slang for "Hey you!") was usually our first word of greeting. Always it was, "Where are you from?" and, "Do you know so and so there?" And, sure enough, someone always knew about friends or relatives from the other's hometown. It seemed that everyone had relatives from Los Angeles.

Our people have the same common spirit. Here were these individuals who had never met before, and yet at the very first contact everyone acted as though they had known each other for a long time.

On the first night at the reception center, all the *palomilla,* (slang for gang) approximately 30, as if by a prearranged plan automatically gathered outside the barracks to get better acquainted. Soon someone brought out a guitar and we began singing songs, old and new, all familiar to us. As the best singers were paired off, the songfest kept getting louder and the tempo picking up.

We were in a happy mood, for we had joy, music, song

—and nobody knew where it came from. Soon there was a bottle of *Fuerte,* (hard liquor). Someone kept yelling, "*que linda es mi raza!*" The hour was late and we must have gotten too loud, the C.O. came down and chased us all off to bed.

Processing took about six days. We filled out insurance and allotment papers, were given I.Q. tests, and were read the Articles of War. Then came the march to the camp barber shop for the G.I. haircuts. Many—especially the younger set felt naked with so little hair left on their noggins. We all protested loudly about the amateur haircut. The young recruits actually felt hurt to shed so much of their hair, for it was the trend to sport a big "*greña*" (hair-do), whether they were *Pachuco* (popular youth-type in those days) or not.

After the hair cut, we marched in line to the Supply Building and suited up in G.I. clothing. With the same fit (usually too large) and wrinkled uniform, we all looked like the proverbial G.I. Joe! The only thing that distinguished us was the fact that we could speak both English and Spanish. We applied our bilingual advantage to the utmost; using Spanish to understand each other better, and to curse the damn Sergeants who kept blowing their whistles every ten minutes.

Most of the Mexican-Americans who were being drafted then were assigned to the Army and put in the Infantry. The saying was, "Mexicans, Oakies, Polacks, and Wops. That's all you see in the Infantry." Actually, Mexican-Americans were in all of the branches—in the Navy, Marines, Air Force and in such specialized units as the Airborne, Armored Infantry, Submarines, Seabees, Combat Engineers, Anti-Aircraft, Artillery, Cavalry, Coast Guard, M.P.'s and the Medics.

After several days of processing and I.Q. tests, we awaited the word that would let us know where we were to be sent. Recruits went out every day by train, bus, or truck to the many training camps that the government had established throughout the U.S. Some eventually would end up in the Air Corps,

Signal Corps, Medics, or in an Army Cooks and Bakers School.

We all took the same tests, for the purpose of finding out which branch of the service one was best fitted for. The only thing we found out about the tests, really, was that perhaps in the early days of the war the results of the I.Q. tests did have a bearing on which unit you were assigned to. But by the years of 1943, '44 and '45, as far as the Army was concerned, you were just a number. The tests had no bearing on where you would be sent and besides, the Infantry needed more men than all the other services combined.

All of us had pipe-dreams of being assigned to the more glamorous branches of the service, such as the Air Corps, Artillery, Signal Corps, or Special Services, and also of being sent to some training camp in some distant state; perhaps even in Texas, where I would have been close to relatives. When we finally "woke up," we discovered that it was to be the same state, and the same branch. That's right, the outfit nobody wanted—the INFANTRY. I bade goodbye to new-found friends, and off we were—to Camp Roberts, California.

REPLACEMENT TRAINING

Of the many training camps activated by Uncle Sam during World War II, none had so many Mexican-American trainees as the IRTC camps at Fanning, Swift, and Bowie in Texas; Robinson in Arkansas; Polk, Claiborne, and Erwin in Louisiana; Blanding, Florida; Croft of South Carolina; Beale and Roberts in California.

These Infantry Replacement Training Centers were set up by the United States Army to train the many replacements that they had long anticipated would be needed to defeat the well-trained German and Japanese Armies, which had been fighting since 1939.

For training his Infantry forces, Uncle Sam picked the most isolated and lonely locations in the South and Southwest.

Places where one would find rugged terrain, high mountains, dry desert, and swampy marshes. Ideal as this may have been for desert training, mountain fighting or jungle warfare tactics, to the raw recruit these places represented a "Hell on earth" and prospects of a disheartening future.

The Infantry Replacements received an intensive 17-week course in all phases of ground fighting. After four months of Infantry training, the recruits then were supposed to be ready for combat duty. These replacements were then sent to the war zones, assigned to some combat unit to replace battle casualties in the front lines, or wherever the need might be.

Camp Roberts, California, was a typical Infantry training center. Here we landed, right in the middle of nowhere, a spread that extended over a large, wide range bordered by high rocky hills and deep ravines; an area that was hot and dusty in the summer, cold and rainy in the winter, a very desolate country. The location was between Los Angeles and San Francisco, but you could swear there was nothing "California" about it.

Here we were to learn Army discipline, where we would be transformed from soft civilians to hard-bitten soldiers, "where the men would be separated from the boys." We heard so much of this that by the time we arrived there, we had a pretty good idea of what was in store for us. The moment the non-coms from the Cadre set eyes on us, we knew pretty well what was running through their minds. They seemed to be saying, "Are we going to put you guys through the wringer!" Many of us had that dumb and befuddled look about us as we glanced around the strange surroundings and you could hardly have blamed the non-coms if they wondered what a dumb-looking bunch of Mexicans we were. Their job was going to be a little harder with us, because not only did they have to convert us from civilians to soldiers, but also from *Mexicans* to Americans.

There were many Mexican-American trainees in Camp Roberts, and no way of telling how many thousands of them had *passed through* there before us. They had been *coming and going* since the early days of peace-time draft, when Uncle Sam had reactivated many old training centers, and after the beginning of the war had opened up many new sites. Many of the combatmen who were then fighting in the Infantry Divisions in both the Pacific and European battlefronts had taken their basic training at Camp Roberts.

In Roberts, the majority of the *raza* (belonging to the same *Latin* race) were from Los Angeles, from well-known neighborhoods such as Maravilla, Flats, Palo Verde, Dog Town, Boyle Heights, Belvedere, Happy Valley, Vernon, Watts, South Los Angeles, Clanton and West Los Angeles. These were the *barrios,* made famous by the gangs, athletic clubs or girl friends they remembered.

April, May, June—1944. Basic training life was a very interesting experience. Finding ourselves in a new setting away from the old surroundings, with new faces, new friends, and everyone in the same boat, put us on equal status. Most impressive was the smooth way that Americans of all nationalities were assimilated in their new life.

For many there was nothing too unusual about living, working and playing together with groups of many different races. We had been doing it back home; in school, where we worked and in the daily social and recreational activities. But there were many who came from various and different types of sectors of the United States where minority groups were kept segregated, or where minority groups were small in number. Here for the first time in their lives they became acquainted and really got to know their fellow countryman of a different nationality and racial background.

Army life afforded many their first experiment in putting into practice a *real* democracy, a simple, quiet democracy effected without any pressure or compromise. We were so engrossed in our new chores of soldier life, and so aware of an uncertain future, that no room was left for anyone to be choosy about his neighbor. No one went about demanding special treatment, or complaining about unequal opportunities.

Here we learned all there was to know about each other. In the course of our continuous association, all characteristics, personal traits and individualisms were openly revealed so that no one could hide anything from the other.

Rich or poor, light or dark, the educated and the ignorant—all were thrown together to accomplish the same objective, mainly that of learning military skills; and all were subjected to the same rude Army discipline. Our inert qualities were discovered and the superficial appearances soon wore off. In the test for the Infantry, only the more basic qualities were needed. What mattered most was that you had to be rough, tough and alert of mind.

What do you do in the Infantry? The song goes on with the words, "You march . . . you march . . . you march." Not only did we march, march, and march, we many times hurried and then waited, slept very little and were kept half-starved. We learned many new curses and risque jokes, made like a jackass with a full field pack, carried rain coats on dry days, none when it rained, played poker and shot dice a lot, went through hundreds of short-arm inspections, got our arms shot full of holes by medics, got "Sick, Lame, and Lazy," went AWOL, and like all the wise-guy recruits, soon learned to "keep our mouths shut, eyes and ears open" and to "never volunteer for anything."

The average Army G.I. went through practically the same cycle of events that occur in all training camps, since there wasn't very much difference in camp life those days. However, we Mexican-Americans had a few extra escapades that we shared among ourselves. As for myself, the moments that I enjoyed and like to remember the most are the times spent with *la Raza* in the early days of Camp Roberts. We were always seeking each other out; we enjoyed our particular type of fun. In the many tiring field problems when the going got rough, we would shout to each other, *"No te rajes!"* (Don't give up.)

Always the older ones were concerned with the young trainees, in a fatherly way, or as a matter of pride. In many instances, when one of them wavered or got downhearted, someone was sure to shout, *"Orale! No dejes que la Raza quede mal."* ("Come now! Don't make the 'Race' look bad.") Not so much as to reprimand, but to give them encouragement.

Had it not been for the many *Chicanos* at Roberts, I probably never would have remembered that dry hole. Every evening after getting back to camp from the long hikes and hard field problems, you could always see them jostling around. Young *"pachuquitos"*—who often bragged of being veterans of the *Pachuco-Zoot-Suit war*[1]—would be wrestling, fighting, cursing, and yelling. No one could figure out how they could generate so much energy. All of us old codgers felt deadly tired after the long hard day, and only after visiting the mess hall for chow would we come back to life.

After chow we would make a bee-line for the PX to fill up with beer, then gather outside to make a party of it. The boys with the *liras* (guitars) would then take over . . . It seemed that wherever we gathered there would be two or three who played a good guitar and sang rather well. Gregorio "Pancho" Ramirez from Austin, Texas, was one of the good entertainers, and was always in demand by the Special Services officers who staged camp shows to entertain the trainees, and by us whenever we had one of the impromtu 'parties' that lasted way into the night.

---

[1]See page 56.

One of the outstanding characteristics of the Mexican is his ability to sing and the songs that he sings. The saying goes that a Mexican *"canta con el alma."* (sings with his soul). There are many songs in Spanish known throughout the world but very few people really understand Mexican folklore ballads. These songs have a feeling that comes from the heart of a humble and proud Race. In his memoirs of the Mexican-American War, Sam Chamberlain tells of hearing the Mexican soldiers who were camped close to the American troops on the eve of the battle of Buena Vista:

> "The American troops actually enjoyed listening to the strumming of guitars and the singing of the Mexicans, and I recall that at the end of nearly every song they always let out a long melancholy yell that seemed to convey pain and suffering in the heart of the individual".[2]

The Mexican and Mexican-American for that matter, has a song for every mood that he happens to be in. When he feels happy, carefree or in love, he is most likely to come out singing a *Ranchera,* a high yelling song of the peasant, or a *Corrido,* a fast ballad. If he is sad or in a reminiscing mood, he will sing a *Bolero* (torch song) or a *Huapango.* If he feels remorseful, angry or jealous, a song of spite and challenge.

The songs we sang in camp embraced all of these different sentiments. We would go through the whole repertoire of the many singers we had in the gang. The astonishing things about so many good voices was that they were found in such small groups. Duets, trios, and quartets, we had them all, and they all sounded very professional.

Sentimental war story writers have always lamented the fact that no soldier song of World War II ever reached the popularity of such songs as "My Buddy" and "Madamoselle

---

[1]*The Mexican War Memoirs of Soldier-Artist Samuel E. Chamberlain,* **Life** Magazine, July 30, 1956, p. 52.

from Armentiers" of World War I. The most popular tune among the G.I.'s in W.W. II, "Lily Marlene," was taken from the Germans by the Allied soldiers at the front. With us it was different, for we had not one but several songs that were popular during the war. One of the most popular was *"Soldado Razo"* (Common Soldier). This song concerns a young Mexican who is going to the warfront, and it expresses Courage and Love to his mother, his sweetheart, to his country and his religion. The words, translated, went something like this:

I leave as a common soldier,
I'm going to join the ranks.
I will be among the Brave boys
who leave their beloved mothers
and sweethearts in tears,
crying for their departure.
I'm leaving for the war, contented.
I have my rifle and gun ready.
When all the shooting is over,
I will return as a Sergeant.
The only one thing I regret,
Is leaving my poor Mother alone.
Oh brunette Virgin, please take care of her.
Watch over her, she is a wonderful person.
Please take care of her till I return.
I will depart at early morn tomorrow,
right at the break of day.
And so . . . hereforth goes another Mexican
who is willing to gamble his life.
And I say goodbye with this song . . .
Long live this Country of mine.

(F.V. Leal)

Jose Mendoza, who saw war service in the Pacific and now operates a guitar shop in Los Angeles, says that *"Soldado Razo"* was Number One of the Spanish Hit Parade during

W.W. II. "Everywhere that Mexicans would gather, here and overseas, they were sure to ask for *"Soldado Razo."* That song was good for one thousand dollars ($1,000) while singing with a trio in Olvera Street at one dollar a song, before and after my enlistment. Another very popular song was *"Vengo a Decirle Adios a Los Muchachos."* (Bidding goodbye to the boys.)

Training, hard as it was under a sweltering California sun, was lightened because of the fun we got out of the obstacle problems and the way we would chide anyone that would not stand up under the hard, vigorous tasks the Cadre put us through. Since most of the fellows were from the Southwest, they were accustomed to the hot and low-humidity weather in Roberts, and consequently, could "take it" better than those that came from cold-weather country, such as the upper Middlewest and Northern States.

On our final twenty-five mile hike that all trainees had to make at the end of the training cycle, we found out how much the constant *vaciladas* and chiding had affected our morale. The long trek was made on a hot day under very dry and stuffy weather, accompanied by an unbearable thirst. We were allowed only one canteen of water, and with clothing sticking to our tired bodies to add to the full discomfort, it was terribly unbearable. The steady pace set by the well-conditioned non-coms soon sapped all the strength out of the GI trainees. We had started in the early, cool morning, and by noon we had gone half the distance with the hot sun at its peak. Trainees began to drop off like flies, with blisters on their feet, cramps in their stomach, or short of wind. Every hour we would get a ten minute break. If we noticed someone of our group about to quit, we would warn him with, *"No se raje, cabron!"* (Don't give up, you goat! (slang) We would make them feel that we were all together and that no one would be permitted to quit.

In the ten minute breaks, all the other GI's laid down and stretched themselves on the ground, dead tired, cursing, and whining. They were surprised—and actually mad—when we stayed on our feet and broke out singing *"La Feria de Las Flores" or* some other peppy *Ranchera.* At the end of the song, as customary, we let out a big long yell, and said, *"Las mas grande el que se raje!"* to curse anyone that quit.

None of the G.I.'s in our group gave up, and we all made it into camp in high spirits, yelling and singing. At last we detected a smile on the faces of the non-coms who came in with us.

IX

D DAY

June 6, 1944. D Day was known in history as the greatest invasion operation of W.W. II, with the largest number of ships participating (4,000), and the biggest number of assault forces (66,000 men) landing in the longest stretch of heavily-defended shoreland, the 1,000 mile Normandy coast between La Havre and Cherbourg.

Every type of modern war weapon was utilized and every branch of service put into use by the American, English, Allies, Germans and Axis Forces. Assembled here were airplanes, Navy ships, transports, assault boats, landing craft, liners, cutters, minesweepers, warships, and gliders. Block-ships were sunk to form breakwaters and huge floating harbors were towed across the channel in sections.

The Navy, Air Force, Coast Guard, Army and Airborne troops all participated with equal effectiveness. Thousands of planes maintained a protective umbrella over the landing area. Airborne troops descended behind enemy lines. Naval guns engaged shore batteries. Mine sweepers drove in through shallow water, blowing up underwater obstacles, then the landing craft began bringing in the largest mass of men and supplies ever attempted in war history.

Catarino "Cato" Cuellar, Lockart, Texas; Raul Rosales and Joe Ramirez of Houston, Texas; Frank P. Martinez and Guillermo "Memo" Terrazas of Los Angeles, California—these were among the many thousands who participated in the memorable D Day landing on the Normandy Beach to open up a western front on the impregnable 'Hitler fortress.'

Both Cuellar and Ramirez were line sergeants in the 2nd Division. Ramirez was reported missing. Cuellar and Terrazas were both badly wounded, but returned later to the front lines. They saw a lot of their buddies killed right next to them trying to make the beach. They'll forever remember the ghastly horrors on the beach that day. They vividly recall how the drivers of the LST's could not get close enough to the beaches because of the heavy fire from the Jerry 88's. They still hear the rattle of the machine guns that raked the shore line downing many of their comrades, who drowned in the deep waters laden down with the heavy gear they carried. Their memory is still saddened by the many dead bodies of American GI's they saw floating in the waters, remembering the many who never got ashore, and the many who died as they set foot on French soil.

Manuel Nuñez, Manny Bernal, 82nd Airborne, "Chuy" Galvan and Mundo Lozano with the 101st 'Screaming Eagles' all from Los Angeles but unknown to each other, were with the many advance troops that parachuted down behind the German lines—the first American combatmen to do ground fighting on French soil.

At 0100 of D Day, the Allied Airborne Paratroopers in the dark of night plunged into space from transport planes and gliders to prepare the way for assault troops that would be landing all over the Normandy coast. They worked behind the lines disrupting communications and supply lines, clearing main causeways and fighting from the very moment they landed. Many of them were shot down by the alerted enemy as they descended. Despite the strange country and the necessity of fighting in the dark, the American Airborne Infantrymen contributed invaluable assistance to the Allied assault troops that landed later that day.

To counteract the long anticipated move, the Germans had built solid defensive positions with concrete-built pillboxes and dug deep ditches to stop the men and armoured vehicles. They moved in railroad guns and built concrete machine gun emplacements on the hilltops; they had crossfire covering the entire beach line. Off the shore, they had floating mines and landing obstacles; along the shore they had buried land mines by the thousands in the sand. Behind their lines they had great concentration of land troops ready to give battle to the landing forces and well-planned synchronized reserves that would move additional Divisions to the front on a moment's notice.

German ack-ack installations filled the sky with flak. The Stukas and Messerschmitts of the Luftwaffe, went out to give battle to the invading airmen. Their manpower far out-numbered ours, and they had the advantage of the higher terrain. It was hard for our combat troops to move uphill, heavily-laden as they were with combat equipment and through waist-deep waters facing the murderous enemy fire. Many lives and vital supplies were lost in the landing.

Back home, the whole Nation awaited anxiously for news of how the invasion had fared. Prayers were offered for the many troops participating. We paid a dear price for this maneuver, but the invasion was a success. The Germans were pushed back, and the war picture took on a new aspect. Everyone in America and throughout the world now felt that it would not be long before Hitler would be defeated.

The 2nd 'Indian Head' Division, which landed on D Day plus one, had many Mexican-Americans from south Texas. The division called Fort Sam Houston their home. Other GI's who participated with the 2nd Division were S/Sgt. Agustin Lucio, San Marcos, Texas, of Co. L, 23rd Regt., and Pedro Rubio, Austin, Texas, who operated on a wounded comrade under heavy enemy fire, removing a bullet from his thigh with a pocket kife. Vincent Gonzales, Rio Hondo, Texas, received the Silver Star for crawling under a sheet of heavy machine gun fire from the high bluffs of Omaha Beach to give first aid to

STAFF SERGEANT AGUSTIN LUCIO
San Marcos, Texas
Silver Star, Bronze Star, Purple Heart and the French Croix de Guerre
European Theatre World War II

two wounded comrades. All of them were wounded in action and sent to ship hospitals. Lucio and Rubio returned to their outfit after being released from the hospital. Gen. Norman D. Cota headed the 29th Division at Omaha Beach.

Once ashore, the ground troops began making headway. They hurled the Nazi defenders out of their positions, blasted them right in their foxholes and pillboxes with flame throwers, automatic weapons, mortars and grenades.

June 11, 1944. The dogged infantrymen with the 1st, 2nd, 4th, 9th and 29th Divisions drove an even seven-mile wedge into the Cherbourg peninsula. By then, additional Infantry Divisions had landed in France to give aid to the fighting Allied forces. Among them were the 79th, direct from England, a division with many Mexican-Americans, many of whom I got to know personally later on. A big tank battle was waged between American and German armored units led by General Von Runsted. Five thousand German prisoners were taken by American forces in this 15-mile Normandy strip.

On June 18th, the 79th moved into the outskirts of the French port of Cherbourg. First Lt. Agustin Barron, El Paso, with the 313th Regiment, Rudy Mesa and Joe Montano, Los Angeles, with the 314th Regiment, were with the foot soldiers of the 79th who relieved the regiments of the 90th Division in the shattered French port, which had been completely destroyed by the war. Meeting stiff opposition that led to bitter hand-to-hand fighting, the Yanks finally took Cherbourg and trapped 30,000 German 'supermen.'

After his return from a base hospital for treatment of wounds received in the D Day landing, Memo Terrazas also joined the 79th and was assigned to the 315th Regiment. He saw heavy action with the 79th at Saint-Lo, Fougeres, Le Mans, and later when the 79th crossed the Seine River. After the crossing of the Seine River, Terrazas was wounded for the second time. He received serious wounds of the head and arms. His side and leg were shattered by artillery blasts. His critical condition required immediate evacuation from the front lines. He was first sent to England, then finally to the U.S. by plane. He remembers 'coming to' in a mental ward of some Army hospital in the States with impaired speech and complete loss of memory.

LAST DAYS AT HOME

June 6th, 1944. D Day in Europe . . . and we were still in dirty old Camp Roberts. Weren't we ever going into the damn war? Some of the younger GI's really felt that way, but not us old family men. With us, the feeling— and wishful thinking —was that somehow the war would be over before we would be sent overseas. If only we were as free as the single men in camp, we would not have to worry about leaving a family behind. It was not easy to tear away from your loved ones.

Basic training had been a vigorous routine. By the end of the 17 weeks, most of us were rounding into shape. Everyone looked 'sharper,' and the drinking bouts we staged by the PX kept getting rougher and rougher. They all ended up in the same way .. . GI's fighting and slugging each other. Everyone was itching to get into the big scrap.

Despite all the talk about what a lousy camp Roberts was, we were beginning to enjoy it there. Things were changing. The non-coms, who at first delighted themselves in browbeating us, started treating us like decent human beings, except for a few duty-bound morons who were always bucking for an extra stripe. Most sergeants and corporals still acted the hard-boiled-type, all we did about it was just look at each other. They would over-do it more when they were within earshot of company officers. A few of us would be invited to the 'private' gambling games in Cadre Sgt. Harris' quarters, where most of the non-coms would take off their stripes to become 'regular guys.'

Mexican-Americans in Roberts still ganged around together, and in addition, we had picked up a lot of '*gabacho*' (Anglo) buddies. For instance there was Tony Despagne, born and raised in Texas, who could understand *chicano* talk better than English, and who was familiar with all our customs; Leonard Muschinsky, a young Polish kid from Brenham, Texas, of all places; and Robert Smargeanian, an Armenian, who got indoctrinated with *pachuco-ism* in East Los Angeles. They, and many others got a bang out of hanging around with the Mexican-American *plebe.* They even learned to eat the 'hot stuff' the fellows used to bring in from town to spice the tasteless (to us) G.I. chow.

Because most of the trainees at Roberts were from the Middle-west and Northern part of the United States, it was not surprising to find many who had never associated or had ever seen a Mexican before. We were amused with the description they gave and the concept they had of a Mexican back in their hometowns. Walt Musick, from South Dakota, was being very frank when he told us, "The only Mexicans we ever saw back home were those that worked in the Railroad and lived in section houses. I always heard that they were not to be trusted, and if you turned your back to them, they would knife you in the back. But these fellows I have known here in Roberts are just like other Americans."

Even the trainees who hailed from Texas were a friendly lot. Back in the old CCC days, every time a Texan and a Mexican crossed paths there was sure to be a brawl. There never was any trace of racial strife in Camp Roberts.

The most appreciated fact about Camp Roberts was that it was close to Los Angeles. Everyone who got a weekend pass made a bee-line to the "City of Angels." Every Saturday afternoon we had to fight for space in cars belonging to some of the comrades who lived in Los Angeles. On week-ends, there was always a steady stream of cars tearing into Los Angeles both on the coast and the inland routes. One chap whose father owned a mortuary drove a hearse into camp and always had a fullhouse going into town.

After the hectic week-ends in Los Angeles, the gang would always gather around to tell of the good times they had in the City and about the many popular night-clubs they had taken in. To hear them say it, everyone of them was a playboy and a great lover. They bragged about the many *'lindas'* and 'shack-up jobs' they had in town.

When at last our company, the 76th, completed the 17-week training cycle, all kinds of 'latrine rumors' began to circulate. Some said we were going to the Pacific, others said that we were going to Europe, and another said—this one we liked—that we were staying in the States and would be given a job to train other Army recruits. Everyone smiled when they heard that one.

Late in July, 1944, our moving-out orders came through. These included a ten-day furlough and specific orders to report to Fort Meade, Maryland, on the East Coast.

My first five days were spent in Los Angeles at home with the wife and three children. I found the great city going full blast with war activity. The whole town was overcrowded with defense workers, *braceros*[1], sailors, marines and soldiers on pass or AWOL.

Out on North Main Street, Provost Sgt. Pete Despart, Chief Little Wolf and Jerry Gioviano were kept busy making room for more G.I.'s in their hotel (the Army stockade) due to the many AWOL's the MP's kept rounding up.

My five days at home went by too soon. It wasn't easy to leave, this time it was different. There were so many things to worry about . . . the wife, the children, Olivia aged 4, David aged 3, Eddie aged 2, they would have to carry on in case I

---

[1]Contract laborers from Mexico.

didn't return . . . Most of our ugly thoughts were put off. We pretended that it was just another short trip, that I would be back in a few days.

There were church services, short visits to near relatives and friends, many goodbyes . . . and off we were.

My next stop was San Antonio, Texas, where I spent the next few days with my mother and sister. San Antonio was about the busiest Army town I had ever seen. There were many Army camps, airfields, and training centers, and towering above all, the gigantic Fort Sam Houston, the U.S. 4th Corp Area Army Headquarters. With so many soldiers around, civilians were a rare sight.

Most surprising to me was the sudden disappearance of all the old *palomilla* I used to know there. They had all gone into the service, many of them had been among the early volunteers. Hardly any of them had been 'deferred' or found 'unfit for Army duty' like where I came from. Even those with three or four dependents were taken in the early part of the draft. No one was classified 'exempt' because of vital defense occupation here.

In such places as Lockhart, San Marcos and Austin, where I spent my early youth, I learned that friends and relatives with whom I had grown up were long since in the service. Many of them had already seen plenty of combat duty overseas. Some had been wounded and were being treated in Army hospitals far away from the combat zones.

At last my short furlough came to an end. Once again it was hard to say goodbye. My mother and sisters were very serious about my going away, but I managed to ease their minds, assuring them that the war was about over and that we would probably be used as occupational troops.

As I boarded the train that was to take me to Washington, D.C., I ran into some of the fellows who were also on their way to Fort Meade. At the S.P. station in San Antonio I met

Joe Ramirez, a short stocky youngster, and Tony Rodriguez, in his late forties, married and father of six. From near-by Austin, there was Gregorio 'Pancho' Ramirez, that very good singer and guitar player who had delighted us in our training days, also Jose T. Ramirez and Jose Nerios, both mature family men and farmers from south Texas. We all had been at Camp Roberts and now had the same destination. When we boarded the train, we found more of the Camp Robert's bunch. Young, recently married, Mike Tapia from Ontario, California; Juan Arlee, an oldster from Pasadena, and Bobby Nunez, Gilbert Villegas, Jimmy Desma, all from Los Angeles. The five of them, all teen-agers, were full of fun and took soldiering, the war, and the going away trip very lightly. From Denver there was Jess Martinez, a quiet married man about 30; Joe Arvisu and Lupe Gonzales from south Arizona, also Carlos Amor and Manuel Davila, two quiet men from the border who hardly spoke in English.

We represented the average Mexican-American replacement group that were being sent out to the war front in those days.

We had all trained together with the 76th Infantry Regiment at Roberts, and now were all going overseas as replacements together, some to never return, and others to just barely make it back . . .

X

THE ETO CAMPAIGN

THE TRIP ACROSS

August, 1944. Fort Meade, Maryland. Replacement troops arrived here daily by the thousands. They came from all sections of the country. The majority were from the IRTC camps of the South, Southwest, Far West, and Middlewest. From such Army replacement camps as Erwin, Swift, Blanding, Robinson, Croft, Hood, Walters, Claiborne, Beale, Gruber, Roberts, and of course, the big Infantry Officer's Candidate School and Airborne training centers at Fort Benning, Georgia.

There was quite a visible contrast between the Mexican-Americans we first met at the reception centers and training camps and the ones we encountered at the staging area centers and ports of embarcation, where we spent our last days before being shipped out of the United States. We never have forgotten how almost everyone of us looked ragged and sloppy in our early recruit days. These GI's here presented an entirely different aspect now. All of them looked sharp and snappy.

We took pride in our appearance and the way we wore the uniform. Besides going to pains to keep it well pressed, many spent their small army pay to buy tailor-made khakis and caps. A favorite trick to improve the G.I. garb was to use rubber bands around the legs inside the trousers so the pants would hang real low giving them the "*pachuco*" look.

Basic training had done a lot to improve the appearance and character of these boys. Back in training camps you hardly ever noticed a non-com among the trainees and since no stripes were earned in training, it was indeed a rare sight to see a rated man. We now had many non-coms and commissioned officers among us. We felt very proud about them.

Fort Meade was a dream camp in those days. The food was good and plentiful, we had no duties to perform and passes were issued freely to Washington D.C., Baltimore and other near-by towns everyday. We had plenty of entertainment; there were stage shows and boxing bouts every afternoon. Every night came bus-load after bus-load of girl hostesses from near-by Washington, Baltimore and Virginia, brought in for the big dances at the club house. We spent much of the time taking in the big dice games and sitting in on the poker sessions. Big games were held in almost every barrack where the boys with the big bankrolls, crooked dice and marked cards were making a daily killing.

In the nearby towns, everything was wide open, bookies, dives, bistros and clip joints did big business. All the citizens, the authorities and female population treated every serviceman like a king. Nothing was too good for us those days. The only bad thing about it was that we knew it would not last. People were only over-nice to us because these would perhaps be our last days in our homeland. Many other GI's who had been there before us had been treated the same way.

At Meade, the big question was where we were to go next. We found out that the longest we would be kept there was six days. Only one thing was certain, we were going overseas and our destination would be the European Theater of Operations; but would it be Italy, France or England for more training?

We were asked to turn in all of our old clothing. New clothing and shoes were issued. Brand new gear and field equipment was also given to us, along with blankets and comforters. Next, we had all our clothing and equipment 'impregnated' to make them weather-proof. Everyone received a gas mask and we were told this was a most essential item overseas.

When they gave us brand new Thompson sub-machine guns full of heavy grease, we were elated over speculation that we would be assigned to a Military Police battalion overseas. We were told to clean them thoroughly as they were to be our weapons from then on. Everyone agreed wholeheartedly that being an M.P. was a softer job than that of a frontline soldier.

Around midnight, we were marched out of the camp with our heavy packs and tommy guns into the near-by railroad station where we boarded a train. In the darkness and with the lights out, it was impossible to tell in which direction the train was headed, but by early morning we knew we were going through Philadelphia. After New Jersey, we made a brief stop in New York City. Our final stop was Providence, Rhode Island. Security regulations made it necessary to have us arrive at our new destination in the dark of night.

Our new location—we learned later—was Camp Myles Standish, a port of embarcation station located close to Boston, Massachusetts, and just out of Taunton. This was to be our last stop in the United States. We were placed 'on alert', and confined to the area, which meant that passes to town would not be issued to anyone.

We were kept in groups, even when we went to the mess hall we would all be marched in together. No chance was given to anyone to be absent without being missed right away.

Once again we had a lot of time on our hands. The only duty we had was "bunk fatigue" and "comforter drill." Everyone spent the time writing letters or gambling. From then on, our post office address was APO, New York, N.Y. This would be our address from now on until we were back home. All mail leaving Myles Standish was being censored, there was no way of telling the folks back home that we were still in the good old U.S.A. and on our way to the E.T.O . . .

By the time we got to the embarcation center, our group had been enlarged. Besides the original gang that had left Camp Roberts together, we now had many other Spanish-speaking GI's assigned to our group in Fort Meade, and since having arrived at Myles Standish we had made many new acquaintances among the others who were also going overseas. Among the new faces were: Rudy Ortiz, whom I had known in Los Angeles where he had been an upholsterer; Frankie Escobar, a well-liked youngster who called Mountain View, California his home. Frankie was a very promising boxer who had scored some good wins in the camp bouts at Meade. He had endeared himself to the other GI's having whacked the daylights out of a loudmouth gambling Texan whom he caught switching a pair of six-ace flats in one of the 'big' games. Escobar made the switch artist give back his loot to all losers in the game. Another was Frank Padilla, a tall good looking lad who hailed from L.A. and claimed to be from the old 38th Street gang. Sgt. Romero Peru, a real *mejicano* came from the state of Sonora, Mexico, with plenty on the ball. In his heavy-accented English he was constantly called upon by the C.O. in charge, to lecture to the many groups that were on their way to Europe about metric equivalents; how the table of measurements in Europe, also used in Mexico, compared to the measurements in the U.S.

Among the others of the newcomers were: Leandro Esquivel, Fort Lupton, Colorado; Benjamin Soto, San Marcos, Texas; Joe Casiano, Corpus Christi, Texas; Luis Gomez, Frankie Arredondo, Carlos Abril, all of Phoenix, Arizona; and Armando Gonzales, a Puerto Rican.

Evenings we would gather at the beer garden behind the big P.X., to discuss the camps where each one of us had taken basic training. Everyone insisted that his camp had been the the worst and the weather there the hottest. An amusing fact we discovered was that the same rumor—or tale—prevailed in all the different camps. This was that in the Pacific, General Douglas McArthur had stated he did not want any more replacements from this or that camp because by the time they had finished basic training there, the trainees were burned out and not fit for combat duty.

In the daytime, when we weren't having inspection or lectures, we were taking shots or getting vaccinated for typhus and colds. We would be taken out on a large lake located amid the camp area where they had built a large model ship. With the whole company taking part, some aboard ship and the rest at the lake's edge, they gave instructions through a loud-speaker as to the correct and incorrect way of embarking and disembarking from a troop ship. Also, the nomenclature of a ship, the different terms used by the Navy with which we had not been familiar in the Army, such as: deck, cabin, the head, fore and aft, ship's store, etc., and to never call the ship a 'boat.' We also went through dry runs of abandoning ship, with full field packs and equipment, in case of disaster or being torpedoed. They would announce a long list of things that were allowed on ship and those that were prohibited. The worst one, according to the low moaning of the crowd, and especially those of us who had gotten the gambling fever, was "gambling aboard ship while enroute is prohibited." This was always topped off with, ". . . so the soldier with the loaded dice may as well throw them away now."

After we had finished the dirty job of cleaning the heavy cosmoline oil from the tommy guns, they made us turn them in. We were then issued regular M-I rifles. This, we presumed, was to be our Number One weapon overseas. We knew then that it couldn't be anything else but infantry duty in the front lines, and not the M.P.'s as we had been hoping.

September, 1944. After our brief stay in Standish, we moved out by train to the Commonwealth Pier, Port of Embarcation in Boston. The going away was made as cheerful as possible

... a military band played patriotic marches, such tunes as "Over There" and "Hail, Hail" ... pretty Red Cross girls with cheerful smiles passed out hot coffee and doughnuts. For security reasons, no one other than military personnel was permitted at the pier. Our embarcation and date of departure was a strict military secret. The ship had been in port for some time, and some of the troops had been aboard for over a week.

Our load consisted of two issues of clothing (fatigues and wool khakis), several pieces of under-clothing, shoes and combat boots, blanket roll, web equipment, mess gear, and a few personal belongings loaded in our duffle bag, besides the uniform we had on. We also had a steel helmet, and plastic helmet liner, field pack, rifle, bayonet, and shovel, an overcoat, a raincoat, plus other small accessories. We could not help but feel like pack mules and it was almost impossible to keep our feet on the ground with such a heavy load on our backs. As we moved near the gang-plank, an Officer would call out the last name of each soldier, and as previously instructed, we would answer out loud with our first name. Huffing and puffing, up the gangplank we ascended. Now and then you could catch a glimpse of a guitar on top of the big packs moving aboard. Another *Chicano* ... I kept remembering the song *"Soldado Razo,"* that part which says, *"aqui va otro mejicano que va jugarse la vida."*[1]

ON THE S.S. WEST POINT—TROOP CARRIER

Our ship was the "West Point," a converted luxury liner. In peacetime it had been known as "The American Beauty" and used for luxury trips from the United States to Europe. After the U.S. entered the war, it had been in constant use carrying troops to combat zones.

[1] "Here goes another Mexican to gamble his life."

There was no luxury on this trip, we were closely packed and accommodations were most uncomfortable. Imagine trying to accommodate 6,000 soldiers in a ship that normally carried 1,500 passengers. All available space was used. Trying to reach the ship's store at night below deck was like walking in a dark room full of logs. Men and equipment were sprawled all over the place, and because of the strict blackout regulations, the ship was pitch dark and you were sure to step on someone's legs or stumble over the G.I.'s who were trying to get some sleep. Many of the intruders were cursed, pushed, and slugged in the dark, and it did not matter if you were an enlisted man or an officer, you were sure to get rough treatment.

The "West Point" sailed down the Boston Harbor. We passed Governor's Island and the big lighthouse, the 'Boston Light,' 15 miles out of Boston. There was a lot of activity in the Boston bay, scores of fishing boats were coming in bringing in their load of fish, schooners and Coast Guard cutters wove in and out of high Atlantic coastal waters. Soon other ships joined us, to be part of the large convoy. We had escort vessels, gunships and other cargo ships. All togther, the convoy numbered close to 25 ships.

The emotions each one of us experienced about being carried away from our homeland is one most difficult to describe. How we felt about leaving our home, our family, and friends, was something no one wanted to discuss . . . We preferred to leave this to the end of day, when more-or-less we would be left to ourselves.

Ever since we had been given the alert to prepare to move out of Myles Standish, we had been going at a rapid pace and full of excitement. Starting out in early morning in a hurry to pack and check all equipment, then having to hurry to and from one formation to another, standing and waiting, and finally walking up the gangplank and being assigned to a particular deck with orders not to leave your bed, which may have been the third one up and highest of the three-decked cots in the crowded quarters. There had been no opportunity for any serious thinking. After eating our first meal that evening, we were well tired and soon dozed off to a good night's sleep, thus ending our first night on the "West Point."

The following day we kept joking and kidding with each other, mostly to embolden one another with a high morale. Towards evening, one by one we would manage to tear away from the group for a few moments alone. I recall going out on deck to watch the sea and gaze at the horizon, then having that old feeling creep in . . .

The day had been so exciting with so many pastimes, such as: exploring the ship's conformations; meeting other passengers and the ship's crew; joining the games on the top deck; enjoying the impromptu entertainment set up by some of the boys; going through fire drills; attending religious services, and reading the many books furnished by Army Intelligence about the customs and languages of the countries we would probably be visiting, like England, France, Italy, and Germany.

At last we found time for a little meditating. "Well, this is it . . ." I began. I tried to remember who had been the person that had assured me that because of my age (32) and number of dependents (4), I would never get to go overseas . . . and because the Allies were at this moment turning the tide in Europe, it would not be necessary for us to go to the ETO. I wondered . . . had I really made a mistake by playing it the smart guy when I left the aircraft defense job at Douglas? Had I outsmarted myself by ignoring the personnel manager who threatened to report me to the draft board for leaving my job? Perhaps the lure of more money in working at a non-essential occupation had been my downfall. I had never really believed that I would be called. Now here I was on my way over, and with the possibility of never returning . . .

What if I were killed? . . . What would happen to my wife,

my three children? My mother? I hated to think of all the suffering they would go through. All the horrible thoughts imaginable would grip me, and before I could find the answers, other thoughts would begin to swirl in. I remembered about us, the Mexican-Americans . . . how the Anglo had pushed and held back our people in the Southwest for the last two generations . . .

"Why fight for America when you have not been treated as an American?"

"Do you really think that in the event the United States wins the war the Mexicans will be given better treatment?"

"Are you really ready to lay down your life for this country?"

And such remarks as, "Can't you see that they are only using you for the dirtiest and most dangerous of all branches, (the Infantry)?"

"Doesn't it look like they are trying to get rid of you because there are too many Mexicans in the United States?"

I tried my best to find honest answers to these questions. It would take a little time and study, but I would always get a reassuring feeling, and in fact, it would serve to cheer me up by going at it with a positive attitude.

Concerning the family, I felt that this was the chance everyone of us had to take, and with unfaltering faith in God, I would surely come out of it alive. Perhaps the war would end by the time we would be sent into action, or there was still a chance that we would be assigned to a non-combat outfit.

About the remarks I had often heard concerning the Mexican-Americans in the United States, I kept thinking and remembered that most of this talk had been made by irresponsible persons, who may have meant well, but they could not comprehend how we Americans of Mexican descent who were born here feel about America. I remembered the remarks Carlos Peña of Austin, Texas, had made in our early days in Texas, in which he pointed out the two choices we Mexicans or Mexican-Americans who live in the United States have to make.

It was during a bitter election compaign for the Governorship of Texas in the late Twenties. One of the candidates had put out literature regarding his opponent which was calculated to swing the Mexican-American vote. This sheet stated that in the course of said candidate's tenure in office, he had made some disparaging remarks concerning Mexicans in Texas. Among some of the statements he had been quoted saying were, "Mexicans here are not the desirable type of citizens for Texas. They are here only for personal gain, they do not contribute anything to this country, and have no desire of becoming American citizens. During World War I most of them fled back into Mexico to avoid giving war service to this country which has been sheltering them. After the war was over they migrated back, to reap the harvest of this great State."

These statements were, of course, untrue, but they had made an alarming effect on the Spanish-speaking population, so much that everyone who had read the sheet was furious and had made up their mind about "*whom* they were going to support."

Along came Carlos Peña, a brilliant young student, well known to all, campaigning for the cause of the person who had been quoted in print as having made the foul remarks about the Mexican people. When Peña was confronted with the sheet by Mexican-Americans in a small town, he held his composure and made this statement, a statement that I have never forgotten: "There are only two things we Mexican-Americans who live in the United States can do in reference to discrimination, prejudice, and injustice to our people. One is to leave the United States and go live in Mexico where we may not live as comfortable as we do here, but we will be among our own people. The other alternative is to become Americans, not only by being American citizens, but *living* and *thinking* 'American'." Then he went on to explain the difference as he, personally, saw it: "We, the Mexican people tend to be too patriotic (for Mexico) and always too conscious *'por la Raza,'* and furthermore, we are too homogenous. If you dare to insult Mexico or *"la Raza,"* whether about someone known to you or in a past incident, you will arouse them one and all.

"On the other hand, here in the *Estados Unidos,* the *Norte Americanos*—call them *Convinencieros* (opportunists) if you will—they are for Business, Money, and Prestige. They are constantly trying to be different from one another. Try to insult them by referring to their country or their racial background and as long as it does not effect their person, their money or their business, they would not deem it necessary to raise any strong objections. It would taken it more as a joke."

Peña's reasons for his campaigning activities in behalf of the disliked candidate—he stated later—were because he honestly thought his candidate was the most qualified of the two, and as far as Mexican-Americans were concerned, he was "the lesser of the two evils."

Although we never adopted all of Peña's philosophy, his remarks did make an impression, and I too had been thoroughly convinced that if we were to live here, we all must strive to be real Americans. For this reason all remarks made by persons who were not concerned with this country could not make me change the feeling I had for my home in America, the country where I was born. All we wanted was a chance to prove how loyal and American we were.

Now, here on the ship the food and beverage we were served was tasteless and skimpy. Only two meals a day were served. Many times we preferred to do without chow when we saw the long line that wound in and out of the cabins like a conga line. We would rather pass the time away enjoying ourselves with such old Mexican card games as *Conquián, Maliá* and *Poka Chica,* games which only we understood. The others would gather around to watch and they asked, "What the hell kind of game is that?"

Poker, Blackjack, and dice games on the trip were not strictly prohibited, but they were allowed on the main deck only. I was lured into the big game and encouraged by the run of good luck that had been with me all through the different camps. The gambling fever had a strong hold on all of us. There had been some pretty big games at Camp Roberts and Fort Meade, but these on the "West Point" were the biggest I had ever seen during my time in the service.

There must have been a cool two thousand dollars in the game, and amid the loud noise and frenzy of excitement, they were pretty reckless with their money. Even counterfeit money was passed from hand to hand with no one bothering to scrutunize it, because no matter what, it was always good for another bet.

Just like any other Army crap game, everyone wanted to get into the action, and the pushing and howling was terrific. To avoid confusion, one partner would act as treasurer and bettor while the other would just throw the galloping dominoes.

I got the biggest thrill of my gambling G.I. life when at the insistence of my dice partner we ran up two singles into a bankroll of five hundred and twelve dollars. We hit for nine straight passes without dragging in any of the winnings! From the fifth pass on, I pleaded with my partner "Faro," a fervent gambler out of New York, to drag in the winnings and split our money and then start over again with two dollars. Faro would not listen. "No, man," he would yell, "We're going to break this game!" Since he had staked me after going broke trying the same thing, I had no other choice but to keep on, and there I was, playing for the highest stakes I ever saw on someone else's money.

The excitement and yelling was mounting. By now everyone gathered around the game was pulling for "Pancho." The try for the one thousand-and-over failed and the excitement ended when we found ourselves gazing at a pair of snake eyes on our try for the tenth pass. We were back where we had started—flat broke.

When not engaged in the games on the top deck, we would gather with the rest of the Mexican-American G.I.'s to pass the time kidding with each other. If anyone of us was caught off guard in a pensive mood, they would start with *"Olvidala!",*[1] or "Those *braceros* are great lovers and the 4-F's are making lots of money and showing the girls a good time back home."

After having been at sea for more than a week, I ran into a funny little surprise that until this day very few of the gang believe. I had known Pvt. Ben "Beetles" Soto ever since we arrived at Fort Meade back in Maryland, and we got to be close friends. He had told me he was from Texas and had trained at Camp Swift. One day on the ship we got to talking about our home towns. He happened to mention that he came from San Marcos, a small town where I had a lot of relatives. When I questioned him about some of the them, imagine my surprise to find out that he was married to my cousin Ida Rosales! When I tried to explain this to the gang, no one would believe it. They all seemed to think that we were just trying to have a little fun.

The many Italians and Polish-Americans we had aboard ship were a loud and boisterous bunch. We had not known many of these back home, but it did not take very long before we were well acquainted with them, and we got along very well together. Finding so many similar characteristics, they immediately took a liking to the *chicanos.* First word they picked up from the gang was *"Ese!",* (hey you). Whenever we got togther, we were in for a lot of ribbing and some awful

---

[1]"Forget her!", meaning that girl or wife left back home.

kidding. They took delight in calling everyone of us *"Pancho,"* presumably for Pancho Villa, the Mexican bandit whose fame spread throughout the world. We would counter with *"Paisan"* for the Italians, and *"Bentibogas"* for the Polish. We got along good with them, also with the other G.I.'s who hailed from the East; from such places as New York, Brooklyn, "Philly," Pittsburgh and Jersey.

After being accustomed to hearing so much of the slow Southern drawl of Texans, Okies, and the guys from the "hills," we found the Brooklyn and "Joi'sey" accents a relief. We began to imitate their speech. We kept imitating them so much, soon we too found ourselves talking in "dese" and "dose."

Through the news release that was picked up by the radio operators, and given out to the passengers via the loudspeakers on the ship, we learned that the Allied Forces were making good headway in France. Americans had made a breakthrough at Saint-Lo, and at the moment, General Patton's tanks were chasing the Germans back into the Rhineland. Our morale shot sky high . . .

"Maybe by the time we arrive in France the war will be over . . ."

"Sure, all we're going to do is police up the area," many a GI was saying.

FRANCE

Late September, 1944. With replacement troops unattached. We first set foot on French soil on Omaha Beach, where three months previously American GI's had made the historic D-Day landing.

Although everything was quiet and the day was clear, much of the evidence of what had happened there was still visible. Litter of wreckage lined the shoreline. The coastline was still cluttered with submerged vessels, many of which had been purposely sunk by Allied advance-landing forces to give protection to the landing troops.

The appalling sight of the beachhead seemed to speak out. It was easy to visualize the great war drama here on June 6th. You could sense that a lot of American blood had been spilled here. Above the high bluff, the foxholes and wrecked concrete dugouts were still there. From these heights, we paused to look down at the shoreline. It was from these well-protected positions that the Germans had stopped the first two waves with their heavy fire. It had indeed required a fighting miracle to take the beach.

We were awed by the many tales we heard from the men who had been there . . . of the many lives lost, of the landing being so costly, of the many dead bodies that for a time lay on the beach and how they had been stacked up six feet high, like cordwood, and later swept into deep holes by giant Army bulldozers . . .

The whole Omaha beach was seething with activity. Supplies and materials were being brought in, unloaded, and piled. Army vehicles shuttled back and forth. Quartermaster and Military Police troops filled the area. Most of the sector occupied by U.S. Army supply-troops was laid out in the city-like blocks, with street signs on every corner. We noted every street was named after some American hero who had lost his life in Normandy. There were Johnson Street, Thompson Avenue, McCoy Street, Jennings Street, O'Neil Street, Castillo Street, Murphy Street, and many others.

We marched out to a bivouac area, about nine miles from the beach. The day was warm and our packs were heavy, but it felt good to get the kinks out of our sea legs. We put up our tents, ate C-rations and prepared for our first night of sleep in France. The night weather got cold, damp and foggy. It was an uncomfortable and bleak first night on the cold Normandy Coast.

As customary, Mexican-Americans in our own group sought out each other for tent mates. You just couldn't keep us apart. Every morning, even those who were camped in another area would come over to us, to be together and partake of the delicious hot coffee that Jose Nerios had brewing.

At the time of our arrival in France, the war picture was taking a good turn in favor of the Allies. Having been deserted by Italy, her big ally, Germany was now having difficulty trying to hold off the enemy. The Russians were driving hard on their eastern front, and American, French, and English forces were closing the gap from the South through the Brenner Pass.

In the Pacific, American combat forces were blasting their way back to the Philippines and into Tokyo. The First Marines and the 81st "Wildcat" Infantry Division were successfully driving the Japanese out of the Palaus in the western Carolines.

In France proper, our troops were making a speedy drive to the Siegfried Line. Since August 15th, the Seventh Army—which included the 3rd, 36th, and 45th Infantry Divisions—had landed practically unopposed in southern France at the Toulon-Marseilles area. They had been driving up the Rhone Valley and had already made contact with General Patton's Third Army units at Autun. English troops had entered Antwerp, and Airborne had landed in Holland. It seemed like Germany would not be able to hold out much longer.

Our morale was sky-high. We felt like American tourists enjoying our first visit abroad. After a few days, we obtained permission to visit the nearby villages. We went to Carenten, Ste. Mere Eglise, Montebourg, and Cherbourg. These war-torn places still held evidence of the recent battle. The towns were crowded with rear echelon troops, special service detachments, Red Cross girls, WACS, Medical personnel, English Tommys, sailors, and, of course, French civilians. After having been wiped out to the bare walls by the German occupation troops, it was a wonder how quickly the French shopkeepers filled their counters with wares for the many English and American *touristes.*

For those of us who spoke Spanish, it was an easy matter to find our way around. With both the French and Spanish languages being so close, it was easy for us to understand such signs and identifications as *brasserie, vins, biere, Hommes* and *Femme.* We didn't need an interpreter to talk with French natives. A familiar and amusing sight that never failed to surprise other American G.I.'s was to watch a Spanish- speaking G.I. carry a running conversation with the French. Although the G.I.'s and many times the French never knew it, they were speaking in French and we were answering in Spanish.

Had someone told us that once we were·in France we would be riding the famous "40 and 8" *(40 hommes e 8 chevaux)* French railroad car, we never would have taken them seriously. But it wasn't very long before we were all crammed into one of them. Compared to U.S. trains, it was like a play train, with its' small engine and a funny little toot-whistle which the engineer constantly tooted.

It seemed to us that someone with a rash sense of humor had found it necessary to have all incoming troops ride to the front in the same rickety old boxcars that the doughboys of W.W. I had used. They barely accommodated the 40 *hommes* (men) or 8 *chevaux* (horses,) let alone 60 men with equipment.

The silly little train traveled back and forth and hardly made any distance. It would go forward four miles and backwards five. Why, no one knew. We surmised it was because the tracks were out or roads had been damaged by shelling.

The trip took longer than anticipated. After a few days on the road, we all looked like the proverbial American hobo with a full growth of beard and faces blackened with soot. It wasn't long before our C-rations and water supply ran out. Everytime the train made a forced stop, we scrounged all over the farmyards for food and water. If the train remained stalled for too long, we built small fires to keep warm, picked berries and apples, and knocked on doors for nourishment around the farm houses.

When we pulled up within a short distance of a United States Army supply depot, a raiding party was organized, headed by the bold Frank Padilla. Under the threat of getting shot by the M.P. guards on duty, they still managed to swipe enough boxes of "K" and "10-in-1" rations to feed all the half-starved G.I.'s and the officers who were in charge.

We finally made it into Le Mans where we were taken to a large tent camp. It was a replacement processing center situated in the woods, five miles out from Le Mans.

Here we enjoyed the luxury of hot meals. By bartering with the natives that came into camp, some of us were lucky enough to taste fresh eggs once again. This was a clean camp with large pyramidal tents to accommodate personnel who would be staying a long time. We passed the time away playing poker and writing letters to the folks back home. I sketched a few drawings of some of the fellows with me. After six or seven days, the groups started to move out. Most of our original gang was separated. About half of the replacements were sent to the Third Army which was then led by General "Blood and Guts" Patton. The rest of us were sent to join the Seventh Army Forces in southern France under General Patch.

From Le Mans we went by truck through the towns of Orleans, Troyes, Chartres, and many other small villages. All these places still had signs of recent fighting. We could see wrecked buildings silhouetted against the skies and streets filled with rubble and debris. All that was left of some of the buildings were drab looking stucco walls with bullet holes and mud splatterings. Many wooden buildings had burned completely to the ground.

Along the countryside, the roads had been torn and large holes were left where many heavy vehicles had passed. Felled trees, burned stumps and sturdy silent trunks whose tops had been blown away by artillery adorned the fields. Empty fox-holes, trenches with abandoned equipment, litter, dead horses, and burned vehicles were more evidence of a total war. A steady splashing drizzle and cold wind added to the bleak appearance of the ravished battlefields. We were now getting close to the frontlines. Now and then we could hear the low rumbles of the long toms which went *Barr-oom!,* with a low hum. We would just look at each other and suddenly the conversation became somber and very serious.

Appropriately, France has been called the "Battlefield of Europe." We were inclined to agree. Every little village was laid out in the same manner; the main artery was a winding street that formed the shape of the letter 'S.' If the town was a little bigger, it would start winding over again in another 'S' shape. From one end of town to the other, the main thorough-fare had the appearance of a wiggling snake. This gave us the impression that in case of enemy attack, the town could be ably defended from block to block because of the layout of the streets. At the entrance of most every town, there would be a tunnel or overpass with adjoining buildings, there-by giving it the appearance of a fort. Further proof that the people of France had envisioned many wars was the fact that even the smallest of family dwellings had sturdy thick walls, and a spacious cellar filled with edibles and barrels of wine.

After a long thirty hours on the road, we finally arrived in Luneville, cold, tired and hungry. Luneville was near the Vosges Mountains, and very close to the German border in eastern France. We unloaded our gear and entered what at one time had been a large auto race track. It was now an Army "Repple Depple" (Replacement Depot). The center area of the track was crowded with pup-tents and G.I.'s moving all around.

These replacement depots flourished all over the fighting

fronts in both the Pacific and European war theatres. Here all infantry replacements, fresh from the states, were pooled together to be assigned and sent later into combat divisions whose lines had been depleted. There were also many soldiers who already had been in combat and recently discharged from nearby Army hospitals. Other combatmen recovering from wounds or illnesses were sent to these repple depples, later to rejoin their outfits or be reassigned to a different unit.

October, 1944. Once again, we *mejicanos* sought the companionship of each other. Our group was beginning to thin out. Back at Le Mans we had parted company with Ben Soto, Jose P. Ramirez, Ruben Ortiz, and Jose Nerios. They had been sent out with the group assigned to the Third Army.

As tentmate at the Luneville camp, I drew Jess J. Martinez. At first I was hesitant about bunking with him. We had been together in basic training at Camp Roberts, but had not sought out each other's company for some unexplained reason. I had become better acquainted with fellows whom I had met after leaving Camp Roberts simply because to me they were more the *Chicano* type. I had rarely seen Martinez pal around with any of our group. To me he had seemed too *agabachado* (Anglo-ized). He had been bunking with one of the men from Roberts who had also left for the Third Army, and I was the first Mexican-American tentmate for him since leaving the states.

I learned a lot from Martinez. I got to understand and admire him. He spoke very little Spanish, but his English was perfect, with no trace of the Spanish accent so commonly found among the Spanish-speaking of the Southwest. Jess was from Denver, Colorado. He was around 25, and had a boyish face with deep-set eyes and a square-set jaw. I found that we had a lot in common. Both of us were married and had small children, one of them named after their father. We talked so much about our own wives and children that we assumed we already knew each other's family.

Jesse was a truck driver back in Denver, hauling coal and produce from around Brighton. His early life experiences were similar to mine. Born in a large and poor family, he had struck out on his own at an early age, had traveled up and down the northwestern states seeking all types of work. He worked in beet farms, at sheep herding, cowpunching, trucking, and mining. Finally, he had married and settled down in Denver. Just when he had begun to earn a good living and making plans for the future, the war broke out and he was drafted into the service.

Every morning we lined up and a sergeant came over with a long list of names, calling out those who had been picked for frontline duty that day. These replacements loaded up on trucks and in no time were frontline bound. Everyone of us hoped our names would not be called next. If called, then we would hope that our buddy would also be called; we hated to be separated at that time. Now more than ever we wanted to stay together.

First to go to the front lines from our group was Sgt. Peru. We had been warned by the camp authorities that downtown Luneville was off-limits to replacements; that if we were caught in town by the M.P.'s we would be sure to be on the next truck for the front.

Peru, an old frontline soldier who had seen combat in the Pacific, and Frank Padilla, took off to town without proper leave. Later that day Padilla made it back with some bottles of cognac for the gang, but Peru got roaring drunk and the M.P.'s had brought him in. Next morning he went up front with a bad hangover.

We finally got to go into Luneville many times. After being in camp for a few days, the camp authorities decided we might as well brush up on more infantry training. We would march across the town to a field for target practice. On the way back, G.I.'s would start dropping out of the line and hide in town, then sneak back into camp at night.

Luneville had been taken over by the 79th Divisional Headquarters. The regimental rear echelon was quartered in large buildings that the Wermacht had used during their long occupation of the town.

The city of Luneville was the last large French city before reaching the German border. It was right on the borderline until W.W. I had changed the French-German border. It was rumored that the city was pro-German and that the town was full of spies, collaborators, and saboteurs. For these reasons, every G.I. visiting there was cautioned to be armed at all times.

Usually the town was full with American G.I.'s. It was wide open and always crowded with soldiers—some who were stationed there, and combatmen on pass or AWOL. All the cafes, bars, cabarets and houses of ill-repute were guarded by the Military Police so as to keep the unruly mob of G.I.'s in hand. Many times we found the place much like a typical movie cowboy town. G.I.'s (enlisted men and officers) armed with 45's, carbines, or rifles roamed the streets. Many drinking bouts and arguments would end with the soldiers shooting it out in the streets.

Martinez' and my luck held out pretty well in the repple depple. Many mornings passed by and our names were not called. Even some of the late arrivals were called to go before many of us. We stayed over three weeks at the replacement depot. The trucks would leave every morning with new loads of replacements to the front to replace the squads that were undermanned because of battle casualties. Every morning, when the non-coms in charge of the camp would start calling out names, Martinez and I would start pulling each other's little finger (An old Mexican custom for good luck).

One by one we began to go . . . Jose R. Ramirez, Esquibel, Tony Rodriguez, Abril, Arrendondo, Gomez, Frankie Escobar, Joe Casiano, and even Frank Padilla, the colorful guy from L.A., "self-styled leader" of the 38th Street gang, "the toughest in South Los Angeles." Finally Jess Martinez and I were the only ones left of the original gang that crossed over in the "West Point". Even though the place was still crowded with G.I.'s, and more arriving everyday, things just weren't the same without all the old gang around. When we could hear the booming noise of the cannon in the nearby battle area, we kept thinking about our friends who had left, hoping and praying that they would be spared. Yes, the war was too close and real now. Things were getting tougher and we were feeling lonelier and lonelier.

S/SGT. LUCIANO ADAMS

Awarded the Congressional Medal of Honor

For conspicuous gallantry and intrepidity at risk of life above and beyond the call of duty on October 28, 1944, near St. Die, France. When his company was stopped in its effort to drive through the Montagne Forest to reopen the supply line to the isolated Third Battalion, Staff Sergeant Adams braved the concentrated fire of machine guns in a lone assault on a force of German troops. Although his company had progressed less than 10 yards and had lost 3 killed and 6 wounded, Sergeant Adams charged forward dodging from tree to tree firing a borrowed BAR from the hip. Despite intense machine gun fire which the enemy directed at him and rifle grenades which struck the trees over his head showering him with broken twigs and branches, Sergeant Adams made his way within ten yards of the machine gun and killed the gunner with a hand grenade. An enemy soldier threw hand grenades at him from a position only ten yards distant; however Sergeant Adams dispatched him with a single burst of BAR fire. Charging into the vortex of enemy fire, he killed another machinegunner at 15 yards range with a hand grenade and forced the surrender of two supporting infantrymen. Although the remainder of the German group concentrated the full force of its automatic weapons' fire in a desperate effort to knock him out, he proceeded through the woods to find and exterminate five more of the enemy. Finally, when the third German machine gun opened up on him at a range of 20 yards, Sergeant Adams killed the gunner with BAR fire. In the course of the action he personally killed nine Germans, eliminated three enemy machine guns, vanquished a specialized force which was armed with automatic weapons and grenade launchers, cleared the woods of hostile elements, and reopened the supply line to the assault companies of the battalion.[1]

Luciano Adams, the Mexican-American with an Anglo name, was born at Port Arthur, Texas on October 26, 1922. Prior to entering the service he lived with his mother, Mrs. Rosa Adams, of 754 San Antonio Street, Port Arthur, Texas. Adams entered the Army on December 21, 1942.

He was sent overseas where he joined the Third Infantry Division. He first saw combat in Anzio where he earned the Combat Infantrymen Badge, was wounded during battle in Italy, and received the Purple Heart. His whirlwind tactics many times before had brought dismay to the opposing Jerries, and on May 23, 1944, he was decorated with the Bronze Star in Italy.

The Third Division was one of the first infantry divisions to see combat in Europe. It was the first committed in Africa

---

[1]War Department Citation, G.O. No. 20, 29 March, 1945.

STAFF SERGEANT LUCIANO ADAMS
Port Arthur, Texas
Congressional Medal of Honor
European Theater World War II

when they landed at Oran in November, 1942. They fought through Sicily and saw rugged fighting at Anzio and Cassino. On August 15, 1944, they spearheaded the invasion of southern France with the Seventh Army. From there they fought through the Rhone Valley and were in a drive into the Vosges Mountains where they encountered heavy German resistance. By then, heavy rains had come to France. In late September winter weather had set in, the nights were damp and cold, making it difficult for the Infantrymen to keep their bodies warm or their feet dry.

The Germans had fallen back and began to put up stronger resistance in the Montagne Forest. Here they had been reinforced by a fresh Mountain Infantry Battalion from the Rhineland; troops which, at the time of the German occupation of France, had used these same wood areas for their training manuevers. Their Granediers and Panzer commanders and non-coms knew every step of the terrain.

In the misty cold undercover of darkness and heavy timber, the Germans infiltrated into the Third Division's defense area, cutting off a vital supply line. Sergeant Adams' company—a unit of the 30th Infantry Regiment was given the mission of reopening the supply line which had been severed by the Germans.

The story of Sgt. Adams' valor is recounted in eyewitness reports by members of his unit:

"Their opening fire wounded the company commander, the executive officer, four enlisted men, and killed three others," related his platoon leader, Lieutenant Frank H. Harrel, whose home is Orlando, Florida. "The enemy was dug in and had established a defense in depths. They were all specialists and carried automatic weapons, machine pistols or grenade launchers.

"One German had climbed into a knocked-out reconnaissance car and was operating its machine gun against us. Three others with machine pistols were raking my platoon front, and our attack was momentarily halted. That's when Sergeant Adams picked a BAR and set off in a one-man wave of destruction. Firing from his hip, he dashed from tree to tree until he was within 10 yards of the nearest enemy machine gun emplacement.

"The Jerry who had been manning the machine gun in the reconnaissance car climbed out and threw several hand grenades at Sergeant Adams, who moved outside the traversing area of the machine gun. While the grenades were exploding all around him, Sgt. Adams killed this German with a short burst of his BAR . . .

"Bullets clipped the branches off the evergreen trees within a few inches of his body. Rifle grenades struck the branches around him. He refused to take cover. A second machine gun operated by the enemy was firing on him from only 10 or 15 yards to his right.

"Sergeant Adams headed for the gun; he threw a grenade, and the explosion killed the gunner. As soon as this emplacement was put out of action, two Krauts servicing the gun came out of the foxhole alongside and surrendered. Into the thickest of fire directed at him, Sergeant Adams advanced with his BAR spraying fire. He killed five more of the enemy in their protected positions. After 50 yards he came abreast a third machine gun which was about 20 yards to his left and firing directly at him. With one long burst from the BAR he put this emplacement out of action.

"With the destruction of the third machine gun emplacement the enemy took off in a complete rout. We drove on through, completely clearing the line of supply." Staff Sergeant Russel Dunham, Brighton, Illinois, who followed directly behind the pathway blazed by Adams, says, "Those Germans were very rugged and had brand new winter equipment and an automatic weapon for every man. Sgt. Adams moved like a tornado, and when he reached the first gun emplacement, the whole pit seemed to go up into the air. The German in the reconniassance car kept the fire on him until he couldn't move the machine gun around anymore. When he let loose with those potato smasher grenades, it looked like the end. Sgt. Adams cooly put a burst of a BAR right through him.

"There was fire and explosions all around him as he went through the woods like a wild man. At the second machine gun he stood and fired from 20 yards, and for a few seconds there was a violent duel between two rapid-fire weapons—the Kraut machine gun and the BAR in Sgt. Adams' hands. All of his bullets seemed to strike the German gunner, the other Krauts took off in panic."

Private First Class John W. Wood, of Norwalk, Iowa, was another who followed in the wake of infantry fighting perfection carried to the enemy by Sgt. Adams. He says, "I tried to get in a shot but he was everywhere. Before we could see the Krauts he'd kill them and move on. It was just a matter of seconds when he started against those dug-in Heines with automatic weapons and left them behind, dead in their holes."

What inspired Luciano Adams to perform such a valorous act? Why did he gamble his life against the German automatic weapons in the woods? He could have stayed behind and ordered one of his men to take the initiative; just as many line sergeants in combat do.

Luciano Adams felt like Jose Martinez did at Attu. Proud of the Aztec blood that flowed through his veins, used to the life of the underdog and of uphill struggles, knowing very little fear . . . it mattered a lot to him that a duty had to be done, and he wasn't going to wait around for someone else to do it.

Sergeant Luciano Adams was the kind of noncom that the infantry combatmen admire . . . a sergeant who would never ask any man to perform any dangerous mission he wasn't capable of doing himself.

THE CROSS OF LORRAINE

October, 1944. The time finally came for our group of replacements, which included Jess Martinez and me, to join the frontline troops. Our group included a couple of experienced combatmen, Cecil Esquivel from Monrovia, California, and Felix Garcia of San Antonio, Texas. Both had seen combat before with the 79th Division, had been hospitalized from wounds and were being sent back to rejoin their unit. On the shoulder of their combat jacket, they wore a patch with the *Cross of Lorraine.* This was the insignia of the 79th Division.

The Cross of Lorraine is a very familiar symbol in France. Godfred De Boullion, Duke of Lorraine, a quiet, pious, hard-fighting knight and a hero of French legend as leader of the First Crusade, wore the cross on his shield more than 800 years ago. To the people of northeast France, it represents a symbol of the Alsace-Lorraine area. Since World War I, after the fall of France, it became the insignia of the French underground forces. The F.F.I. (Free French forces of the Interior) did daring work during the German occupation and also gave the Allies considerable assistance during the invasion; they used the insignia consistently whenever they could.

Time and again we would pass by some building where some *Maqui* (Free French fighter), in defiance of the Germans, had crudely painted the Lorraine Cross on a wall or fence visible to all passers-by. Often it was written in blood alongside the body of a dead German who had been slain by the Maqui.

The 79th Division had adopted the Cross of Lorraine ever since W.W. I, when the 79th had seen combat action in the Lorraine campaign. This was the division we had been assigned to. The 79th first landed in France at Utah Beach on D-Day plus 6 and went into action right away, helping to rid Cherbourg of the enemy. Many Mexican-American boys were in the original outfit that fought through Normandy, Saint-Lo, and across the Seine.

Since then, after losing many via the casualty route, they had taken in a lot of newly-arrived infantry troops as replacements. The men of the 79th had been in combat since their first day in Normandy, without rest, they had been through many "Death Valleys," "Purple Heart Alleys," and "Bloody Ridges." They earned their share of glory, as did many other infantry divisions in France.

At the time we joined the 79th at the front, they were waging a torrid battle against the Germans in the woods of the Foret de Parroy, just outside Luneville. We were taken by trucks in the direction of the noise of battle, and the ride was the craziest one I ever had. They waited till darkness to go into the danger area. Instead of slowing down and proceeding cautiously, the drivers picked up speed and careened crazily over the muddy roads, disregarding the perils of reckless driving, and obviously too concerned with the more imminent danger of booming shells, whizzing bullets and foul-smelling smoke that filled the area. Too many convoys had met with disaster coming to the front, the drivers didn't feel like staying around any longer than necessary. They yelled at us to unload, turned around quickly and took off instantly.

Back at the replacement depot, we had been instructed to leave all personal belongings and take only the most useful things for frontline duty. We left there our duffle bag, the extra clothing and equipment, including that supposedly indispensable piece of equipment—according to stateside talk—our gas masks. This we left atop a big pile at the 'repple depple'. For frontline duty we were left with two blankets, a shelter half, an overcoat, a raincoat, a canteen, a trenching tool, rifle and bayonet. On our back we carried a light pack consisting of only the most essential things for personal use, such as mess kit, cup, toothbrush and powder, soap, razor and blades, toilet paper, metal mirror, pencils, writing and sketch paper.

Martinez and I parted company in the darkness and there was no time to say goodbye. Garcia and Esquivel were taken back to their outfit, which was Co. E of the 313th Regiment. The rest of us replacements of that day were sent to Co. I, in the Third Battalion. All of our original gang had been split up . . . I was the only Mexican-American assigned to Company I.

One could tell it was the frontline by the continuous blasts and noise of the artillery barrages. Being new at the front, it was very hard for us to distinguish between "incoming" and "outgoing mail." To make sure, we replacements didn't take any chances; as soon as we heard the thunder, it was "hit the dirt!" . . . and we felt silly because we couldn't tell the difference. We were the only ones dropping to the ground when it was "outgoing mail." The old-timers just stood there looking at us.

Item Company was on reserve and we dug-in there in the forest. The weather was cold, wet, and miserable. On the first night I couldn't get any sleep. It was very cold and the damn noise kept me on the jump.

By early morning it started to snow; when we woke up, a thick blanket of white covered the forest. We felt a little warmer under the snow that covered us in our foxholes. As daylight appeared, we were all up and around eating cold K rations that were sent up. I started to walk about and get acquainted with the other men of my platoon. The majority were from the South; they came from Tennessee, Virginia, the Carolinas and Alabama. Not very many of the Latin type in the company. The only two I got to know were Sgt. Tony Marquez from Los Angeles, *(de la Alpine),* and another Jess Martinez. Only this Martinez was from Detroit and didn't speak a word of Spanish. The other Jess Martinez was by then a bi-lingual expert.

THE FIRST TIME IN COMBAT ACTION[1]

I have heard that we will go into the line today, we are to attack. Although no order has been received yet the men can sense it. Everyone is mad . . . the men keep cursing and complaining about the long-awaited rest they have been promised.

"The only rest we'll get is when we get killed off," commented a veteran of the line.

"And now they're asking us to attack again. Guess they want to get rid of a few more (of us) before giving us that rest," remarked another old timer.

We leave our bedrolls and overcoats. A sergeant starts issuing ammo for our rifles to all the squad. We get two filled-bandoliers that we string around our necks and cross under each arm. I have to smile when I remember the pictures I used to see of "Pancho Villa" with bandoliers wrapped around his body . . . More clips of ammo for our M-I's, hand grenades, water, K rations, emergency rations, a thick bar of chocolate that every G.I. quickly bites into, sulfa and plasma for our first aid dressings . . .

We snap the safety off our rifles, and though we feel far from it, we are supposed to be ready to go.

Our line of departure is the top of a small rise. Down below at the bottom of the slope is a road, close to that is a small creek, from there on, the ground begins to rise again and a wooded section begins . . . that's where the Jerries are supposed to be. We are to attack the woods . . .

H-Hour is to be 1000. *About twenty minutes of, our artillery turns the full power of their fury into the German positions in the woods. Soon the big mortars* (81 *mm's*) *open up and all the other attacking companies also go in. More artillery fire and anti-tank guns . . . the hills echo with the tremendous roar of the heavy guns.*

---

[1]From personal notes taken at the front.

Things are happening too fast for me. There is no one to tell me anything of what I am supposed to do . . . what to watch for . . . who to shoot at . . . when to "open up" . . . nothing at all. The others in the squad have been in action before, and they know what the score is . . . I'm just a green replacement and I feel inadequate. I suppose I should have learned all there is to it back at the training camp, but somhow I feel lost . . . I keep looking around to see if I can get any signs or instructions from any of the others, but no one seems to notice me, they're all too preoccupied with their own selves . . .

Now it's our turn to go in. Two scouts move up in front. I recognize Jess "Detroit" Martinez as one of them . . . being of short stature, he has been picked for first scout because he represents a small target. Two riflemen move up front to cover the scouts, then a sergeant with a carbine, the BAR man—usually a guy with a lot of guts—and an ammo carrier with a rifle for the BAR man, more M-I riflemen, a bazooka man, a light machine gun man and an assistant with 45's, a medic who goes unarmed, the tail end (that's me) and a buck sergeant. Behind us there's a runner with a walkie-talkie and the First Sergeant, way back there's a Lieutenant and other officers who are playing it safe . . .

It's hard for me to explain the feeling I have. My heart's beating faster, there's an empty feeling at the pit of my stomach, and I start getting a cold sweat . . . Suddenly I wish I were somewhere else. I keep thinking that I should have kept my defense job . . . and who was the wise guy that said we would never see action, that we were here only to "police the place . . ."

Smoke shells explode near the woods, and the whole area is clouded with smoke. The Germans know what this means—the infantry is attacking—and they're ready for us. We go down the hill into a gully and the Jerries open up, they throw everything at us but the kitchen sink — murderous artillery, self-propelled guns, machine guns, mortars, burp guns, 88mm's, and all other kinds of small arms fire. Men get hit right and left . . . several cries of "Medic!" come from both sides. The only hope we have for safety is to reach a small stone wall just below the woods, they have us "zeroed in."

It seems like we'll never make it. but we finally do and we catch up with some of the others who were ahead of us. The riflemen are going around the corner of the stone wall and are exchanging fire at close range with the enemy. One by one they leave the protected wall . . . only Sgt. Jack[1] and I are left. We look at each other . . . he is just as scared as I am, but it's my turn to go. As I turn the corner I am surprised to see the other riflemen "frozen," hugging the ground for protection—I do likewise. The Staff Sergeant gets up and yells, "Come on everybody, lets have some firepower!" We all rise and everyone fires in unison. I fire at the direction of the enemy, but you never can tell if you hit anyone.

We jump in a trench and follow the others who are turning along the trench. As I turn to my right, I am startled and surprised, all of a sudden, I see him—my first dead German! . . . how frightening and grotesque he looks! . . . and I can't keep my eyes off him. His arms are stretched outward and his eyes are wide open . . . he has a bullet hole in his left temple where the blood still trickles out . . . his face is turning pale-blue, his mouth is open . . . He is still standing behind his machine gun which has been broken—supported by the trench wall.

REST AND REGROUP

October 29. After only a few days, I was lucky to go back with the combat veterans of the 79th, who had seen 128 hard days in the front lines. They were finally getting their much-deserved rest. The 44th Infantry Division, just in from the States, relieved us in the Foret de Parroy area.

---

[1]Fictitious name.

Utmost care and secrecy was maintained during the change-over. If the enemy had the slightest suspicion of what was taking place, they could have ordered an all-out attack. One at a time, the men in the foxholes were relieved and a new man took his place. Then we marched in small groups to the lines where trucks were waiting.

Yet, in spite of these precautions, it was reported that in an area close to a village where the infantry doughs of the 44th had just got ready to turn in for the night, loud-speakers were turned on, loudly blaring out this message: "Welcome to the battlefront 44th Division! We know that you men just recently arrived from the U.S. The members of the 79th pulled out because they lost most of their men . . . they have left you holding the bag. You too haven't got a chance against the powerful German Army. Why suffer out in the cold, wet foxholes? Give yourselves up now. You will be treated well. We have warm food, cognac, and a warm bed for you. Don't stay out in the cold and get killed!" A mere sample of the psychological program German intelligence had worked up.

It was a tired, dirty and unkempt—but happy—bunch of infantry-men that arrived at the Rosieres rest area on a cold November night. For the first time in many months, we had hot baths, shaves, clean clothes, and peace of mind. What a change this made to the men who had been in the line. Soon we all began to look alive again. The commanding Colonel of the 313th came over to make a speech to the front line G.I.'s—and what a beauty of a speech it was.

Colonel "Black" Sam was both admired and hated by the men. He was a real soldier, a handsome West Pointer from Alabama with a granite-like chin, and ice cold courage.[1] His speech went something like this: "Men of the 79th, you have done a

---

[1]McCardell, Lee, *They Wrote Their Story in Blood,* Saturday Evening Post, December 21, 1946, p. 26.

great job. Go out and get drunk, raise hell, and have a good time, you have earned it—we will be doing the same."

Passes were given freely to nearby towns. All the towns and villages quickly sprang to life. Every where you went, the beer hall, taverns, and cafes were full of men from the 79th. Pro stations were set up by headquarters and the "cat houses" did landslide business—guarded by the M.P.'s of course.

The shoulder patch we wore with the 79th was a silver cross of Lorraine on a blue shield. As we marched through French villages, the natives often mistook us for French because of the patch; especially the Mexican-Americans whom they mistook for French Moroccans, since there were a lot of Moroccans with the French Army fighting right alongside the 79th. Many times we were addressed by the natives in French.

Somehow I didn't feel at home in Company I. I kept worrying about how the fellows who had been with me since back in the States were doing. They were all mostly in the Second Battalion. I asked Lt. Houston, the C.O. of Co. I, for a transfer to the Second Battalion as soon as there was an opening. The chance finally came. Lt. Houston called me in to ask if I still wanted the transfer. I bid goodbye to Sgt. Marquez and Martinez and soon found myself in Co. E.

In the Second Battalion I found Tony Rodriguez, Joe Ramirez, "Denver" Jess Martinez, both Franks, (Padilla and Escobar), Abril, Gonzales and the rest. We were all like long-lost brothers and felt very happy to be together—and to find each other in one piece again. It felt good to hear the familiar nicknames I had heard before—*Ese, Tio, Viejo, Ruko,* or *Morin,* no matter what they called me, I was glad to hear it and glad to be back together with them.

Missing among the old gang were Arredondo and Nerios. I learned the sad news that they had both been KIA. It was Nerios whom we missed the most. He had been with us since our basic days back in California. While at Omaha Beach and at the Le Mans replacement camp, we had gotten used to having him come around every morning. He would come very early, remain outside of our tent, and start making us some hot G.I. coffee. He would then wake us by yelling, "*Levantensen, viejas flojas!*" (Get up, lazy old ladies)!

Nerios was a well-mannered, quiet, old-timer who was very well liked by everyone. He hailed from George West, Texas. I had felt very bad about having been drafted because I had three small children, but when I learned that Nerios was the father of eight, I really felt sorry for him, you can imagine how badly we all felt when we heard the bad news.

"Easy" Company was more like it. Here I found both Esquivel and little Felix Garcia, the two who had been with me on the crazy ride to the front from the repple depple. Also another G.I. whom I met for the first time, Lawrence Perchez, a well-liked youngster in his early twenties. He called Ontario, California, his home.

New replacements arriving fresh from the states were assigned to the companies that were under-strength. These new men had the same questions we had when we first talked to the men who had been in combat. All wanted to know what it felt like to face the enemy . . . what would be the best method of survival at the front . . . and how much danger did you have to face out there? . . .

Being in the front lines for only a short period, I did not feel qualified to answer their many questions, but Co. E had a lot of men who were well qualified to do so. They had been in the outfit all the way since the 79th was activated back in the states. Most had been wounded at one time or another. They remembered every battle in which E Company had participated. These men knew what infantry fighting was all about . . .

Every evening at twilight, they gathered around a fire to talk about what they had been through, about the many American combatmen who had shown exceptional courage—*guts* as they called it—on the battlefield . . . they had become legendary heroes among their comrades in the infantry.

It was surprising to hear them extol the bravery of the Mexican-American infantryman. Up to now I had never pictured any of our group as having outstanding qualities for infantry-combat. I was under the impression that many of them had gone to war reluctantly and would not aspire to be standouts, having been more of the followers than the leader type, they —in my opinion, preferred to stay in the background. Many had done this in their civilian life, and with danger lurking everywhere now, they would be justified to continue in their role of followers. But the men in E Company were really proud of their Mexican-American comrades.

At the rest camp, we talked about everything pertaining to the war. We weren't pessimistic over the chances of the Allies defeating the Germans, but at the same time we weren't over-optimistic. We realized that the Germans were a tough foe, and with the fighting getting closer to Germany, he was going to be a lot tougher. Our men gave a lot of credit to the German soldier as a fighter, and they admitted that the Wermacht was a properly trained army, in many instances better disciplined than our army.

The main subject of combatmen was "bitching." This was Number One issue in all conversations. They were always complaining about everything, and they felt that they had every right to do so. They would bitch about the Army, the chow, about having to fight while the civilians back home were getting rich on defense jobs and in the black market. They would complain about the rear echelon troops—enjoying the fruits of victory that rightfully belonged to the fighting men, about the Air Corps and Navy fighting a soft war and enjoying hot food and warm blankets while the infantry had cold rations and slept in muddy foxholes . . . They even complained about other combat divisions whom they claimed did not fight well against the enemy . . . about the Army brass, how incompetent some of them were, how they depended on the foot soldier to do the dirty fighting and then claimed all the glory for themselves.

When Division Headquarters issued orders for all units to resume infantry training and "dry run" night problems, the GI's really started to bitch—and loud, too! This was probably what tipped off the division brass that the men were ready to go back into the campaign.

As every GI knows, nothing good ever lasts long for the Infantry. The wonderful rest was over. It had been a much-needed tonic and a good morale booster. Soon all units were alerted. It was no secret to the men of the 79th that we would go into the Parroy forest again. We had heard that the 44th Division had been having a rough go, and had lost a lot of ground that we had fought for and won . . .

New winter clothing was issued. We received heavy underwear, woolen khaki uniforms, new-type combat jackets, woolen sox and gloves, new snow-pac rubber boots, and a new type of combat shoes that made an instant hit with all the infantrymen. Actually they weren't too new, we had seen officers back in the states and rear echelon troops in combat zones sporting these ankle-high shoes that were copied after those of the German infantry and tank men.

November 12, 1944. We moved out again. The way things were going, it would not be long before we would force the enemy to surrender, or so said the "Star and Stripes," the Army newspaper delivered daily at the front. The Germans were now fighting with their backs to the wall. Our troops had driven them back to the Rhine where they would make their last stand. The way Uncle Sam was bringing in men and materiél, it would not be long now before all was over. We had bright hopes of getting home for Christmas. We felt there was not much of the job left . . . and the quicker we did it, the sooner we'd get out of the blood duel.

We were now racing down the Alsace-Lorraine and all along the road there was evidence that "Jerry" was on the run. Dead horses and abandoned field pieces testified to the debacle. We were feeling in high spirits.

Traveling by trucks we went at a pretty fast clip, when suddenly they fired on us. The trucks stopped immediately and we scattered like frightened chickens. There was a town nearby and we were ordered to go in, find the enemy, and engage him. We moved in very cautiously; there was a lot of fire exchanged and few casualties at the edge of town. Someone cried, "There they are, in that tower!" This was located at the center of the town. More fire was exchanged and the battle picked up in intensity. At last we had them surrounded atop the big tower. It was then that we heard them, first in Spanish, then in English: "Don't shoot! We're G.I.'s too!" We had been battling with a squad from Company G, who were also fired upon on the other side of town, and had been sent out to locate the enemy too. Having suffered no serious casualties in the snafu battle, we regrouped, boarded the trucks again, and sped down the Alsace-Lorraine countryside.

Our Regiment, the 313th, was next assigned to a task force. This force consisted of light, fast trucks and jeeps, all fully armed. We raced at a fast clip up and down the mountain roads in the Vosges, bypassing many small pockets of resistance until we entered the Saverne Gap. Our next big battles with the Germans were alongside our allies, the French 2nd Armored Forces in the outskirts of Strasbourg on the German border.

S/SGT. MACARIO GARCIA

Awarded the Congressional Medal of Honor

Staff Sergeant Macario Garcia, (then PFC), while an acting squad leader of Company B, 22nd Infantry, on November 20, 1944, near Grosshau, Germany, single handedly assaulted two enemy machine gun emplacements. Attacking prepared positions on a wooded hill, which could be approached only through meager cover, his company was pinned down by intense machine gun fire, and subjected to a concentrated artillery and mortar barrage. Although painfully wounded, he refused to be evacuated and on his own initiative crawled forward along until he reach a position near an enemy emplacement. Hurling grenades he boldly assaulted the position, destroyed the gun, and with his rifle, killed three of the enemy who attempted to escape. When he rejoined his company, a second machine gun opened fire and again the intrepid soldier went forward, utterly disregarding his own safety. He stormed the position and destroyed the gun, killed three more Germans and captured four prisoners. He fought on with his unit until the objective was taken and only then did he permit himself to be removed for medical care. Private Garcia's conspicuous heroism, his inspiring, courageous conduct and his complete disregard for his personal safety wiped out two enemy emplacements and enabled his company to advance and secure its objective.[1]

Macario Garcia, the third Mexican-American to win the Medal of Honor in World War II, a "real" *mejicano,* was born in Villa Costaño, in the border state of Coahuila, Mexico, January 2, 1920.

In his early life, Macario Garcia traveled up and down the state of Texas working on farms and in cotton fields. He knew the hard rigors of back-breaking labor under a hot Texas sun from personal experience. Forced to spend his youth working in the fields to help support the family, Macario had very little time for schooling, yet he did manage to reach the tenth grade;

---

[1]War Department Citation G.O. No. 74, September 1, 1945.

STAFF SERGEANT MACARIO GARCIA
Sugarland, Texas
Congressional Medal of Honor
European Theater World War II

considered good for Mexican-American farm workers in Texas.

Even though he was still a Mexican citizen, when war came to the United States, Garcia was eager to answer the call when Uncle Sam beckoned him. On November 11, 1942, he joined the Army at Sugarland, where he was living with his mother, Mrs. Josefa Martinez Garcia.

In the Army, Garcia found many friends and discovered a more attractive democracy than the one he had been exposed to as a civilian. He enjoyed this new feeling and began to appreciate more the things this country offered him. When he was offered the opportunity to become a United States citizen in the Armed Forces, he quickly signed the papers and was readily sworn in. It wasn't long after he became an American citizen that Garcia found himself overseas in the Infantry. He joined the Fourth Division on June 8th on the Normandy beachhead where he saw his first day in action.

The Fourth, known as the "Ivy" Division, derived from the Roman numerals IV, landed in Utah Beach on D-Day. There, on D-Day plus 2, Macario Garcia joined the 22nd Regiment as a replacement. He was with them when they effected the relief of the 82nd Airborne, which had been cut off at Ste. Mere Eglise for 36 hours.

After having a hand in the capture of Cherbourg, Garcia next figured in the capture of Paris with the Fourth in early September. Later they were the first American troops to crack the Siegfried Line. On September 11th, a patrol of the 22nd Regiment became one of the first units to cross the German border.

In the thick of the fighting and with the Wermacht putting on stiff resistance, on September 16, the anniversary date of Mexico's Independence, Marcario Garcia earned the reputation of the "fearless Mexican" when he went out and captured a machine gun and the German gunner. This daring exploit earned him the Bronze Star Medal.

By mid-November, with some of the worst winter weather hitting Europe, Macario and the men of the Fourth found themselves doing battle with the enemy in the dark thickets of the Hürtgen Forest. The Germans had been told to hold the Hürtgen Forest even if it meant fighting to the last man. For 21 days the infantrymen of the 28th, 26th, 8th, 3rd Armored, and 4th Divisions gave battle to the fanatical foe in the green thickets of the Hürtgen.

Garcia went through the Hürtgen mud and splintered paths, and roadblocks interdicted with deadly machine gun fire. He well remembers the bitter cold, the heavy-mined and booby-trapped paths, and the smell of death that lingered on for many days afterward.

In the Hürtgen Battle, the Germans tried every kind of obstacle imaginable, and, aided by a continuous cold rain, they kept launching counterattack after counterattack. But the dogged American Infantry pushed on slowly and at great cost, until they emerged from the impenetrable green, cold and exhausted when at last they reached the outskirts of Grosshau.

It was here where Garcia launched his one-man assault on the German Army. When the two advance platoons of Sergeant Garcia's company were almost to their objective, they were pinned down by enemy machine gun and rifle fire. Many of the men were wounded and the enemy immediately placed mortar and artillery fire on the troops. The support platoon then was committed and also pinned down. Among the casualties in the support platoon was Sergeant Garcia, who was wounded on the right shoulder by a shell fragment.

Sergeant Garcia, on his own volition, worked his way forward twice to get back at the Germans. Although wounded, he managed to destroy two enemy positions.

Says his company commander, First Lieutenant Tony Bizzaro, Bradford, Pennsylvania, "Only then with the withering automatic fire which covered all feasible routes of approach for the company eradicated by Sergeant Garcia, did the remaining 35 men of the company drive on to their objective."

THE RHINELAND CAMPAIGN

December, 1944, with the 313th Infantry Regiment: Allied forces were now driving hard towards the Rhine. The Germans were retreating fast into the Siegfied Line. Along the Allied front things did not look so good as they had back in November, when through "Stars and Stripes" we learned of the many large gains made by the 1st, 3rd, and 9th Armies. Things had looked so good then that we had anticipated being home for Christmas.

It was mid-December and the possibility of being home for Christmas did not look very promising now. "Jerry" was putting up desperate resistance and fighting with fanatical fury. The Allies were now knocking on his front door. He had been preparing for the day when he would have to fight off an invading enemy in his homeland.

Many combatmen remember those early days of the Rhineland Campaign in the 7th Army sector under the command of General Patch. Fighting alongside the 79th Division were the French Second Army and the following United States Infantry Divisions which had many Mexican-Americans in their combat ranks: the 3rd which had been in since the African campaign; the famous 36th from Texas, known for the many *chicanos* it had, who alongside with the 45th were veterans of the Italian campaign; the 26th, 44th, and 100th Infantry Divisions were also part of the 7th Army group.

Only a handful of our gang remained in our regiment, the 313th. Many of the boys who had been original members of the Cross of Lorraine outfit, since the division had left the States, had disappeared via the casualty route. A lot of them, along with hundreds of other frontline men, were back in some hospital in the rear, recovering from battle wounds. Some were in England and many had been flown to the States if the injury was considered severe. Many had been killed or captured. The 79th had been kept busy in its drive towards the Rhine. The combat troops had gone right back where we left off since that well-earned rest back in November.

In E Company, of the 313th, we were down to our last few Mexicans. There was Esquibel, a quiet, mannered, plump farmer from the Colorado hills; Esquivel (*spelled with a 'V'*), the fierce-looking dark-eyed Californian; Perchez, a youngster around 20 years of age; Garcia and myself. Everyone of them had been original members of the 79th; I had joined them as a replacement in October.

December 12. By now we had become seasoned Infantry-combat veterans. Since emerging out of the hellish *Foret de Parroy,* we had been on the go, pushing through ankle-deep mud on rain-soaked roads along the Alsace plains and up and down the Vosges Mountains. After the capture of Blamont, located on the south-end sector of the IV Corps, we began to run into a little stiffer opposition. In the small village of Greis, we were forced to spend three weeks living in cellars because of continuous artillery barrages by the Germans.

In every encounter we had with the Wermacht, we had gained our objective, and had captured many of the enemy with very few dead. It had been almost the same pattern at Blamont, Greis, Hagenau, Bischwiller and Naudorf. After all the major battles for the 313th, following heavy casualties, "Jerry" pulled out and we would take a large bunch of POW's that came out with their hands up yelling, "Kamrad! Kamrad!"; but they were either old broken-down *soldats* wearing long overcoats of no use for the infantry, or young punks too young for any fighting. We knew the Wermacht had a lot of able-bodied infantrymen. Where were they? We had a feeling that the Germans were bringing in these old men and when ready to pull an effective retreat, they would bring them up to go out and surrender.

After our first few times in combat together, we could not help but notice the change in the outlook and personal feelings between our fellow-G.I.'s and ourselves. This also was noticeable between the officers and enlisted men. Sharing combat experiences had served to draw us closer together more than we had ever been before.

In our early days overseas, most Mexican-Americans tended to band together. We would seek each other out because we spoke the same language, sang the same songs, etc. Most of us had known each other since back in the States. Sometimes, on rare occasions, when we were in the presence of someone who was not the friendly type, or who was disliked by one of the group, we deliberately ignored the *gabacho* (Anglo). The meanest stunt that was pulled many times to insult those we did not want around was to suddenly change all the conversation to nothing but Spanish.

As for the kind of treatment we received from the *gabachos* —as we used to call them—I can truthfully say that we were never treated badly. At the front we were all on equal terms. We were accepted just like any other G.I. No one ever referred to us as being "different Americans," except for a few smart-alecks who used to make us feel uncomfortable by insisting on calling us such names as "Pancho," "Mex," or "Joe" instead of by our last name, which was the proper way with all the other men in the platoons. Others were great kidders and were constantly showing off their limited Spanish with such words as *amigo, señor, mañana, poco-loco, etc.* Most of these words have now become part of everyday language.

The officers always kept to themselves in accordance with military custom. They ate and billeted apart from the enlisted men. While not as strict as back in the States with saluting and all of that, they did demand and got respect from all the enlisted personnel and were always addressed as "Sir," whether we approved of them or not.

Some of the officers took a special liking to us. They appreciated the docile and mild-mannered *Latinos* from the Southwest. Many of the CO's were greatly admired by all of their men. There was nothing the men wouldn't do for some of their leaders. Whenever a unit or company would lose such a leader, it had a demoralizing effect on the entire company. One such man was Lt. Marty Bachiero[1], an officer in the 313th.

Lt. Bachiero was a well-liked young officer of Italian descent. Just recently he had taken over Company E, having arrived as a replacement officer at about the same time our bunch from Camp Roberts joined the 79th. Bachiero hailed from San Francisco, California, and had been an arranger with a dance band in civilian days. The young Lieutenant was in his early twenties. He had soft brown eyes and a ready smile about him at all times. All the men in our platoon thought he was tops.

The following is a last-day account of the beloved "Bachi," (as we all learned to call him), taken from notes at the front:

With the 313th. *Easy Company is below full strength. More replacements have been brought in, but it seems like we're losing them quicker than they can bring them in. We have lost Captain Dale, and the company is now being led by Fleming, the Executive Officer. Our platoon is led by Lt. Bachiero, a young Italian-American from California. Bachi is an amiable easy-going person. He's always telling us that he is just a plain G.I. at heart, and that he doesn't care for the officers' way of life. The other officers of the company are always getting after Bachi to stay back, to sleep at the C.P. with them; but Bachi would rather be up front sleeping in the mudholes among the*

[1]Fictitious name.

G.I.'s and with his foxhole mate, little Felix Garcia, whom he nicknamed "Pinchey."

Bachi has always shown partiality to the Spanish-speaking G.I.'s in our squad, which were the two Esquibels, Perchez and myself. Once in a while he speaks to us in Spanish too.

December 14th. *We come in about midnight into a small village close to the German border. After a long march, dead-tired and hungry, we pull off our packs and lay down on the cold cement floor of an empty barn and begin munching some cold K-rations. Those of us who do not get guard duty fall into heavy slumber. No sooner do we begin to stretch our legs and enjoy sound sleep, when one of the guards comes in to awake the whole company with orders to move out again.*

"Oh, my aching G.I. back!" . . . everyone protests loudly. If you have never heard tired doughs put their thoughts into loud-voiced epithets, then you've really missed something.

We are told that we are to engage the enemy in close combat. The order is to fix bayonets . . . and me without a bayonet! (I was one of the smart ones that threw my bayonet away because I found little use for it and I didn't like to have it scraping against my legs in the long marches we made.)

We are to attack Lauterberg, a town beyond the Lauter River which is the German border, and beyond it is the vaunted Seigfried Line. F and G Companies are to attack from the Southeast, making junction with the 3rd Battalion at a church in the center of town. Utmost secrecy is to be preserved, the tanks and artillery are not to start until the assault commences just at first daylight.

Because we have the longest route, our battalion moves out at 0245 hours. We move out as softly as possible. In the darkness of the cold night you can barely make out what is in front of you. You have to put out your hand to touch whoever is ahead of you—sometimes you can't keep from stumbling into one of the slow moving men in front of you.

It's pitch dark, and we hope to catch them (the enemy) by surprise. Just before daybreak we reach the edge of the town ... not a sound from the "Boche"[1] ... either they haven't heard us or they are waiting for us to get closer. Perchez, our first scout, signals for us to advance. He jumps a small creek and we follow him. Now we are in an open field. Then it happens ... we are like sitting ducks and they open up on us with fire from above, at the edge of town. They have heavy machine gun nests placed at each side of the field and they wait just long enough for us to get within their cross-fire range. Frontal fire and fire from above rakes the field, and we are trapped!

Too late to go back ... and the machine guns are too far to try to knock out. Men fall in front of me, to my right, and my left ... I can hear the agonizing plea, "Help, I'm hit," and from some other felled comrade, "Ay, Madre mia!" It's terrifying to hear your buddies pleading when they're hit ... but you can't do much when you are told, "Leave them alone! The Medics will take care of them."

I hear Staff Sergeant Griff above all the commotion, "Everyone, the machine gun on the left!" We all concentrate our fire on the gun position to our left ... soon it is silenced. The other machine gun pulls out to another position and we advance to the left. As we crawl along the brush, around the gun nest, we learn that they are positioned all around the town's edge. They have long trenches running from one dugout to another, and keep us under fire by shifting to the next gun position as we go around them.

We now find tree protection; we arise and go into full attack ... My M-I is jammed ... it does not eject the spent cartridges due to a wet shell. I throw it away. I have to go back to get a rifle from one of the comrades who has fallen. There

---

[1]French slangword for German.

behind a tree I am surprised to find Lt. Bachi with a very frightened look in his face!

"What's the matter, Bachi? You're not scared?"... I only mean it as a joke, but he has taken it as an insult. He comes out from behind, stands erect and orders, with a twist of anger in his voice, "Let's go!" I can't figure Bachi out ... everytime we had been in action against the enemy he has been there right alongside of us. Everyone always admired his great courage ...

We go back to the front together where the Jerries are still holding off our attack.

There is a small creek that is in front of the advance troops. The same creek that Perchez had jumped over earlier this morning. Further up Sgt. Griff is the only one across the creek. The Krauts are laying a sheet of heavy fire. The rest of the squad is about ready to jump across . . . Griff, who is protected by the rise of the ground is around a bend, and the fire is over his head. He is motioning to the men where to jump, and to keep their heads down. It is our turn to go next ... We are kneeling behind a clump of brush and a wooden fence. Lt. Bachi starts to rise to get a better view ..."Bachi!" I yell, "Stay down!"... too late. An enemy gunner has been waiting for another head to pop up above the fence. His body topples over me and falls on my side. A shiver runs through me when I see his mortal wound; he has been hit right above and between his eyes. It must have been an automatic weapon, probably AP[1] ammo. The top of his head is torn off, his brains spill out ... there is still a quiver in the membrane.

ARTILLERY AID

At long last our heavy-weapon platoons come into action behind us. Their heavy thunder sounds like sweet music to our ears. After a few grenades thrown at the enemy, coupled with

---

[1]Armor piercing ammunition.

the heavy fire on their tails, the Jerries finally give up their positions and pull out. It is 1500 hours when we finally enter the town of Lauterberg.

It had been a long day and the good Lord had been good to me indeed. Those of us who had come through without a scratch were very thankful to be alive, but regretted very deeply the death of Bachi. The beloved Lieutenant's death had a demoralizing effect on the whole company.

On that day, after the shooting died down, a squad of volunteers who had been close to him, went out to look for Lt. Bachi's body.

We found him just the way I had last seen him. We took off his pack and stripped him of all his valuables, which included his wrist watch, ring, a picture of his wife and children, personal letters, cigarettes, and several pairs of dry socks he carried.

All valuables and his personal items were turned over to the officer of the company to be mailed to his wife. The cigarettes and dry socks were passed out to his friends, just as Bachi would have wanted it.

Bachi must've had a feeling that this was going to be his day. Many combat men often got that feeling. It was surprising how often the feeling became a reality.

THE COMBAT INFANTRYMAN

With the 313th in Southern France. The German officer looked every bit the fighting leader he was supposed to be. His neat trim uniform, his arrogant features, his straight posture, shiny boots and the military air about him: in fact, compared to him, we looked more like the prisoners than he did. He felt proud that his men had fought so well and had held off the enemy for so long against such tremendous odds. Now he wanted to see for himself what sort of creatures were the "Ami soldats"[1] that had defeated such brave fighters as his

Grenadier forces; these "Amerikaner gangsters" that would not retreat when there was no advance, who would not give up when they were hopelessly trapped, the reckless fools who would dare to match their inferior weapons against the Wermacht's!

Anxiety filled his features as the G.I.'s neared the house where we were holding him at bay. Here they came now. First on the scene was Pfc. Bill "Brownie" Brown, a stubby, short-sized, freckle-faced country boy from Oklahoma. He had his rifle pointed down low and walked with lazy long strides. The German officer gave him a quick glance and turned his eyes to the next G.I. strolling in. This one was a tall, pimple-faced, lazy-looking G.I. who wore thick-lensed glasses and looked puzzled, and nothing at all like a fighter. He was Pvt. Henderson, a new replacement from Ohio. Next came a short little Mexican, smaller than Pfc. Brown. He wore no helmet and his thick, curly, black hair extended over his forehead, making him look like a *borrego*(lamb). This was Pfc. Garcia from Texas. A strain of unbelief filled the officer's eyes . . . Surely these sloppy looking infantrymen weren't the *"Amerikaner"* killers . . . Where were the men that had defeated his brave fighters? Two more men came. Tall, lanky, grim-faced Pfc. Davis and tobacco-chewing Sgt. Jones from Tennessee and Kentucky. A dark-complexioned, bowlegged character followed—another Mexican. This dark eyed, rugged-looking individual with black hair was Sgt. Esquivel from California. Their clothes were tattered and torn, their faces were very dirty and grimy. They looked more beaten than the defeated German soldiers. The German officer looked around, puzzled . . . but where??? Surely not these . . .

Apparently, he had seen pictures of the neatly-uniformed U.S. Air Force men, the rugged-looking Marines and the trim-

---

[1]German nickname for American soldiers.

looking young U.S. Navy sailors. He had not heard about the old familiar saying that went something like this, "Mexicans, Okies, Polacks, and Wops. That's all you see in the Infantry" . . . Well, this was the Infantry. *The Combat Infantry,* please.

"The Queen of Battles" they call the Infantry, and the job they give you as an infantry-combatman is equally despised by one and all, no matter what army you're in because there's nothing 'royal' about it. Not only do you hate it because to live in it you have to forget all about human principles and it's either kill or be killed, and you are taught that you *have* to kill your fellow-man as if he had no right on this earth, you also hate it because if you should start getting too soft about the human race you are most likely to wind up getting killed by this same human you feel so sorry for.

The life of a combatman is more animal than it is human—it has to be. You live in filth, sleep in a mud-filled earth-hole and exist on the bare necessities of life. You live in continuous nerve-shattering fear of the enemy and his ultra-superior death-dealing weapons. Not only does the enemy and his weapons make life unpleasant for you, the terrain also comes in for its share of bother—with you having to battle through thick forests or jungles, high rocky hills and mountains, open plains, hedge-rows, hot deserts, and through shattered villages and towns, risking falling plaster, brick, and debris, not to mention sniper fire. Then there are the elements. The hot sun, rain, sleet, snow, earth-freezing blue cold . . . it is always severe weather at the front, no matter what.

All the latest weapons of modern warfare are fired point-blank at the infantry, and .all that an infantryman can fight back with is a small-arms weapon, and most likely—for the U.S. Infantryman—a M-1 30 calibre U.S. Garand, semi-automatic rifle, a weapon which is apt to become defective from constant use or through faulty neglect.

It's amazing how similiar the daily routine is for all infantrymen. How relatively close they follow the same pattern when at the front lines. A regular day for an infantryman at the battle zone would begin as follows:

You awake in the early morning just at the end of a beautiful dream about all the niceties you had at home—a soft bed, clean sheets, and the love of a woman—you hear soft whispering . . . *someone* is calling softly . . . No, it is not your loved one back home, it is the squad leader!! Then you discover the fact that you are in the same old muddy hole; your body aches all over, and you feel the tired weariness of sleeping with all your clothes on in the hard, cold, rocky ground, and you are still very much in the war.

There is a bad taste in your mouth; your face feels thick with dirt, grease, and grime; your hair is thick from lack of grooming; and you can hardly stand the nauseating body odors. You yearn for a cigarette, but you can't smoke unless you get back under the blanket. A cup of coffee would taste just wonderful right now, but you don't dare light a fire that will make telltale smoke . . . so you open up a can of cold K-rations and start munching, washing the food down with cold water from your canteen.

The artillery guns that had quieted down in the wee hours of the morn are also awakening. They begin to increase their salvos and once again they start to harrass you. You hear that the enemy moved up a lot of stuff last night and they may attack any moment now. You must prepare yourself for an attack. You check your rifle, your ammo, and your gear . . . then you wait . . . There's no telling how long you have to wait—you do a lot of waiting in the infantry—but this time you are glad to wait; the more you wait the better you feel.

The C.O. gets a message from battalion and he sends a runner with a message for the First Sarge; he sends for the platoon sergeants and they pass the word around that we are to attack. The platoon will attack with our squad leading the attack. Why does it always have to be your squad, your platoon, your company? It always seems that way . . . Then they just tell you "Get ready," and that's all—nothing else. They never tell you more. We ask questions, but all we get for an answer is, "It beats the Hell out of me!" . . . our guess is that they don't want you to know much in case you get captured by the enemy.

Now it is time to go . . . Everyone is told to put on their pack and be ready to move out. Then you do more waiting; this time you hate the waiting. Your whole insides move around . . . you feel like having a bowel movement . . . Here and there G.I.'s go back of bushes or behind trees. Everyone has the same sickly feeling. You try to figure out which would be preferable—to attack or be attacked? I'd hate to be caught in a foxhole in the middle of a fanatical attack—so common with the enemy—but then, too, I would hate to be in an attack against a well-dug-in German company, who have plenty of automatic weapons and are backed up by the mighty 88's. I would hate to be in either one, but, anyway here we go now. The scouts move out in different areas along the line. We are just plain 904 riflemen, and we are "expendable," which means if we are caught in a predicament it may be necessary to sacrifice us in order to save the rest of the platoon, the company, or the position which is worth more to battle strategists than you are. You then begin to wonder . . . *Will I get it today? . . . or will my luck hold out once more? Will there be a bullet with my name on it?* Or, *Have I pressed my luck a wee bit too much?* You pray a little . . . *Dear God, please spare me today* . . . Do you feel afraid? *Everyone* is afraid—you just can't help it. You are now in the line of departure, and you can't help but to go into one of the stages of battle participation.

There are four stages you go through when you face the enemy. The stages you go through are:

First—a mild anticipation when you learn the order has been

given to go into combat. You know there will be danger; you wish you didn't have to go along; but still, you hate to miss out on it.

Second—as you leave the line of departure you get a cold fear. Sweat rolls off your skin. Your stomach feels empty and your intestines start twisting and twirling. You begin to wonder if you are going to be able to stand the gaff.

Third—when you are within sight and range of the enemy and the shooting starts, you get a panicky feeling. You look for cover; you hit the dirt or start digging a little with your trenching tool. The instinct of self-preservation engulfs you as the shooting and noise picks up momentum. You "freeze" . . . you look back and usually you have to be urged on by one of your comrades or the squad leader. If you recover quickly from this, you go on into the fourth stage, otherwise you are liable to "crack-up," or uncontrollably start doing cowardly acts . . .

The fourth stage—usually at the heat of battle. Suddenly you regain your composure. You get a warm feeling . . . your nerves get settled and you can think better. You feel there's someone behind you, you get *courage,* you realize that the enemy in front of you is just as scared as you are and maybe more so. Our weapons are just as effective as his, and we have more of them. There is yelling, and before you realize it you are yelling too! Then, as an old Mexican saying goes, "*Quien dijo miedo? Y alcabo para morir nacimos.*"[1] And if you see one of your comrades "get it," you might fly into a blind rage, ignoring the danger and trying the impossible—as many of our CMH heroes did—or you may feel so tired of the war that you actually don't care anymore . . . you become indifferent to everything . . . You do not even seek cover . . .

When the battle is over, you seek out a position to dig in—

---

[1] "Why be afraid? Anyway we were born to die."

you anticipate a counter-attack. You dig like hell because you want to have some protection when they start throwing stuff at you. The sergeant marks out the perimeter of defense. He sets up an outpost, two or three of the men in the farthest out position from our lines, with a telephone to relay any movement of the enemy to the C.P.

If the enemy does not counter-attack, you get a feeling of security. You begin to arrange things around your foxhole. You have time to dig deeper; you get logs, branches and leaves for protection and to camouflage your foxhole.

Just when you are getting set to enjoy a brief respite in your "safe" foxhole, the order comes to get ready to move out again. The enemy apparently has retreated and our objective has been secured. Now Regiment or Division Headquarters has decided on another objective for our platoon today.

So, once more you put on your pack, check your piece and ammo, and set out in quest of the enemy. There is no enemy in sight, but we are to seek him and try to reach another objective further away. We are now on a forced march. It is to be only a "short march"—about 5 or 10 miles is a short march if you're in the infantry. We march in columns, each platoon keeping about 20 feet apart. You lock your piece . . . no enemy in sight . . . you throw your rifle astraddle over your shoulder "rabbit-huntin' " style. You come to the edge of a town and march right through the main thoroughfare.

The natives come out to greet you. They rave and shout; they shower you with gifts, flowers, and bottles of cognac; they call you a hero; *Les liberatoures!* This is the great moment for the infantry. You enjoy the smiling faces of friendly people. To the young girls and small children you are the great American Hero. There are invitations to come in and visit them in their living quarters. The G.I.'s, who are the daring type, break ranks to stay behind, risking disciplinary action later. Most of us continue the march to the end of the town and into the country, through rocky and dusty roads, and into woods. It is late now. The day is about to end. You can feel the long hard day all over your bones. Your legs are weary and your feet sore. We are now closing in on the enemy. If we are close enough we might engage him again, or perhaps the C.O. may decide it is better to dig in at this point and send out a reconnaissance patrol to feel out the enemy's strength.

If feels mighty good to take off your pack and lay down your fighting gear. When you take off the heavy helmet, your head feels like a feather. Now you will light a cigarette, lie down, and rest . . . but only for a little while, for there is work to do. Rations and water have to be brought up. If it's your turn you will have to go way back five or eight miles where the supply trucks have pulled up. You'll have to struggle with heavy supplies, 5-gallon cans of water, boxes, cans of ration, and bedrolls (if available) in the darkness, up the hills and through the woods.

As darkness sets in, the C.O. sends a runner out with the password for the night to the sergeants. Each sergeant passes it along to the different squads. "Password for tonight will be 'Hollywood Man.' You had better not forget it or misquote it because if you should get lost and stumble into one of the other company's area where nervous sentries have itchy trigger fingers, your life won't be worth two cents.

You get rations, water for tonight and tomorrow, and water for your own canteen. If you're not picked for an early hour of guard duty, you get set to enjoy the luxury of a night under the stars in the open—even tho' your bed might be rocky, damp, and uncomfortable—where you can shower your face with dirt, and rocks crawl under your body at the slightest movement or shift of your body.

Tomorrow will be another day. In all the other parts of the world, the morrow might be a new and different day, but to the combat infantryman at the front, tomorrow will not be any different from that of today—just as today was no different from yesterday. And there is no end to it, unless your Division is pulled out for a rest, or if the impossible should happen—*the enemy might surrender and the war would cease.*

Everyone else feels pity for the combat infantryman, but the combatman does not feel self pity. In fact, the combat infantryman possesses a proud feeling that not many can understand . . . proof of this is the pride they have of the *Combat Infantryman's Badge.* The badge that is the most prized possession of of the combat infantryman.

When a replacement, or any infantry soldier for that matter, goes through his first experience of actual combat against the enemy and he comes through in exemplary manner, his name will be put in for the "*Combat Infantryman's Badge*" by the C.O. This award differs from the ordinary "Infantryman's Badge" that is awarded to all soldiers who complete a rigorous course in Infantry training. With the combat badge goes an extra ten dollars monthly combat pay. But it means more than that to the infantryman who has been in the front lines. It means—*Pride.* They wear the badge with pride because they know that to get a combat badge you have to *earn* it. When combatmen see it on the uniform of another G.I., they give instant recognition to the wearer, and a mutual feeling of comradeship is expressed by one another. They know what the wearer has been through, they can understand this more than anyone else.

THE GERMAN BREAKTHROUGH

Mid-December, 1944. The U.S. First and Third Army groups were positioned along the Siegfried Line. The Ninth was facing the Roer River and the Seventh (the group we were in) was driving towards the Rhine in southern France.

The Third Army was fighting near Metz. Farther north, near Aachen, the First and Ninth were "just holding" defensive positions. All these Army groups had been pushing for the Rhine over difficult terrain, across swollen rivers, and in severe weather against a stiffening foe.

On the morning of December 16th, the German Army, under their brilliant General Von Runsted, launched their greatest counteroffensive of World War II against American divisions situated in the Ardennes sector, an 88-mile front along eastern Belgium and Luxemburg.

Very few people know how close the Germans came to pushing the Allies back into Normandy and into the sea. Even before the Germans launched their counteroffensive in the Ardennes, the G.I.'s at the front pointed out what an easy matter it would be for the Jerries to drive through France again because there was no one to stop them behind the lines once they broke through Allied troops at the front.

The only combat-tested fighting Divisions between the Rhine and Normandy were the 82nd and 101st Paratroop Divisions. who were in reserve, enjoying the sights of Paris and preparing for some happy celebrations during the Christmas and New Year's holidays. A few untested Infantry Divisions, fresh from stateside were in reserve. One of them, the 106th "Golden Lion" Division, was moved up into the front around mid-December and because their men were without any previous battle experience, they were moved into a supposedly "quiet" sector of the Ardennes. Then it happened . . .

The VIII Corps' front, which had been relatively quiet since the latter part of September, suddenly flared up. A concentrated infantry-tank attack was opened at 0800 hours on the 16th of December on the north flank of the VIII Corps. The 106th Division and the 10th Calvary groups were attacked by a mass of infantry and tanks. Alfred Guerra, Sacramento, California, a rifleman with the 3rd Battalion, 42nd Regiment of the 106th Division, was one of the untested frontline soldiers who met the might of the Germans' offensive head-on, at the start of Von Runsted's Ardennes attack.

"We were dug in along the wooded ridge of the Schee Eifel, near the city of St. Vith," says Guerra. "On the foggy morning of the 16th, the Germans began their attack with a tremendous artillery barrage, then came enemy tanks, hundreds of them, followed by hordes of infantrymen." Guerra continues, "The Jerries further confused us with their many English-speaking soldiers disguised in captured American M.P. uniforms."

The 28th Division, commanded by Major General Norman D. Cota, and the 2nd, the 4th, and the 9th Armored were the only combat divisions along the 75-mile front from Monshau to Trier, where the Panzers struck their heaviest blow. Von Runsted assembled 20 divisions of what was considered to be the cream of the German Army. These elite troops were bolstered by the 6th SS Armored which were brought in all the way from the Russian front. The group was composed of battle-toughened, young fanatics, fully indoctrinated with German patriotism.

The ground was frozen and the Germans went along at a rapid pace. They struck with speed along weak American positions. The 28th Division was attacked by two Panzer divisions, a Parachute Division and three Infantry Divisions riding on tanks along the ridge road just west of the Our River. In three hours the 28th was forced to withdraw. The 4th Infantry and the 9th Armored were also heavily attacked, but these were diversionary attacks by the enemy to prevent the Americans from shifting troops to plug the gap further north, near St. Vith and Bastogne, which was the German objective.

In Belgium, on the southern half of the First Army sector, Lupe Naranjo, of Agua Dulce, Texas, Alan Diaz of Laredo, Agustin Lucio of San Marcos, and Tom Castro of San Antonio —all sergeants and squad leaders in the 23rd Regiment of the 2nd Division—along with Sgt. Jose Lopez of Brownsville, Texas, (whose story is related in the following chapter) were stationed just south of the First Army sector and also met head-on the fury of the German thrust.

In the breakthrough, a large force of Germans attacked them near the twin towns of Rockeroth and Krinkelt. The role played by some of the men in the 2nd Division in the German breakthrough is revealed in the "Jose Lopez" story.

SGT. JOSE M. LOPEZ

Awarded The Congressional Medal of Honor

Krinkelt, Belgium, December 17th, 1944. On his own initiative, he carried his heavy machine gun from Company K's right flank to its left, in order to protect that flank which was in danger of being overrun by advancing enemy infantry supported by tanks.

Occupying a shallow hole offering no protection above his waist, he cut down a group of ten Germans. Ignoring enemy fire from an advancing tank, he held his position and cut down 25 more enemy infantry attempting to turn his flank. Glancing to his right he saw a large number of infantry swarming in from the front. Although dazed and shaken from enemy artillery fire which had crashed into the ground only a few yards away, he realized that his position soon would be outflanked. Again, alone, he carried his machine gun to a position to the right rear of the sector; enemy tanks and infantry were forcing a withdrawal. Blown over backwards by the concussion of enemy fire, he immediately reset his gun and continued his fire. Single-handed, he held off the German horde until he was satisfied his company had effected its retirement.

Again he loaded his gun on his back and in a hail of small arms fire he ran to a point where a few of his comrades were attempting to set up another defense against the onrushing enemy. He fired from this position until his ammunition was exhausted. Still carrying his gun, he fell back with his small group to Krinkelt.

Sergeant Lopez' gallantry and intrepidity on a seemingly suicidal mission in which he killed at least *100* of the enemy, was almost solely responsible for allowing Company K to avoid being enveloped, to withdraw successfully, and to give other forces coming in support time to build a line which repelled the enemy drive.[1]

Jose M. Lopez, of Brownsville, Texas, was the 4th American of Mexican descent to be awarded the Congressional Medal of Honor. The short, stocky, Mexican-American was a machine gunner with K Company of the 23rd Regiment, 2nd Division. He has the distinction of having killed more enemy soldiers than any other American in the ETO or Pacific Theaters in World War II.

Not even Sgt. York of World War I fame comes close to the number of enemy killed or personally destroyed. Lopez is credited with having killed over 100 German soldiers in the Krinkelt Wald, near Belgium on December 17, 1944.

Next to Lopez was S/Sgt. John C. Sjorgen of Rockyford, Michigan, who personally killed 43 Japanese near San Jose Hacienda, Negros, while serving with the 40th Division in the Philippines on May 23, 1945. Then stands Sgt. Veto R. Bertoldo of Decatur, Illinois, who destroyed 40 Germans in Hatten, France, with the 42nd Division on January 9-10, 1945.

All Mexican-Americans are very proud of Jose M. Lopez. Not only because he won the Congressional Medal but because of the way he accomplished this unprecedented task.

Lopez first landed in France with the 2nd Division on D-Day plus-one at St. Laurent-sur-Mer in Normandy. He was in the thick of hedgerow fighting around Saint-Lo and in the breakthrough out of Normandy. In Brest, he fought against the

---

[1]War Department Citation, G.O. No. 47, June 18, 1945.

SERGEANT JOSE M. LOPEZ
Brownsville, Texas
Congressional Medal of Honor
European Theater World War II

tough 3rd Parachute German Division where the 2nd battled for 39 days before they took the ravished city. On July 29th, he received the Purple Heart for being wounded in action.

While fighting near the Siegfreid Line around St. Vith, Lopez was awarded the Bronze Star Medal for conspicuous gallantry against the enemy.

On December 17, 1944, the second day of the German breakthrough, near the town of Rockeroth, Lopez and other men of K and L companies from the 23rd Regiment were ordered to protect an exposed left flank as the German infantry came on with two light tanks. Lopez set up his machine gun to protect the withdrawal of the other troops and began firing.

The Germans wasted no time in returning Lopez' fire, riddling the area with burp guns, rifle, and tank fire. A Tiger tank appeared at the road junction and fired point-blank at Lopez' exposed position. The long barrel of the 88 seemed to reach halfway to his foxhole, but Lopez continued to fire.[1]

The woods echoed with the rapid staccato of the hot lead he was pouring, and smoke erupted from his water-cooled barrel that was now burning up. Over the noise of Lopez' machine gun, Captain Walsh shouted to his men to withdraw, but Lopez ignored him and continued to fire. He cut down a group of the Jerries that were advancing toward him—backed up by a Tiger tank. Ignoring the tank fire, he held his position.

To the rear of the sector, enemy tanks and infantry were forcing a withdrawal . . . now he was almost alone facing the enemy. Rifle and tank fire kept hitting all around him. Then came hand grenades . . . One of the grenades landed right in his foxhole.

The action is described by his comrades as follows:

"Twice, when the Germans were overrunning his position,

[1]MacDonald, Charles Brown, *Company Commander,* Infantry Journal Press, Washington, D.C., 1947, p. 187.

he picked up his machine gun and withdrew to set it up and continue the "fight," Private First Class Leo J. Albert, 419 River Street, Paterson, New Jersey, reported. "The Germans were supported by tanks. Twice, fire from the gun of the first tank plowed up the ground close to his position, but he continued firing his machine."

Lieutenant Paul E. Burkhardt, of Fairground Road, Xenia, Ohio, said the engagement lasted from 11:30 a.m. until 6:00 p.m. "After beating off an attack from the flank, killing at least 35 Germans, Sergeant Lopez was forced to withdraw with his machine gun after tank fire had twice struck his position," reported the Lieutenant.

"Alone in holding up the advance, he was the target of every German weapon, but disregarding the intense fire, he again set up his weapon and continued firing. Another tank approached to within 50 yards and its 88mm was swung around, turned directly on him . . . but he kept his fire on the advancing enemy.

"A shell from the 88 struck his position and he was blown backward away from his gun, still he staggered back to it, reset it, and continued firing.

"All during this time ammunition bearers were forced to toss boxes of ammunition to him because of the tremendous volume of enemy fire being poured into his position. When his reformed and reinforced company returned to the attack, they drove the enemy from the area."

Born in Mission, Texas, on June 1, 1912, Lopez, his wife Emilia, and his six-year-old stepson, Juan P. Lopez, lived in Brownsville. He entered the Army from his home there on April 8, 1942. It is a shame that very few Americans have heard of the record Lopez holds, and the daring exploits that won him the Congressional Medal of Honor. Yet others who did less have been glorified more. Even though he has been given little recognition here, Lopez feels very satisfied because the people of Mexico have all heard of his courageous achievement and is well known to them. They remember him when he was guest of President Aleman in Mexico City in 1948, where he was feted and awarded the Aztec Eagle, the highest honor medal of the Southern Republic, and he later toured that country as a guest.

HITTING THE SIEGFRIED LINE

December 17th—with the 313th. After having taken Lauterberg, the 79th moved into the Hagenau Forest to attack the Siegfreid Line. Plans were made to push the 3rd Battalion and the 1st Battalion and advance to the North as a reconnaissance force, because no one was sure about the enemy's situation. Our battalion, the 2nd, was to patrol and protect the 3rd's left flank.

We moved out about 8:30 in the morning. As we entered the woods, I noticed a neatly lettered sign placed along the bank of the Lauter River, which read: "You are now entering Germany—Courtesy of the 79th Division." I studied the sign; it was obvious that it had been lettered by a professional, probably some T-5 back at safe quarters in the rear. *Why couldn't I have a soft job like that of painting signs* (my profession in civilian life), *instead of the role of a combat infantryman, which did not offer a very bright future?*

For the first time in many battles E Company was not to lead the regimental attack. We couldn't believe it. Everyone in our company swore that we always spearheaded the attacks for our regiment. This time we were put in reserve, as a supporting unit. We dug in at the edge of the woods. It was a thick-wooded area on the North side of Lauterberg, where fresh trails had been cut through and new roads opened by the combat engineers. When "George" Company passed by, I went out to look for my old buddies—most of whom had been together since shipping out from the states. I saw and talked to some for the last time . . . Tony Rodriguez, the short, little *viejito* (old man) from San Antonio; the "great" Padilla, *"El Azote de la 38,"* always full of life and a lot of personality. "Hey Padilla!" I yelled. Everyone knew the light complexioned Mexican from the southside of Los Angeles. He was a big favorite with most of the regiment. There was also Joe Casiano, Padilla's competitor in wine, women, and song. Missing were: Gonzales, the Puerto-Rican; Luis Gomez; Carlos Abril; and Jess Martinez, my old buddy. Martinez had gone back with a small wound. The attacking company moved on in "full strength" with plenty of anti-tank guns, tanks, and jeeps. They were followed by the Combat Engineers.

We rested our weary bodies all day. I resumed my frontline sketching, wrote notes and some V-letters for the folks back home and cleaned my Garand rifle. Next day we were up early and soon had a poker game going. We could hear a lot of shooting and felt good about being on reserve.

A jeep, made into a make-shift ambulance with two bodies on the top, passed by on the road. The jeep had come from the direction of the "Line" where we could hear a lot of artillery firing.

The first jeep did not cause much attention, as we were too engrossed with our card game. When jeep after jeep with wounded bodies followed out of the woods in quick succession, we began to take notice. We realized then that something bad was going on out there at the 'line'. We soon learned from one of the jeep drivers that G Company had run into an anti-tank ditch which was too long and too deep for any tank to cross. As George Company was trying to cross, the Jerries had let loose a tremendous artillery and mortar barrage. The battalion's history of that day is reported as follows:

> ... the 3rd Battalion had reached the anti-tank ditch which was well covered with artillery and machine-gun fire. It was approximately twenty feet wide and ten to

> fifteen feet deep in places, adequately stopping any tracked vehicle. Beyond it, between it and the pillboxes, was a band of barbed wire twenty to thirty feet deep, completing an obstacle the like of which the Regiment had not encountered since Cherbourg.[1]

When the 2nd Battalion was stopped cold and the 314th Regiment met the same fate on the left of them, we knew for sure that this was it. We had encountered the famed Siegfreid Line!

In trying to take the pillboxes, G Company suffered terrible losses. Only 23 men were left of the original attacking company. Then we heard the word we always hated to hear . . . we were to relieve G Company. We were to try to crack the Siegfreid Line where George Company had failed.

That afternoon we held religious services. Joe Catalano, our Medic, a chubby little Italian from Pittsburgh, had made sure this part of our preparation was not forgotten. Joe was a devout Catholic, he always brought out rosaries and prayer books to the Mexican-American boys in our group—most of whom were Catholic. He would pray with us and give us words of encouragement. Everyone felt more religious than ever. And those who never believed before surely did believe now.

We moved out about 1600 hours. My notes of that period described what followed:

There is litter strewn all around the foxholes that have been dug by the men from George Company. Battered helmets, crushed canteens, empty ration boxes, unexploded grenades, rifles, and bandoliers are scattered around. The whole area is a mess. The First Sergeant assigns the men to each position. He tells me, "Yours is the last hole. Shoot anyone you see in front of it."

The noise is terrific. Over the din of the thunderous blasts

---

[1]*History of the 313th Infantry in World War II,* Infantry Journal Press, Washington, D.C., 1947, p. 147.

we can hear yelling of someone giving orders or soldiers shouting questions. The artillery pounds the earth with a loud, heavy thunder . . . trees burst and broken branches add to the danger of each barrage. An empty tank is afire and exploding its ammo close to the ditch; the foul smell of powder fills the air . . .

Tonight a green replacement; just recently arrived from the states, was brought to my foxhole. He is "Joe Sarcino," a very nervous G.I. from New York. He is about 20 *and so fat he looks funny.*

Enemy artillery continues to roll in. It comes from the North, Northeast, and from the East. They are even sending it out from the east bank of the Rhine, which is Southeast. In between artillery barrages we get showers of mortars . . . We are so close to them that we can actually hear the click of mortars when each round is fired.

Joe and I take hourly turns at guard during the night. He is so nervous and afraid, I feel sorry for him—he keeps praying continually with a rosary in his hands. Why do they send green kids to a hot spot like this? . . . I can't sleep knowing that he is untried and afraid.

December 19*th. Next day the nightmarish hell continues . . . we are losing men and the squad is getting low. No one dares to venture out of his foxhole because any little movement brings another barrage—they have us well spotted. Bailey gets hit by "tree burst" . . . Murphy's leg is blown off . . . Others go out quickly when they get direct hits . . . Oh, for one of those million dollar wounds . . .*

Night comes and we're still sweating blood. The cold weather is so miserable that we have to cut down watches to half-hour turns. We have a couple of skimpy blankets to wrap around our feet when we sleep. I can't sleep when it's my turn, and I can hardly stay awake during my watch. Joe has a marvelous way of falling into a heavy slumber right away. I have to awaken him when he starts snoring loud for fear the enemy will hear him. They are around close to our hole . . . They come every night to probe our positions . . . they are so close that we can hear them move about . . . we dare not fire at them so that they will not learn our location . . . Once in a while we let go a grenade.

On the next morning, December 20th, we find ammo and rations that someone tossed out at us. No one dares to go out of his hole . . . the only way I can tell we are not alone is by calling out to the next hole where Esquivel and Gobles are. I can't stand it any longer—I just have to take a chance and go out to answer a call of nature . . . It doesn't take long . . . they are throwing shells again. I jump back in the hole holding my pants up with my hand . . . you can't even stick your head out. To urinate—we use the K ration boxes and hurl them out.

On that night I spend the darkest moments of my GI life. It seems that the only target they have now is our foxhole. Rounds of artillery begin to come in our immediate direction. The first one is short and falls a few feet up in front of us . . . the earth shakes and we shake with it . . . The dirt walls of our foxhole cave in . . . we start digging out frantically. The next hits a little past our hole . . . more dirt and our shovels are doing double duty . . . Now they're "zeroing in" on us! . . . the next one will be a direct hit. Joe prays and groans, he pleads to the skies . . . "If you want to live, do more digging and less praying," I tell him. Oh my God! What am I saying? I had better do some praying myself. This is going to be it . . .

The next round is close to our left. They are only prolonging this agony and fear that we have. Next one is to the right and It's coming in fast now. The next one will be for effect 1 *am sure . . . No more traction . . . no more elevation . . . They are on the target now. I know we'll be goners after this one. We stop our digging now. We are both praying hard and pleading with God.*

I remember the 23rd Psalm, it goes something like this: "Yea, tho I walk through the valley in the shadow of Death, I will fear no evil, for Thou art with me . . ." It fits just the way that I feel. I keep remembering my family, my wife, my mother, my children . . . What will become of them? I get the sudden notion to dash out and run over to the next foxhole; perhaps then I will be missed . . . I try . . . but I can't move, as we are stuck in the soft dirt that has crumpled around us.

The finisher comes . . . we flinch . . . we are splattered with dirt, tree branches and rocks . . . But miraculously we escape out of the brink of death . . . Thank God they have missed us. Our prayers have been answered.

The rounds continue, but to the right of our position—that is the target they are now concentrating on. The assault continues all next day. I am now near exhaustion . . . I can feel my nerves on the verge of a breakdown. We have had several "crack-ups" and I suppose I will be the next one. I have a nauseating headache, and feel shaky all over.

I begin to feel demoralized. The constant pounding we're receiving keeps us in a frenzy. I can't see how we're ever going to get out of this living hell. If the Germans were to attack us in full force, they could easily take us all as prisoners.

Early that night Sgt. Buck crawls to our hole and calls us out in a low voice. He tells us, "Don't make any noise. We're pulling out when it gets dark. Get all your gear ready." I couldn't believe it, but what else could we do? We weren't getting anywhere . . . May as well give up the ghost.

On December 21st, we moved out about midnight. We moved out silently, and sadly we took down the sign that said we were going into Germany, "courtesy of the 79th." It was midnight and the weather was below freezing, but we were actually feeling good about leaving.

Later we learned the Germans had started an offensive in the Ardennes. All replacements and ammunition were being diverted to that critical area, where they had top priority on all incoming men and materiél. This was the reason we had abandoned our fight near the ditch, or so they told us, but they could never convince me. I knew better . . . the Siegfreid Line had stopped us cold and "Jerry" had beat the hell out of us. This was one time the American Army had retreated . . .

THE BULGE

The Battle of the Bulge was the turning point of the German breakthrough. The fighting took place during some of Europe's worse winter weather, with rain, snow, and ice hampering the fighting men in the Ardennes where the historic battle was fought.

For the first twenty-four hours the Jerries made long gains. The ground was frozen solid and the German *blietzkrieg* went along at a rapid pace. Had not the Germans failed in their attempt to capture 3,000,000 gallons of gasoline stored near the Malmedy and Spa dumps, "Jerry" would have gone all the way to Normandy. To fight off the enemy while American trucks rolled out of Spa with load after load of the precious gasoline, the First Division exhausted all their front-line troops, and then had to throw in their headquarters troops. M.P.'s, cooks, clerks, motorized cavalrymen, chemical and anti- aircraft troops—all had to go out and fight as Infantry against the onrushing Germans, some of these had never fired a rifle since their basic training days.

Following close on the heels of their armored spearheads, the Germans had strong columns of Infantry, tanks and artillery, with fanatical German soldiers yelling their heads off. These Jerries were playing for keeps, no more trying to wound the enemy and capture prisoners. They were determined to kill all enemy on sight and not to take any prisoners. The massacre at Malmedy, where almost 200 Americans who surrendered were stripped of their arms, lined up along a snow-laden field and then sprayed cold bloodedly with machine gun fire by both officers and unranked privates, was an example of their intentions.

Supreme Headquarters, frantic over the German successes, alerted all available forces and rushed them in to stop the powerful German offensive. British and Canadian troops came in from Holland. The U.S. 9th and 1st Army troops were thrown into the battle area; two Airborne Divisions, the 82nd and the 101st, fought as ground troops. Patton's 3rd Army had to give up its attack at the Saar to send troops to the embattled area. Things got so desperate that Army Chiefs saw fit to bring in replacements direct from the training camps in the United States to the front lines by air.

Bastogne was the center of the roughest fighting. For nine days the 101st, the 9th Armored, and miscellaneous troops known as Force Snafu (cooks, clerks, etc.), fought alongside the infantry holding the Germans to a standstill.

Christmas day the Germans made their final attempt to take Bastogne. The 502nd Regiment held and very few tanks went through. Patton's troops, the 4th Armored Division and the 4th, 5th, 26th, and 80th Infantry Divisions, had to battle for four days before they could break through to relieve the weary troops. The 4th, 26th, 28th, and the 101st had a lot of Mexican-American boys that gave their lives in the Battle of the Bulge.

Among them was Fernando Peña, well-remembered in East Los Angeles where he grew up. He, along with Abe Sandoval, also of Los Angeles, fought around Bastogne with the 326 A/B Engineers of the 101st. Their C.O. was Lt. Edmundo Brash[1] who didn't know then that Peña was married to his cousin Rosie who lived in Los Angeles. "Had I known he was your husband," he told her, after he found out, "I never would have sent him on the suicide mission where he lost his life."

---

[1]Now an attorney in Phoenix, Arizona.

Peña was killed when he and three other paratroopers made a jump in hostile territory in Belgium, on January 1, 1945. His body was blown to bits when he and three others seeking cover jumped into a booby-trapped foxhole. This was to have been Peña's last jump overseas. After the 5th jump he was eligible for home rotation.

By now, everyone knows of the many *Chicanos* that were in both the 82nd and the 101st Airborne. "Chuy" Galvan, Mundo Lozano, and Chris Samaniego, from Los Angeles, and Bert Duran of Fullerton, California, were with the 82nd, to mention a few. These two Airborne Divisions were right in the thick of the Bulge fighting. They are discussed in the "Paratrooper Chapter."

On December 27th, the Americans went into the offensive . . . The Bulge was now a confusing mess of attack, counterattack and counter-counterattacks. As the weather cleared, the heavy bombers in the European Theater, the big flying Fortresses and Liberators went into action. They pounded German columns and supply lines silhouetted against the snow and turned the tide.

HELL AT RIEPERTSWEILER

December 26, 1944. In the 7th Army Sector with the 313th Infantry Regiment Southern France. It was Christmas and American troops were still locked in battle with the Germans at Bastogne. Troops in the 1st, 3rd, and 9th Army groups were busily engaged trying to stem the tide of the over-whelming Nazi Stormtroopers who threatened to break through in the Ardennes sector.

By contrast, those of us in the 7th Army, stationed along the Vosges in the Alsace-Lorraine, were holding defensive positions with very little activity in the front lines. We eagerly awaited to hear news about the German break-through up north. At Oberseebach, where the 313th Regiment of the 79th was billeted, we were enjoying a nice Christmas week. We had been taking things easy since pulling out of the front where we had abandoned the attempt to cross the Siegfreid Line in our sector. The regiment was put in reserve and our sole duty was to go by truck every day to the edge of town where we all busied ourselves digging defensive trenches, replicas of those used in W.W. I. At the end of day the "W.P.A." G.I.'s would put away their trenching tools and truck back into town for some hot chow and another night of tall tales, of front line rumors and "a night of peaceful sleep."

Christmas Day we received our gift packages from back home which had been in the mail since early November. It was a big thrill to receive something from the folks back in the States. Every G.I. was happy to share his goodies with others. Most of the packages contained the same item, as there wasn't very much the combat soldier was allowed at the front.

A typical sample of what we got were my two packages. From my mother and sisters in San Antonio I received a can of Gebhart's beans and tamales, a can of chile sauce, a can of hot chili peppers, a couple of pounds of broken home-baked cookies, a pound of nuts and candies, a comb, a mirror and razor blades, shaving soap, (not much chance of using these at the front), and a pocket-size New Testment with a bullet-proof metal front cover.

From the wife and the kids there was a can of hot chile sauce and one of *chiles jalapeños*[1], another couple of pounds of broken home-baked cookies, candies, fruits and nuts, a latest snapshot of my sons, David and Eddie, a sketch pad, drawing pencils, and gum erasers, playing cards and dice (requested since back at the replacement depot).

Needless to say, all the "hot" stuff was quickly devoured by the G.I.'s who were possessed by that wolfish craving for hot

---

[1]Pickled chile peppers extra hot—originating in Jalapa, Mexico.

seasoning—not only the Mexican-Americans but many other G.I.'s who had picked up the taste during our long associations. There were also a few who out of curiosity ventured a taste only to tear away yelling bloody murder and crying for water!

At Oberseebach we had strict news-blackout. No one could tell for sure how the American forces were faring against the enemy up in the Ardennes. The only thing that was being spread around were rumors, and most of them weren't very cheerful. We had an idea of how bad things were going because we weren't getting additional supplies nor any replacements to bring our platoons up to company strength. Only the artillery units were getting in ammunition, and even that was being rationed.

December 31, New Years Eve. The first real news we heard about the German breakthrough was that they were attempting a breakthrough in our sector. Historians record the activities of those days in that sector as follows:

> Besides the offensive in the Bulge, Von Runsted sought once more to trick the Allies with a drive to recover the Alsace-Lorraine[1] as the new year (1945) dawned.

The surprise blow in our area was struck only thirty kilometers from Oberseebach on New Years Eve of 1945. The Germans caught an armored task force that was spread thin in a large sector; they easily broke through and captured tanks, jeeps, halftracks and threw the defenders in confusion. Troops were needed badly to prevent the enemy from exploiting his successes.

On that New Years Eve I happened to be pulling guard on the midnight-to-1 shift around the CP quarters. It was a

---

[1]*Pictorial History of W.W. II, Vol. I, The War in Europe,* Veterans of Foreign Wars, Memorial Edition, Veterans' Historical Book Service, Inc., Series No. 3511, Washington, D.C., 1951, p. 315.

beautiful moonlight night and my hopes were very high about the incoming New Year. I felt sure that 1945 would be the year the war would end, and with a little luck we would all be able to get back to our loved ones at home.

My moments of wishful thinking were interrupted by the sounds of footsteps and a moving object that I distinguished by moonlight as a G.I., approached at a fast pace. As he came closer, I recognized him as a company runner known as "Tiger". Trying to catch his breath, he delivered a message he had from the C.O. It was from Regimental Headquarters with orders that our Second Battalion must get set to go into action. The Germans had dropped paratroopers behind our lines, isolating the 45th Division who were manning that area.

All the men were awakened and hasty preparations were made to pull out immediately. At exactly 0100 hours in the early morning of January 1st, 1945, we set out to bring relief to the 45th Division. *What a hell of a way to begin the New Year.*

On the first day of 1945, we foot soldiers found ourselves once again doing the same things we had been doing in 1944 . . . marching out—reluctantly—with the Infantry. The men were bitter. We all felt disappointed that the war had not been terminated before the arrival of the New Year. The weather had worsened, the sky was dark and gloomy. Still smarting over the pounding we had taken in our attempt to go through the Siegfried Line, now having to battle the Jerries once again over the same ground we had shed blood for once before; being quite undermanned with all platoons still under full company strength, and facing severe cold—all of this had reduced our morale to the lowest ebb. This was undoubtedly the most low-spirited squad we had ever moved out with.

We reached the outskirts of Riepertsweiler, a small village close to the German border. Company E was put in reserve on the first night. The ground was frozen solid and it was very hard to dig in—so most of us slept on the top of the ground in the few blankets and sleeping bags that were available. The night was cold and unbearable—it was impossible to get any sleep. Most of us just walked around and stomped our feet to keep them from freezing.

We were up very early next morning. The water in our canteens was frozen; our rations had to be eaten without any coffee or water to drink or wash up. It was near noon before the water melted enough so we could get our first drink. We spent the rest of the day checking our gear and making sure our weapons were in working order.

Only a trio of Mexican-Americans remained in the platoon now. The three were Felix Garcia, Esquivel, and myself. Since the battle of the Siegfried Line, most of my *chicano* buddies had disappeared from the ranks. They had either been captured, killed in action, or wounded by the enemy. Gone was Larry Perchez, Leandro Esquibel; and from the other companies, Tony Rodriguez, Joe Casiano, Luis Gomez, Frankie Escobar, and Armando Gonzales—the Puerto-Rican. We also learned that Frank "The Great" Padilla was missing.

We were stunned to hear about Padilla. It was hard to believe the report that Frank had been KIA. "Oh, no . . ." we said. Those who knew him didn't want to believe it. I recalled the many times we had battled for different towns, where we drove the enemy out . . . and after entering the town we would see Padilla among the crowd of French people that came out to greet us. He was usually with a couple of French cuties—one in each arm—shouting to us in French . . . He had either been one of the first in town or had sneaked in the night before. The last time I had talked to him he told me that he had made a contact with a Spaniard who was living in Luneville who could arrange to have him, Frankie Escobar and myself take off and hide out in Spain. There we could pass for Spaniards and stay for the "duration,"... because this war is getting too damn rough," he said. I didn't know what to make of it. You never could tell if he was kidding or not, and Frank was one of the most daring and brave men I ever knew.

That afternoon we moved in to Riepertsweiler and prepared to go into attack. We were to make an attempt to relieve elements of the 45th Division which were cut off north of the town.

Riepertsweiler is a village in a narrow valley of the Vosges Mountains close to the German border. The Vosges run generally northeast and southwest, cutting Alsace off from the rest of France. These consist of five or six heavily wooded ridges with very steep sides, strewn with rocky cliffs and gorges. Here was where the Germans had decided to launch their breakthrough of the Seventh Army area.

The regiment was ordered to attack and seize the mountain passages at their northern exits. Line of departure was about 5 kilometers north of the village. As usual, or so we felt, the Second Battalion was to be the attacking battalion, and again it was E Company who had been chosen to lead the attack. *Same old butterflies in our stomachs.* We moved out at about 1700 hours with one column on the east ridge and another on the west ridge. In between we could see two TD's (small tank destroyers) on the narrow road which wound around the bend about fifty feet below. They were to support the attack.

The ridge was thick with trees. Felix Garcia, the short and rugged little combat veteran, was first scout for our squad. Our company had split up, half of them going with the attacking unit to the other ridge. Buck-Sgt. Jack was our only non-com. S/Sgt. Bill Griffith of St. Louis, was in charge of the squad on the other ridge.

It was dusk and we dreaded the idea of fighting in pitch darkness, especially when our squad consisted of only 18 men.

The road formed a round curve and we kept going around the bend. We had made about 15 kilometers when our misgivings proved correct. Here began one of the most disastrous debacles of my battle days. I saw Garcia, our first scout, come running around the bend shouting at the top of his lungs, "Go back, everybody! It's a trap!" He had a wild look about him. At first we thought he had "cracked up." The other riflemen ahead had turned back and were following Garcia hurriedly. We were puzzled. There was shouting and yelling, but no organization. From them we learned there were two Tiger tanks and hundreds of German infantrymen. We looked down the road searching for the TD's that were to give us support. The two TD's were making a U-turn and heading back to town! Being no match for the giant Tiger tanks, they were taking off.

Darkness had set in when the chase began. More Germans swooped down on our left flank which was unprotected. Everything was soon disorganized within our ranks. No one knew who was who, or where to go. The Germans came down, yelling and firing burp guns on the left flank, and along the hillside the tanks opened up on us with their big guns. Everyone pulled back, retreating from tree to tree. Lt. Ferguson, from F Company, tried in vain to get some of us to form a line of protection on our left flank. We took up the positions, but when the horde of Germans came over the high ground pouring heavy fire at us—one by one we were forced to abandon our lonely positions. This angered Lt. Ferguson, but he too was forced to move out of his temporary post.

It was really a shame to be chased without putting up any kind of resistance. But what could we do? No one would back you up. Not even the officers could control the fleeing G.I.'s Soon we were all fleeing . . . the odds were too big, and the law of self preservation had won out over all of us. Down and down we descended until we were on the road. We joined another bunch of frantic G.I.'s. Like us, they were fleeing, trying to elude the big cannon of the booming Tiger tanks which kept firing at anything that moved as it came around the bend.

Many other G.I.'s from the other units joined us at the foot of the ridge. They too had been chased off by the superior numbers of the enemy. Everyone was heading back to Riepertsweiler. We moved back fast and quietly to keep from being overrun by the attacking German infantrymen who were now being very bold, shouting loud orders, telling their men where to head us off, caring little about being heard or getting spotted in the dark.

We all scattered and finally managed to get back to the village. Three of us from E Company and one from F Company stuck together but none of us knew just where to go. By now the town was getting shelled from three sides. Only the south end entrance—where Americans were still bringing in troops and supplies was not being shelled, but someone had set fire to the buildings nearby. We decided to go to what we thought was the safest place, the battalion aid station where the Medics were housed. When we got there, we found the place full of wounded men who were being evacuated to another building because the aid station had also been set on fire.

The Jerries came into the raging village right behind us and were all around outside in the streets. By shouting in English and with the aid of darkness, amid the confusion, it was easy for them to sneak in and knock down our unsuspecting forward outposts from the rear. Someone reported that the Germans had seized an American tank, turned it around and had opened up on the other American tanks and the G.I.'s that were near.

Among the bunch at the aid station we met a squad leader from E Company. He volunteered to take us to the company CP which was located at the north end of the village. At the CP we were immediately assigned to guard the approaches. Only a handful of E Company were there—mostly noncoms.

Among them was Sgt. Griffith, our platoon leader. That night we stayed indoors sharing our house with a heavy-weapons platoon of the 313th. Tired, cold, and hungry, we soon dozed off into heavy slumber while the fighting raged on during the night.

LAST DAY AT THE FRONT

The situation of the last day at the front for me began the morning of January 3, 1945, our second day in Riepertsweiler; and the day after we had been turned back by the crashing German infantry hordes in our ill-fated attempt to bring aid to the encircled 45th Division. The town was full of German soldiers who had sneaked in, and collaborators who lived there. Our outposts were overrun. There were no guards out on the streets, most of the men being holed up in the small buildings throughout the town.

There was poor communication between the units and very little organization. Most of the American G.I.'s slept indoors to keep out of the severe cold. Snow fell all through the night.

When we awoke that morning, many of us were startled and surprised to learn we had Jerries for next-door neighbors instead of the Yanks who had been there before. The Germans had all the entrances to the village sealed off—only the jeeps with white flags and the Red Cross symbol of the Medics were being let through. They were not allowing supplies to enter.

All vehicles coming in were captured or wrecked by the Jerries. At our CP we had a clear view from our windows as we watched the proceedings at the town's south entrance, which was about one mile across open space. There were loud yells and excitement when we saw a jeep carrying the mail being overturned and all our letters and packages set on fire.

On that morning I was assigned to a squad that was ordered to guard defensive positions atop the ridge close by, in order to keep the Germans from coming over from the side—the only side where the Jerries had not appeared. Our squad was small. It consisted of only six riflemen and a heavy-machine-gunner and his assistant, with the sergeant from heavy-weapons platoon in charge.

We had climbed a short distance on the rocky hillside when I spied a German lookout who quickly hid behind a tree! Everyone wondered what the hell I was firing at; they could not see anyone and no one had answered my fire. A short while later another Jerry appeared to our left, behind some big boulders. I could see him clearly but the others could not; he was wearing an all-black uniform similar to those of the S.S. troops. He stopped abruptly, then I saw him wave to the others behind him to hold it up. We opened up on him and began to dig in hastily.

"I got him!" said Adams, a kid from Pittsburgh, gleefully exclaiming, as if he had just bagged a deer or a rabbit. We saw him hit the ground, but he was far from dead. At the next instant he fired at us and put a bullet right between the eyes of the machine gun Sergeant, who was set up next to us. The German scout raised up and motioned to the others to advance . . . large numbers of infantrymen soon appeared—then all Hell's fire opened up.

The machine gunner's assistant grabbed the heavy gun but he didn't even get a chance to fire it. The same black-garbed German hurled a potato-smasher (grenade) right into his hole. The concussion killed the assistant gunner, the loud bang left a lingering din in our ears and burned—powder smell over the area. They came charging, moving closer to our positions, and things were getting hotter. Without a leader and once more facing big odds, Adams and I in our half-dug holes both got the same idea . . . "Let's get the Hell out of here!", I said. Down the line the others were doing the same.

We had just barely started to roll ourselves down, when the

Jerries were upon our former positions. They jumped into the half-started holes and turned our own heavy machine gun on us. Down the hill we rolled, with Jerries firing point blank at us. How they managed to miss us is beyond me.

Everyone does crazy things in the heat of battle. I remember losing my rifle as we were rolling over and over trying to dodge the fire, I stopped rolling, stood up, climbed a few steps up to recover my rifle, and I still didn't get hit. The gang back at the CP down gave us enought fire support to enable us to make it back safe to the small house where we had billeted. Only four of us made it back safely.

Late that afternoon, Lt. Johnson from the weapons platoon ordered a patrol be sent out to look for evidence of any Germans in our former positions, and to find out how large a force there was on the hillside. Those of us remaining from the original eight that had been in those holes knew damned well that the hillside was full of Jerries because we had seen and battled them at close quarters. We were anxious to hear what the patrol would find out.

The patrol came back and made a surprising report! That 'no enemy had been sighted.' All four of us looked at each other with puzzlement—we knew someone was lying.[1]

When the First Sergeant hollered out, "All right, you guys who were out there in those holes, get set to go back there." There was a lot of commotion and running back and forth by the G.I.'s who had been there and whom the sergeant was referring to. None of us relished the idea of going back on that hill. There were four small houses close together where we were staying and the sergeant had a hell of a time finding the men

---

[1]Many times some of the patrols at the front would "goof off" when they were sent out to probe the enemy. To keep out of danger, they would kill time in some safe location, then go back to the company and report, "No enemy in sight."

who had been on the hill before, as it was already getting dark.

He approached me and asked if I was one of them. I was honest and foolish enough to reply, "Yes, I was." I felt a little annoyed. The others had left me holding the bag and I didn't like the idea that out of the four of us I was the only one they could find. I was told that I would have to take a squad to man the holes on the hill, because I was the only one that knew where the positions were located.

First, I tried to reason with the sergeant that it would be suicide to go out there with a small squad, because I knew that the place was full of Germans, and we needed a full attacking force to drive them out. But it didn't work.

"The patrol reported that the Germans were gone!", the First Sergeant snapped.

"You're crazy if you think I'm going out there with a small squad," I retorted.

Staff Sergeant Griffith, my old friend, taunted me, "What's the matter? Don't tell me you're yellow, Morin!" He might have been kidding, but it made me mad. Suddenly, I remembered what I had been told back in my basic training days about the infantry. The SOP (standard order of procedure) was that no patrol is sent out on a mission unless it is led by a sergeant —I was only a PFC.

"I'll tell you how yellow I am," I challenged, "I'll go if you'll lead the squad. You're a sergeant, I'm only a poor PFC."

Sgt. Griffith did not have to go, as he was in charge of the men in E Company—he was the highest ranking noncom in the CP and we were short of squad leaders—but he immediately accepted. "Let's go!", he said, hurriedly picking up his rifle. There was no backing out now for either Griffith or myself. But neither one of us were using our heads; it was more of a dare.

THE MILLION DOLLAR WOUND

Being the only one in the squad who knew the exact location of the holes, I took the lead. Slowly we began to trek uphill. From what I could remember, the positions we once had abandoned must have been about 150 yards ahead, on the hill. We kept climbing up, hiding behind the trees and boulders. When we had gone about a hundred yards, I could make out the forms of the German sentries silhouetted against the sky. There they were, just as I had suspected. The hills were swarming with Jerries!

I was stuck now . . . there wasn't anything I could do about it. I couldn't halt, go back and try to explain to Griffith about the German sentries above us. He would only think that I was still trying to back out.

Doggedly, and as quietly as possible, we continued to climb. I had the darndest feeling—I knew this was going to be 'it.' It was getting darker. On and on we climbed. We were getting closer to them now. I was trying to judge the distance where I had spotted the silhouettes.*Must be about twenty-five feet further up.* I turned to make the silence sign to Sgt. Griffith. He came up behind a tree and nudged me with the butt of his rifle to keep going. I searched my soul for courage. *Well, here goes . . .* I stepped out from behind the tree, when suddenly in the darkness I heard a weak, scared voice blurt, *"Achtung! Wer is dort!"* Jesus! I had overestimated the location of the first foxhole! *What should I do? If I open fire, I'll be a sitting duck.* Quickly, I turned around and jumped back, trying to find cover, when they opened up all down the line. Rifles, burp guns, machine guns and grenades blasted off at the same instant, their fire lighted the night.

The next thing I remember I was flying through space and my legs were burning up. I rolled downhill once again, just like I had done that afternoon. A machine gun opened up right above me. About every fifth shot was a tracer bullet—it would light up the area. I had landed in a soft spot of the hillside which offered very little protection. They knew I had been hit and that I was close by. I could hear them moving about. I kept crawling downhill on my stomach until I made it back near the small shack at the bottom where we were housed. I felt both my legs—they were soggy and wet with blood—then I discovered that they could not hold me up, so I lay back in the snow that was piled up there. I tried to make myself as comfortable as possible.

I must have lain there in the snow for more than an hour. I remember being cold from shock and loss of blood, and having to eat snow to fill my dry mouth. The house where we had been staying seemed abandoned. I cried out, "Medic! . . . Medic! . . . Help!", but no one answered.

Finally one of our men came to the window and asked, "Who is it?"

"It's me, Morin."

"Who?"

"Pancho!", I pleaded. I didn't care for that name but it didn't matter right now, just so he could not mistake me for a German.

"I'll get you a Medic." It had finally dawned on him who I was.

The other G.I.'s now were all in the last of the four houses. No wonder the Medics had not come after me. They had their hands full with the other wounded. Everyone had been hit except Sgt. Griffith. What a rabbit's foot he carried—all through the campaign 'and never scratched. He smiled when he saw me, ignoring our little squabble, "Well Morin, you got your *million dollar wound!*" This is the type of wound that all the frontline G.I.'s dream about—not serious enough to kill you, and not slight enough to send you back to the front. I was hurting too much to enjoy Griff's slight humor.

It had been a hand grenade that had done the damage and one of our own grenades at that! I recalled that we had been exchanging fire with the Jerries in the afternoon when one of the squad leaders had crawled up close to us. He had left ammo and grenades just outside our foxholes. In our hurry to get out of there, no one bothered to pick them up. (The Germans preferred to use our grenades because of the fragmentation, theirs being a concussion grenade).

A Medic took a knife and cut my trousers. He applied sulfa and plasma, and did his best to make everything comfortable for me. Then all the wounded were removed to the aid station. I was still in a state of shock. The 'Doc' who examined me at the aid station noticed this—he took out a bottle of good whiskey and gave me a drink . . . This helped a little, but the pain was still sharp. I was sure I would lose both legs.

My wounds were dressed again. I was given more blood plasma. Then we were put on a jeep and taken to a station hospital located in Strasbourg. There I lost track of time. When I came to, it was the 5th of January. A pretty young lady was standing over my bed. I thought it was a dream . . . until I tried to move. Then I discovered that both of my legs were in a plaster cast.

The young lady was an American Red Cross worker who aptly reconstructed all the events leading to my being there. She volunteered to help in whatever I needed. She wrote some letters for me and tried to cheer me up, but I was in no mood for joy. I felt very bitter. I was angry and remorseful . . . I was mad at the goddammed war, angry at the glory-seeking Generals who would sacrifice needless lives to satisfy their aims. I felt sorry for all the infantrymen—even the enemy frontline men. All the suffering we endured, the bitter weather, the long marches, cold rations, going through one battle after another, facing danger every moment . . . I remembered all my buddies who had given their lives . . . Nerios . . . Padilla . . . Abril . . . Arredondo . . . Gomez . . . Gonzales . . . They would not be going back to their families anymore. And the others who would go back half-crippled, battle scarred and maimed . . . Esquibel, Perchez, Ramirez, the two Martinez', Peru, Soto, Escobar, Rodriguez . . . these were just in our outfit alone, and there were hundreds of infantry outfits like ours. I blamed everyone for our plight . . . Hitler, Mussolini, Stalin, Churchill, Tojo, Roosevelt—they were all the same, warmongers, all. To hell with all of them!

After my departure from the warfront, the war in the ETO continued for another 5 months. The Germans put up their strongest final battles in the 7th Army group's area against ground troops of the Divisions that had a large number of Mexican-Americans, both replacements and old veterans. These included the 3rd, 36th, 45th, and the 79th. Two more of our boys arrived among the new troops in time to participate in some of the heavy fighting, particularly in the last big battles. Both were awarded the Congressional Medal of Honor. They were Jose F. Valdez and Silvestre Herrera.

PVT. JOSE F. VALDEZ

Awarded The Congressional Medal of Honor. (Posthumously)

Rosenkrantz, France, January 25th, 1945. Valdez, a rifleman in Company B, 7th Regiment, 3rd Division, was in an outpost with five other infantryman near the town of Rosenkrantz, in France, when the Germans launched a counterattack with overwhelming strength. From his position near the woods and 500 yards beyond the American lines he observed a hostile tank seventy five yards away; the nineteen year old lad immediately went into action with his BAR. He raked the tank with automatic fire until it withdrew. Soon afterwards he saw three Germans stealthily approaching through the woods. Scorning cover as the enemy soldiers opened up with heavy automatic weapon fire from a range of 30 yards, Valdez waited for them to get closer; then to get a better range he jumped out of his hole and engaged all three of them in a fire fight. At thirty yards they exchanged heavy automatic fire and Valdez killed all three of them.

The enemy quickly launched another attack with two full companies of infantrymen; they were determined to break through the outpost and to drive into the American line. Blasting the patrol with tremendous concentration of automatic and rifle fire, they began an encircle movement which forced the patrol leader to order a withdrawal. Despite the terrible odds, Valdez immediately volunteered to cover the withdrawal; and as the patrol, one by one plunged through the hail of bullets to reach the American lines, the slightly built kid from Utah fired burst after burst of his BAR into the swarming Germans, and on came, more and more of them. Three of his comrades were wounded in their dash for safety. Valdez himself was struck by a bullet that entered his stomach, passed through his body and emerged from his back. Overcoming agonizing pain, he regained control of himself and resumed his firing position, delivering a protective screen of bullets until all others of the patrol were safe. By field telephone he called for artillery and mortar fire on the Germans and corrected the range until he had shells falling within fifty yards of his own position.

For fifteen minutes he *refused* to be dislodged by more than 200 of the enemy; then seeing that the barrage had broken the counterattack, he dragged himself back to his own lines where medics worked frantically to stop his bleeding, but the loss of blood had been too much; he died as a result of his wounds.

PVT. JOSE F. VALDEZ
Governador, New Mexico
Congressional Medal of Honor
European Theater World War II

> Throught his valiant, intrepid stand and at the cost of his own life, Valdez made it possible for his comrades to escape and was directly responsible for repulsing an attack by vastly superior forces.[1]

Sacrifices such as these, especially of such a young life as Jose Valdez, is what has made our country such a great and strong nation. We, the Spanish-speaking people, and other Americans as well, feel very proud to know that he was one of our own.

The 19-year-old boyish-looking young infantryman who was born in Governador, New Mexico, was one of the youngest American soldiers to win the Congressional Medal of Honor. He earned the highest military award when he single-handed, though slowly bleeding to death, fought off an attack by two German companies of S.S. troops in the Vosges Mountains section.

PFC. SILVESTRE HERRERA

Awarded the Congressional Medal of Honor

> Private First Class Silvestre S. Herrera, Company E., 142nd Infantry Regiment, 36th Division, advanced with a platoon along a wooded road near Mertzwiller, France, on March 15, 1945, until stopped by heavy enemy machine gun fire. As the rest of the unit took cover, he made a one man frontal assault on a strong point and captured eight soldiers.
>
> When the platoon resumed its advance and was subjected to fire from a second emplacement beyond an extensive minefield, Private Herrera again moved forward, disregarding the danger of exploding mines, to attack the position. He stepped on a mine and had both feet

[1]War Department Citation, G.O. No. 16, 8 February 1946.

> severed; but despite intense pain and unchecked loss of blood, he pinned down the enemy with accurate rifle fire while a friendly squad captured the enemy gun by skirting the mine field and rushing in from the flank.
>
> The magnificent courage, extraordinary heroism, and willing self-sacrifice displayed by Private Herrera resulted in the capture of two enemy strong points and the taking of eight prisoners.[1]

Silvestre Herrera is a symbol of determination and courage manifested by the Mexican-American infantryman during World War II.

His Award of the Congressional Medal of Honor came after one of the utmost demostrations of bravery ever witnessed by a squad of infantrymen on the battlefield.

He was the eighth Mexican-American to be awarded the Congressional Medal of Honor in W.W. II. Herrera was born in El Paso, July 17, 1917. He entered the Army January 13, 1944. His wife, Mrs. Ramona Herrera, and their three children, Mary, Elva, and Silvestre, live in Phoenix, Arizona. Herrera formerly was a farm worker in El Paso. He was awarded the Combat Infantryman Badge November 10, 1944, after proving himself in combat.

Following are eye-witness accounts of Private Herrera's actions in Mertswiller, by Private Henry Van Dyke, Millville, New Jersey:

"The whole area was thickly mined and every step had to be carefully taken. Just as we got the push going again, another machine gun opened up from a fortified emplacement. Private Herrera went after that gun as he had the other. He charged straight ahead, knowing there were mines every inch of the

---

[1]War Department Citation, G.O. No. 75, 5 September 1945. *The Medal of Honor,* official publication, Department of the Army, U.S. Government Printing Office, Washington, D.C., 1948, p. 359.

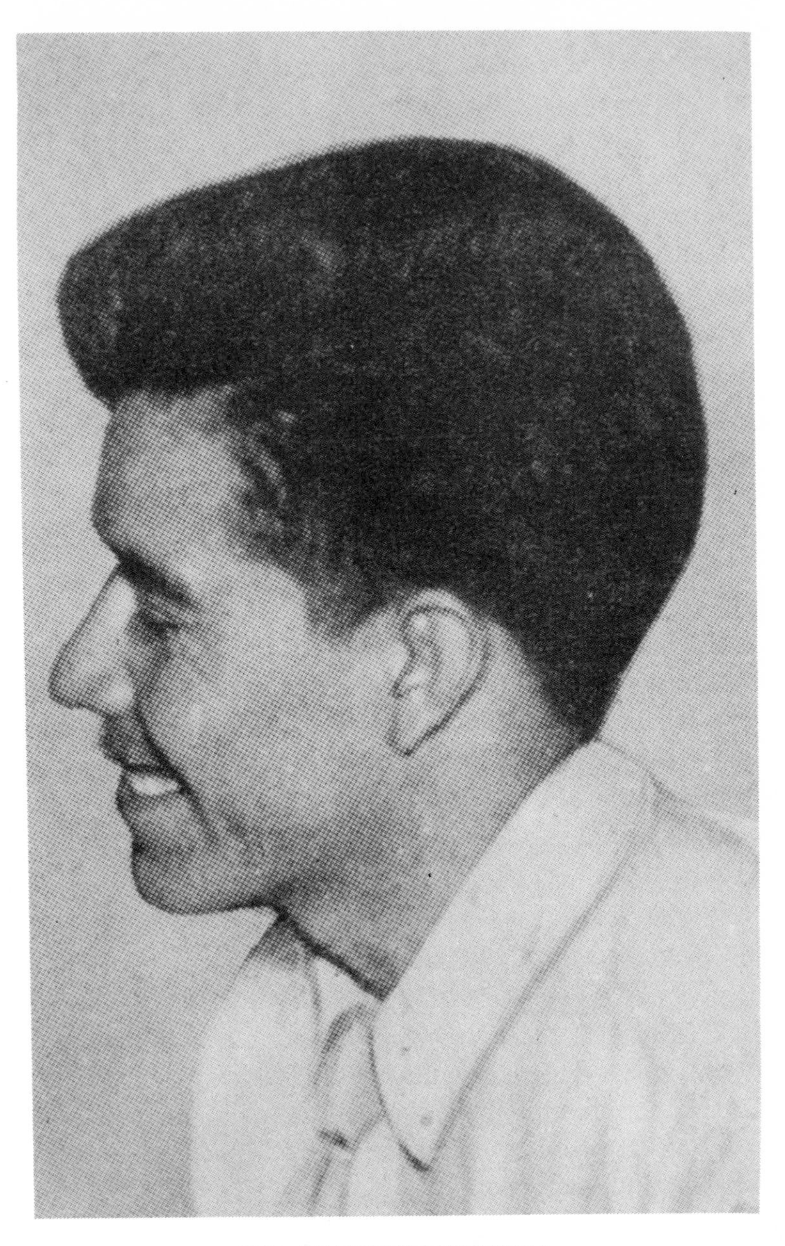

PFC. SILVESTRE HERRERA
Phoenix, Arizona
Congressional Medal of Honor
European Theater World War II

way. Again the German machine gun fire was played on him, without any effect. But about half way to the position there was an explosion, and he fell. We could see that a mine had *blown off both of his feet. But he didn't quit.* He kept his rifle pumping fire into the German position. The Germans couldn't raise their heads."

(Private Van Dyke's account refers to an attack made by Private Herrera's Company after having been once checked by the enemy during which time Private Herrera upset the opposing enemy machine gun and captured eight Germans).

Another report by Staff Sergeant Richard B. Davis, Washington, Iowa:

"He made repeated and deliberate efforts to draw the fire of the enemy machine gun by rising to his knees to fire into the German position. His fire kept the Germans pinned down, and while they kept all their attention on him, a squad from our company was able to work around the position and make the kill. Weakened from loss of blood that was pouring from the stumps of his legs, he kept up his fight until the position had been won."

Silvestre Herrera was a member of the 142nd Infantry Regiment in the famous "T" Texas 36th Division. He joined the 36th as a replacement while they were still busy fighting in the Mediterranean (Italy). He fought along-side the 79th in the Alsace-Lorraine; in fact, when the 79th stormed the town of Birschwiller, the 36th was right along. When the 79th took a pasting in trying to crash through the Siegfried Line, the 36th and the 45th—both fighting Divisions from the Southwest with a lot of Chicanos—were thrown into battle and came through with magnificent support.

"To welcome home Pfc. Silvestre S. Herrera, Governor Osborn of Arizona declared August 24, 1945, to be "HERRERA DAY." Herrera did not stand when he received his Congressional Medal of Honor from President Truman, for he had left his legs along a wooded road near Mertzwiller, France, on March 15 of that same year. By public contribution, Phoenix raised a fund of ten thousand dollars to provide this hero with a home.[3]"

---

[3]Griffith, Beatrice, "*American Me,*" Houghton Mifflin, Company, Boston, Mass., 1948, Page 265.

XI

IN THE PACIFIC

During the hard fighting days of front-line action against the Germans and other Axis forces in Africa, Sicily, Italy, France and Germany, Uncle Sam's fighting G.I.'s had also seen long days of combat on the other side of the world, where they faced an enemy just as stubborn and even more fanatic—the Japanese.

Since the early days of Jose Sanchez[1] and Jose P. Martinez[2], Mexican-Americans figured in many battle units that met and defeated the Japanese with the fighting taking place in the most remote places of the South Pacific. They fought with the Navy in the sea battles of Midway and the Coral Sea, and took part in many bloody encounters with the Marines in such places as Guadalcanal, Bougainville and Tarawa.

The largest number of our combatmen served in infantry units of National Guard Divisions that had been sent into the Pacific since early 1942. Regular Army Divisions, numbers one to ten, such as the 1st, 2nd, and 3rd Divisions, were assigned to the European Theatre with the exception of the 7th, which was first in Alaska, then re-assigned to the South Pacific. The National Guard Divisions from the 24th to the 50th were scattered in both the European and Pacific war zones. These Divisions had more Spanish-speaking soldiers than the old Regular outfits. The early Guard outfits in the Pacific were 25th, 27th, 37th and 43rd Divisions. They fought in Guadal-

[1]See p. 27.
[2]See p. 34.

canal, New Guinea, Rendova, New Georgia, Vella Lavella and Bougainville in late 1942 and 1943.

Many of our boys drafted or volunteered early in the war, trained in IRTC camps all over the United States. They were then assigned to newly-activated divisions in the higher numbers, such as the 85th, 86th, 87th and 88th. Most of these outfits were made up strictly of draftees, or selective service recruits. Many more Mexican-Americans joined combat outfits as replacements. Just as in Europe, most of the infantry divisions in the Pacific were brought up to full strength from time to time with new replacements fresh from the States. Many of the GI's who had taken basic training together with us at the IRTC centers had parted ways at the end of training, some going to the ETO, others to the Pacific. By the fall of 1943, American forces in the Pacific stepped up their offensive in the battles of beachheads. Their island-hopping campaign slowly drove the enemy closer to the land of the Rising Sun. In early 1944 the Japanese were driven out—or bypassed—in the island of Saipan, and after bitter struggles at Kwajalein, Nemur and Eunebi. Next came the Marshall Islands and the liberation of Guam where many of our G.I.'s distinguished themselves in fighting with the 7th, 27th, 32nd, and 77th Infantry Divisions; also the 11th Airborne and with the First Cavalry which originated out of Fort Bliss with their many Spanish-speaking *Caballeros.* Our soldiers gave a good account of themselves in all these units. A popular rumor in those days was that General McArthur had expressed approval of the fighting men of Mexican extraction from the Southwest. He had been quoted as having said, *"Send us more of these Mexican boys; they make good jungle fighters."*

The war in the Pacific was very different from the one in the ETO. In Europe most of the fighting took place in civilized countries, in the outskirts of cities and towns and inside many villages and populated towns. When we fought in rocky mountain country and heavly-wooded forests, at the end of fighting or in the next town we found the natives welcoming us as liberators. Sometimes there was wine, sometimes there were women, sometimes both. Often the Germans left large stocks of liquor and rations behind in their hurry to move out to another area.

In the Pacific, amphibious landings had to be made on each island, where everyone of them was stubbornly defended. After the battles were over it would break your heart to see that the whole place wasn't worth one-tenth of the sweat, blood and lives it had taken to capture the islands No rations (edible), no liquor. Of the women, nobody knew their language and they were not much on the glamorous side, although after being stuck on some island for so long, many a lonely G.I. was heard to mutter, "They're not so bad looking," or "They're not so dark."

October, 1944—The war in the Pacific had not been a picnic. United States combat forces had suffered more than 100,000 casualties. 15,000 had been killed in action and 30,000 wounded. 16,000 were missing or taken prisoners since the start of the fighting.[1] By fall of 1944, General McArthur was well on his way to his history-making return to the Philippines. On the Islands, the famous "Tiger of Malaya", General Yamashita, awaited him with the Japanese 16th Army well entrenched in and around the archipelago.

With their sea power broken in naval battles off the Leyte coast, the Japanese became even more determined to stop their foe. The Philippines must be held at all costs; it was now do or die. Loss of the Islands would mean that United States planes would be within striking distance of Tokyo. General Yamashita hurriedly rushed in reinforcements for the inevitable showdown battle. Among the reinforcements were the notorious

---

[1]VFW, *War in The Pacific;* History of WW II, Veteran's Historical Book Ser.; USA, P. 206.

STAFF SERGEANT JOEY M. OLMOS
Los Angeles, California
Bronze Star
Luzon, Philippine Islands World War II

First and Eighth Infantry Divisions from Manchuria. Japanese planes, ships, armor and Infantry began to pile up in narrow Ormoc Strait.

December 7th, the third anniversary of Pearl Harbor, the 77th Division landed three miles south of Ormoc. By December 10, fourth day of the invasion, the 77th and 7th Divisions had captured Ormoc, wiping out the garrison there to the last man in bitter fighting. General McArthur caught the enemy by surprise when he by-passed the Philippines area held by the Japanese on December 15th and landed on the island of Mindoro, 155 miles south of Manila. During the first days of January, 1945, three more landings were made; one of these was General Walter Kruger's 6th Army group which swept ashore at Buenavista on the small island of Marinduque, putting our G.I.'s ten miles from Luzon and one hundred from the Philippine Capital, Manila.

One of the principal units in the Sixth Army that made the landing at Buenavista was the 37th Division which has much to do with our next Medal of Honor winner, Cleto Rodriguez.

PVT. CLETO RODRIGUEZ

Awarded the Congressional Medal of Honor

Manila, Philippine Islands, February 9, 1945. He was an automatic rifleman when his unit attacked the strongly defended Paco Railroad Station during the battle for Manila, Philippine Islands, while making a frontal assault across an open field, his platoon was halted 100 yards from the station by intense enemy fire. On his own initiative he left the platoon accompained by a comrade, and continued forward to a house 60 yards from the objective. Although under constant enemy observation the two men remained in this position for an hour firing at targets of opportunity, killing more than 35 hostile soldiers and wounding many more. Moving closer to the station and discovering a group of Japanese replacements attempting to reach the pillboxes, they opened heavy fire, killing more than 40 and stopped all subsequent attempts to man the emplacements. Enemy fire became more intense as they advanced within 20 yards of the station. Then, covered by his companion, Pvt. Rodriguez boldly moved up to a building and threw five grenades through a doorway, killing seven Japanese, destroying a 20-mm gun and wrecking a heavy machine gun. With their ammunition running low the two men started to return to the American lines, alternatively providing cover fire for each other's withdrawal. During this movement, Private Rodriguez' companion was killed. In 2½ hours of fierce fighting the intrepid team killed more than 82 Japanese, completely disorganized their defense and paved the way for subsequent defeat of the enemy at this strong point. Two days later, Private Rodriguez again enabled his comrades to advance when he single-handedly killed six Japanese and destroyed a well-placed 20-mm gun. By his outstanding skill with weapons, gallant determination to destroy the enemy, his heroic courage in facing tremendous odds, Private Rodriguez, on two occasions, materially aided the advance of our troops in Manila.[3]

Cleto Rodriguez was another Mexican-American soldier who brought fame and honor to our fighting men. The soft-spoken, medium-build Texan was a sharpshooting BAR man with Co. B., 148 Regiment of the 37th "Buckeye" Division.

He was the 5th American of Mexican descent to win the Medal of Honor and the first Spanish-speaking G.I. to win the highest award in the South Pacific.

Rodriguez was born and raised in San Marcos (Hays County, Texas), where he attended elementary school before moving to

---

[3]War Department Citation, G.O. No. 97, 1 November, 1945.

STAFF SERGEANT CLETO RODRIGUEZ
San Antonio, Texas
Congressional Medal of Honor
South Pacific World War II

San Antonio in search of employment. He worked at the Gunter Hotel and as a newsboy before joining the service in early 1944.

Both Rodriguez and his buddy, John M. Reece of Oklahoma City, earned the Medal of Honor about the same time, as they both put up a heroic stand against the Japanese stronghold, together killing 82 of the enemy during the return of American forces to the Philippines.

The two were members of the second Regiment of the 148th Infantry in the 37th. The 37th formed part of the 6th Army group which invaded Luzon in January, 1945, under the command of General Walter Kruger. Other combat units with the 6th included the 40th, 43rd, 38th and elements of the 24th. Infantry Divisions and the 11th Airborne, and later were joined by the famed First Cavalry.

The 37th, 1st Cavalry and 11th Airborne Combat group composed a task force that was given the job of securing Manila. The First Cavalry crashed into the outer limits of the city and the 37th broke in from the north. Fierce hand-to-hand fighting developed in the Philippine Capital which had been set afire by the Japanese. Destruction of the Pasig River bridge held up the 37th's advance. The enemy soldiers that held the Paco railroad station determined to hold the station at all cost, had built pillboxes containing heavy machine guns. Between these they had placed 20-mm dual-purpose guns. All around the station they had dugouts well manned, and surrounded by sandbags and large clip-fed 37-mm machine guns.

A rifle squad of Co. B, second platoon in the 148th Regiment, was pinned down by heavy rifle fire from the 300 enemy soldiers that held the Paco railroad station. This was the setting for the two infantry combatmen, Rodriguez and Reece, who had earned respect of their company in previous encounters against the Japanese, to move out and perform their heroic deeds, as stated in the War Department's citation.

Their brave act was witnessed by the whole company back in the American lines. The platoon Commander decided then to put in John Reece's name for the Congressional Medal of Honor, posthumously. It was hard for the commander to leave Rodriguez name out at that time; but the two could not earn the same medal for the same act, he judged. Ten days later, Rodriguez once again demonstrated his great valor when single-handed he killed six more enemy soldiers and destroyed a well-emplaced 20-mm gun, allowing his comrades to advance. His Commander promptly put in Rodriguez' name for the Congressional Medal also.

Cleto Rodriguez, promoted to Staff Sargeant, was awarded the Congressional Medal of Honor by President Truman at Washington and later was given a hero's welcome and the keys to the city of San Antonio, Texas. The following is a newspaper account of the welcoming ceremonies at the Alamo City.

CITY HONORS MEDAL OF HONOR WINNER

With the city council chamber overflowing in corridors of two floors, San Antonio Tuesday expressed its gratitude to Cleto Rodriguez, the newsboy who went to war and returned a hero.

City officials, khaki-clad buddies and mantilla-covered neighbors jammed the chamber to render official plaudits to the 22-year-old Congressional Medal of Honor winner and proclaim "Cleto Rodriguez Day."

TALLY OF 82 JAPANESE

In paying tribute to the technical sergeant, who with a buddy killed 82 Japanese in Manila, Mayor Mauermann said, "It is our desire to acknowledge a debt of gratitude to Cleto Rodriguez for his heroic action beyond the call of duty. We shall remember and forever cherish in our hearts his patriotism, zeal and love of country. We shall recall that he was ready to lay down his life for his country."

In the name of the Republic of Mexico, the new consul general, Gustavo Ortiz Hernan, saluted Rodriguez as, "A Hero of the glorious American Army, the symbol of the hope of the world." Terming the day one of pride for Mexico, Ortiz declared;

"The foundations of our history tremble with joy because the blood of the forefathers of our country has flown again in the veins of Cleto Rodriguez."

Obviously ill at ease, the medal winner expressed appreciation for the reception saying:

"I am indeed happy to have had the great privilege of serving our country in the global war, and I thank God for the victory achieved by our nation and its Allies. I wish to ask you to be good enough to join me in a moment of silent prayer to the memory of my buddy, Johnny Reece, and all my other comrades in arms who died for our country."

Rodriguez was referring to his companion on the day they killed 82 of the enemy. Reece was killed in action.

Following the moment of silence throngs gathered around for personal congratulations. Other speakers during the ceremony included Brig. Gen. Michael F. Davis, commander of the San Antonio district personnel distribution center; Col. John E. Grose, commanding officer of the Special Troops, Fourth Army, and C.W. Miller, president of the San Antonio Chamber of Commerce.

Among those attending were the full city council, Commissioners, P. L. Anderson, Pall Steffler, Henry Heins, Alfred Callaghan and Joel S. Quiñones, Mexican Consular Official, Rodriguez' aunt and uncle, Mr. and Mrs. Regino Hernandez, and Rodriguez' fiancee, Miss Flora Muñoz.[4]

[4]From the San Antonio Light, October 23, 1945.

THE PARATROOPERS

On May 10th, 1940, the first large scale Airborne attack in modern warfare had been used when the German machine dropped thousands of armed parachutists in their invasion of Holland. This type of assault troops intrigued military minds all over the world. United States and Great Britian were the next to come out with large airborne combat troops.

Thousands of our young men were attracted by this new style of soldiering. Everyone wanted to be a "Paratrooper." There were so many volunteers that Army Chiefs of Staff decided to make a separate branch out of the Airborne.

Throughout the southwest our young men took well to the Airborne. Since the early days of the draft, newly inducted Mexican-Americans requested and got assignment to the Airborne Infantry. Many of these men soon found themselves at Fort Benning for the roughest and most intensive jump training of the Airborne.

Why did so many of them volunteer for this service? They had various reasons for choosing the rugged life of the Paratrooper. Among some of the reasons given were: 1. The mere fact that it was a new and different branch. 2. They went for the paratroopers' emblem, uniform, jump boots, and jump jacket in a big way. 3. They wanted to find out how it felt to jump out of an airplane and go flying into space. 4. The physical requirements for the Airborne fitted them to a "T" —young, alert, tough, daring, and short stature—the latter alone had eliminated many young Mexican-Americans from other branches of their choosing. 5. Then there was the extra pay, and above all they welcomed the chance to prove to everyone that they could take it as well as dish it out.

Many soldiers resented the glorification of such glamorized service branches as the Air Corps, the Navy, and the Marines. When it became apparent to them that they were doomed to the sad G.I. life of the unpopular Infantry—literally speaking —they jumped at the chance of transferring over to the Airborne.

It took a lot of strict discipline, in addition to hard, rigorous training, to convert a green trainee into a rough-and-ready paratrooper. The volunteer trainees withstood the hard tests that separated the men from the boys at jump school. Few, if any, of our boys failed to pass the grade. Most of them still cherish their Airborne medal and even today keep it in a well-protected place. They were so proud of their 'wings' that many went so far as to have the emblem tatooed on their chest to forever remind them of the hard way they earned it. The browbeating they took from the "gorilla" instructors, the "mock tower," the "sweat shed," and most of all, their first jump; not to mention the daring jumps into unknown enemy-held territory during combat and the tough enemy they tangled with on the battlefield and at close combat.

When the strenuous seventeen weeks of the training course were finished, they joined and fought with exceptional courage, with such well-known outfits as the "All-American" 82nd; the "Screaming Eagles" of the 101st; "The Angels" of the 11th; and the 17th Airborne Divisions. They saw combat in such places as Africa, Tunisia, Anzio, Salerno, Nijmegen, Bastogne, Across the Rhine, Leyte and Manila, and spearheaded invasions of Sicily, Normandy, Holland, and Corregidor. On Luzon they raided the Los Baños prison camp and liberated what was left of Allied prison internees.

With the 504 Airborne Infantry regiment of the 82nd, the first American Parachute Division to pull a large-scale night operation (Gela, Sicily, July, 1943), was Andrew Kirker of Santa Ana, California, as previously mentioned, and the five Carrillo brothers of Los Angeles.

Manuel Bernal, Jess Talamentes, Los Angeles, and Ray Burt, Del Rio, Texas, were wounded in action when they fought with the 82nd in France, Holland, and Germany. Wounded in action with the 101st were Ray Marin, Alex Hernandez, Sandy Sandoval, Mundo Lozano and Shui Galvan, all in the D-Day landing on Normandy and ground fighting at Bastogne with the "Screaming Eagles."

These troopers will tell you how they were dropped from 1000 feet instead of the usual 500 when the plane pilots refused to get down any lower because of the heavy flak that covered the skies. They remember how helpless they felt being shot at by the many German guns as they descended on the outskirts of the small villages of St. Mere Eglise and Carentan, and others in the Normandy section.

In the Pacific, troopers who were with the 11th Airborne, saw combat in Leyte in November of 1944 when General McArthur made his historic return to the Philippines. The 503 Parachute Regimental Combat team was made into a Regimental Combat Batallion and many "Chicano" troopers made the jump with them at Corregidor on February 17, 1945. They had difficulty trying to land on the small 50 x 150 landing strip area,which was supposed to have been a golf course. Many of them landed on the rocky cliffs where they were carried by the strong winds on D-Day.

Among the Mexican-American paratroopers of the 503, RCT from the Los Angeles area were Ignacio "Pini" Martinez, Art Sanchez, and Jess Estrada of Co. C, and two other "Chueys," Jess Perez and Jesse Castillo of Co. C. Airborne Engineers. On February 18th, Castillo, a machine gunner with the engineers, was sent to escort medics who were taking blood plasma to the front lines.

They were assaulted by Japanese snipers as they made their way through the brush. As Castillo made a reach for his machine gun, which had been knocked down by a direct hit, another shot from an enemy sniper put a bullet through his head below his temple. The bullet shot out both his eyes, leaving him sightless and writhing in pain. Assisted back to the rear by his buddy, Jess Perez, Castillo was quickly evacuated for medical treatment.

Another outstanding *Chicano* trooper who earned glory with the "Angels of the 11th," in Luzon was Manny Perez, the kid from Chicago. He was with the 11th when the contingent landed in Manila to fight as ground troops and conquer the famous capital of the Philippines. After having secured Manila, they next turned their attention to Luzon. On January 25th the 11th, along with the 37th Infantry Division and the 1st Cavalry, made an unopposed landing at Nasugubu, south of Manila. Three days later, on January 31st, they jumped to Tagatay ridge on the Cavite area. It was here that Manny Perez made his greatest contribution to his country.

PVT. MANUEL PEREZ, JR.

Awarded the Congressional Medal of Honor. (Posthumously)

Fort William McKinley, Luzon, Philippine Islands, 13 Feb. 1945. He was leading scout for Campany A, which had destroyed 11 of 12 pillboxes in a strongly fortified sector defending the approach to enemy-held Fort William McKinley on Luzon, Philippine Islands. In the reduction of these pillboxes, he killed five Japanese in the open and blasted others in pillboxes with grenades. Realizing the urgent need for taking the last emplacement, which contained two twin-mount .50-caliber dual-purpose machine guns, he took a circuitous route to within 20 yards of the position, killing four of the enemy in his advance. He threw a grenade into the pillbox, and, as the crew started withdrawing through a tunnel just to the rear of the emplacement, shot and killed four before exhausting his clip. He had reloaded and killed four more when an escaping Japanese threw his rifle with fixed bayonet at him. In warding off this thrust, his own rifle was knocked

> to the ground. Seizing the Jap rifle, he continued firing, killed two more of the enemy. He rushed the remaining Japanese, killed three of them with the butt of the rifle and entered the pillbox, where he bayoneted the one surviving hostile soldier. Single-handedly, he killed 18 of the enemy in neutralizing the position that had held up the advance of his entire company. Through his courageous determination and heroic disregard of brave danger, Private Perez made possible the successful advance of his unit toward a valuable objective and provided a lasting inspiration for his comrades.[5]

Manny Perez of Chicago, Illinois, was a whirlwind paratrooper who never let up regardless of how tough the enemy or how large the odds. He was the 7th Mexican-American to be awarded the Medal of Honor, for his stirring display of valor. A month after being recommended for the CMH medal, Perez gave his life in another performance of bravery on the battlefield. Manny Perez died fighting another battle in defense of his buddies and his country.

It was on March 14, while out on patrol in enemy territory above Luzon. The patrol ran into a well-manned Japanese outpost. Facing heavy rifle and machine gun fire, Perez immediately volunteered to protect a withdrawal. He was mortally wounded while exchanging fire with the enemy.

Manny was born in Oklahoma City on March 3, 1923. He was inducted into the army. He volunteered for the Airborne Infantry and was assigned to Co. A, 511 Parchute Infantry of the 11th Airborne.

His body was brought back for burial in the place of his birth, Oklahoma City, where he was buried with high military honors. His father Manuel Sr., now lives in Nuevo Laredo, Tamaulipas, Mexico.

---

[5]War Department Citation, G.O. No. 124, 27 Dec., 1945.

PFC. MANUEL PEREZ, JR.
Chicago, Illinois
Congressional Medal of Honor
South Pacific World War II

S/SGT. YSMAEL VILLEGAS

Awarded the Congressional Medal of Honor (Posthumously)

Villa Verde Trail, Luzon, Philippine Islands. 20 March, 1945. Staff Sergeant Ysmael R. Villegas was a squad leader in Company F, 127th Infantry, 32nd Division. When his unit, in a forward position, clashed with an enemy strongly entrenched in connected caves and foxholes on commanding ground, he moved boldly from man to man, in the face of bursting grenades and demolition charges, through heavy machine gun and rifle fire, to bolster the spirit of his comrades.

Inspired by his gallantry, his men pressed forward to the crest of the hill. Numerous enemy riflemen, refusing to flee, continued to fire from their foxholes. Sergeant Villegas, with complete disregard for his own safety and the bullets which kicked up the dirt at his feet, charged an enemy position and firing at point-blank range, killed the Japanese in the foxhole.

He rushed a second foxhole while bullets missed him by inches, and killed one more of the enemy. In rapid succession he charged a third, a fourth and a fifth foxhole, each time destroying the enemy within. The fire against him increased in intensity, but he pressed onward to attack a sixth position.

As he neared his goal, he was hit and killed by enemy fire. Through his heroism and indomitable fighting spirit, Sergeant Villegas, at the cost of his life, inspired his men to a determined attack in which they swept the enemy from the field.[6]

The story of Staff Sergeant "Smiley" Villegas depicts the story of many of our quiet, unnoticed, humble young men who

---

[6]War Department Citation, G.O. No. 89, 19 October, 1945.

STAFF SERGEANT YSMAEL R. VILLEGAS
Casablanca, California
Congressional Medal of Honor
South Pacific World War II

rose to great heights in performance of their duty and devotion to their country.

Before the war, Villegas was practically an unknown. He lived and worked in Casablanca, a small community in the outskirts of Riverside, California.

His heroic actions in a daring sacrifice in the Villa Verde Trail, on Luzon, where he earned the Medal of Honor, brought respect and pride to his family, his friends, his hometown and most of all, his people.

The 21-year-old Infantryman, a veteran of Philippine Islands fighting of the 32nd (Red Arrow) Infantry Division, was an orange picker in the groves that surrounded his home at Casablanca before he entered the Army.

A squad leader, Sergeant Villegas died while attracting to himself the full force of the enemy fire-power to give the men of his squad an opportunity to move into the enemy foxhole positions. First Lieutenant William A. Newburn, of Selma, California, who was moving up with his company behind the forward squad led by Sergeant Villegas says: "Running like a football player, he charged the first Japanese and killed him with his rifle. All the enemy weapons were brought to bear on him. The bullets caused dirt to spurt up at his feet. He whirled and headed for another foxhole, stood over it, killed the Japanese rifleman, and then headed for another. In this way, he killed five of the enemy.

"Heading for the sixth foxhole, he had allowed every Jap on that hill a chance to get a bead on him. He went down in a tornado of fire." But as the youthful squad leader fell, the battle was lost by the Japanese hill defenders.

First Lieutenant William D. Zahniser, whose home is in Edinboro, Pennsylvania, reported: "The men were so incensed at his death, they charged the position and couldn't be stopped. They had moved in close while the enemy was concentrating fire on the Sergeant and they swept through the strong point, driving the enemy before them. When their charge was over, 75 Japanese lay dead in their foxholes."

The fighting took place March 20th, 1945, during the period of fanatical resistance that characterized the struggles for each hill captured by the Red Arrow Division. Only three weeks before, on March 1st, Sergeant Villegas had been presented the Silver Star for his gallantry in combat in destroying a Japanese machine gun nest.

Sergeant Villegas was born at Casablanca on March 21st, 1924, and lived there with his wife, Mrs. Lillie Sanchez Villegas and his parents, Mr. and Mrs. Dario Villegas.

PFC. DAVID GONZALES[1]

Awarded the Congressional Medal of Honor (Posthumously)

Villa Verde Trail, Luzon, Philippine Islands, 25 April, 1945. Private First Class, Company A, 127th Infantry, 32nd Infantry Division. He was pinned down with his company. As enemy fire swept the area, making any movement extremely hazardous, a 500-pound bomb smashed into the company's perimeter, burying 5 men with its explosion. Private Gonzales, without hesitation, seized an entrenching tool and under a hail of fire crawled 15 yards to his entombed comrades, where his commanding officer, who had also rushed forward, was beginning to dig the men out. Nearing his goal, he saw the officer struck and instantly killed by machine gun fire. Undismayed, he set to work swiftly and surely with his hands and the entrenching tool while enemy sniper and machine gun bullets struck all about him. He succeeded in digging one of the men out of the pile of rock and sand. To dig faster he stood up regardless of the greater danger from so exposing himself. He extricated a second man, and then another. As he completed the liberation of the third, he was hit and mortally wounded, but the comrades for

[1]Picture not available.

> whom he so gallantly gave his life were safely evacuated. Private Gonzales, valiant and intrepid conduct exemplified the highest tradition of the military service.[7]

While the heroic action displayed in winning the Congressional Medal of Honor by David Gonzales was different in nature, it is of the same calibre found only in the very bravest of men. Taking action as only brave men do, Private First Class David Gonzales distinguished himself above and beyond the call of duty, when without regard to his own safety he gallantly laid down his own life in rescuing three of his buddies.

Gonzales succeeded in rescuing three of the entombed soldiers as they sprayed the very soil into which he was digging. Before he could save the other two, he fell mortally wounded and died later that day. The other two buried soldiers were saved later when the intense enemy fire had subsided.

Two eyewitness accounts to Private Gonzales' amazing self-sacrifice reveal the story. One by Second Lieutenant Frank M. Reehoff, a technical sergeant at that time, from Flint, Michigan:

"Our perimeter was receiving extremely heavy machine gun and sniper fire, "Sergeant Reehoff related, "which made all the movement very hazardous, if not impossible. Suddenly a 500-pound bomb dropped on our perimeter, burying five men. Private Gonzales, disregarding his own safety, crawled out 15 yards under heavy fire, and made for the spot where the men were entombed.

"Our commanding officer, also running to the spot, reached it first, but he was killed as he started to dig the men out."

Second Lieutenant William W. Kouts, who was also a technical sergeant at that time, from St. Cloud, Minnesota, continued the story: "Although enemy sniper and machine gun fire was narrowly missing him," sergeant Kouts reported, "and he

---

[8]War Department Citation, G.O. No. 115, 8 Dec. 1945.

had seen what had happened to his commanding officer, Private Gonzales never hesitated but started to dig the men out.

"While bullets continued to fly about him, he dug out the three men before he was wounded so badly that he died a few hours later."

First Lieutenant Benjamin Ring, Flint, Michigan, who commanded Private Gonzales' outfit, Company A, 127th Infantry Regiment, said, "All three of the men he had rescued recovered after brief hospitalization and returned to duty. The other two were rescued later when the enemy fire became less intense."

"It was the bravest thing I have ever seen a man do," said Sergeant Reehoff, and Sergeant Kouts added, "It is a sure thing that if it weren't for Private Gonzales the three men would not be alive today."

David Gonzales was born June 9, 1923, in Pacoima. Before entering the Army March 31, 1944, at Fort McArthur, California, he worked in Southern California as a drill operator. He received his basic infantry training at Camp Roberts, from April to September 1, 1944, and departed for overseas service as an infantry replacement in December, 1944, being assigned to the Red Arrow Division. Private Gonzales was awarded the Combat Infantryman Badge February 1, 1945, for exemplary conduct and action against the enemy.

Just three days later, another Mexican-American added still further glory to the billiant war record of Uncle Sam's Spanish-speaking soldiers. He was Alejandro Ruiz and hails from the plains of New Mexico.

SGT. ALEJANDRO RUIZ

Awarded the Congressional Medal of Honor

Okinawa, Ryukyu Islands, April 28, 1945. Sergeant Alejandro Renteria Ruiz, Company A, 165th Infantry, 27th Division. When his unit was stopped by a skillfully camouflaged enemy pillbox, he displayed conspicuous

> gallantry and intrepidity above and beyond the call of duty. His squad, suddenly brought under a hail of machine gun fire and a vicious grenade attack, was pinned down. Jumping to his feet, Private Ruiz seized an automatic rifle and lunged through the flying grenades, rifle and automatic fire for the top of the emplacement. When an enemy soldier charged him, his rifle jammed. Undaunted, Private Ruiz whirled on his assailant and clubbed him down. Then he ran back through bullets and grenades, seized more ammunition and another automatic rifle, and again made for the pillbox. Enemy fire now was concentrated on him, but he charged on, miraculously to the top. Leaping from one opening to another, he sent burst after burst into the pillbox, killing 12 of the enemy and completely destroying the position. Private Ruiz's heroic conduct, in the face of overwhelming odds, saved the lives of many comrades and eliminated an obstacle that long would have checked his unit's advance.[7]

New Mexico's contribution to the ranks of CMH Heroes, Alex Ruiz, displayed more of the bravery and intrepidity so common with the Mexican-American G.I.'s of World War II on the high ridges of Okinawa on the 28th of April, 1945.

The tall and handsome lad from the "Land of Enchantment" was born in Loving, New Mexico, on June 24, 1922. Before enlisting in the Army he was engaged in truck hauling. He entered the service on September 9, 1943; he was inducted at Fort Bliss and took basic training at Camp Roberts.

This young infantryman who fought and clubbed his way in and out of a Japanese stronghold on the high ridges of Okinawa was the 11th Mexican-American to be awarded the Congressional Medal of Honor in World War II.

In April, 1945, Company A, 165th Infantry Regiment was

---

[7]War Department Citation, G.O. No. 60, 26 June, 1926.

SERGEANT ALEJANDRO R. RUIZ
Loving, New Mexico
Congressional Medal of Honor
South Pacific World War II

assigned the job of cleaning up the remnants of a battalion of Japanese who were firmly entrenched in a network of underground fortifications commanding a series of ridges known as Item Pocket. Their defensive position was strengthened on the crest of the main ridge, by well-camouflaged concrete pillboxes, connected to the underground tunnels and caves.

The platoon in which the then Private Ruiz was a rifleman was given the task, on April 28th, of capturing the ridge.

"This ridge was about 150 feet high, and dropped sharply away from the crest on both sides," said First Lieutenant Mathew C. Masem of Brooklyn, New York, commander of the platoon.

Progress was hindered by jagged rocks and constant rifle fire. Three small pinnacles about 30 yards apart dominated the crest. Members of the assault platoon, who witnessed Ruiz' gallantry, continue the story of the action:

"We worked around the first pinnacle without a mishap," said Technical Sergeant Frank Distefano of The Bronx, New York, "and started toward the second when we learned it was a well-constructed pillbox. Almost immediately the enemy opened up with machine guns, rifle fire, and grenades."

The platoon was trapped. The Japanese had held their fire until the Americans circled a deep coral cut from which a man unaided could not climb out. To retreat the way they had entered would have meant silhouetting themselves against the sky. In a few minutes every man in the two assault squads, except Ruiz and his squad leader, were wounded by nearly 100 grenades directed at them by the fanatical Japanese soldiers.

Staff Sergeant Peter J. Bulger, of the Bronx, stated that six of his squad members were casualties of this attack. Staff Sergeant Ivan A. Coley of Evansville, Indiana, saw Private Ruiz grab an automatic rifle from a fallen man and rush through the excessively-heavy fire to the pillbox. "As he fired into one of the emplacements, the weapon jammed, so he clubbed an assailant with the otherwise useless weapon."

According to Sergeant Presley B. Land of Fort Worth, Texas, who was himself later killed in action, Ruiz ran back to the rest of the squad for another Browning Automatic Rifle and for more ammunition. He retraced his steps through the deadly hail of lead, and again climbed on top of the enemy bastion.

"Private Ruiz moved from position to position, firing into apertures while covering the advance of his squad. The rest of the platoon were so inspired by his actions that they wiped out the enemy position," stated Sergeant Joe J. Bacay of Falfa, Colorado.

XII

THE MEXICAN-AMERICAN MARINES

World War II gave birth to many a witty saying or slogan that became popular with the fighting men. Some of the clever quips were born by mere accident; others were carefully thought up.

Towards the end of the war we heard an ingenious phrase that became very popular and was often repeated by fighting men in the Pacific. It is said that it started in the Philippines.

During a big welcome parade staged by the Filipinos in honor of General McArthur on his famous return to that area of the war, somebody posted a large hand-lettered sign that read:

"With God's help, and a few Marines, McArthur returned to the Philippines."

Get a hard-core Army man and a loyal Marine and for sure the two will start to argue not only as to which of the two outfits is the better one, but also which is the worse of the two.

Not wanting to get involved in any arguments, I would like to repeat some of the opinions that have been ex-expressed. Actually the enemy (the Japanese) had a lot to do with it. During WW II, when the U.S. Marines landed on many of the enemy-held islands in the Pacific, the Japanese defenders came out to engage them. After a few days of hostilities—and seeing the futility of it all, the enemy "made for the hills" or sought refuge in caves. After the hard battles had quieted down and very few of the enemy could be found, the combat Marines were pulled out, the island was called "secured," then Army troops were brought to "mop-up" and occupy the Islands. Each had been trained for a certain purpose and they both excelled in this respect.

No sooner had the Marines left, than the hidden Japanese soldiers came out of the caves and launched a heavy attack on the newcomers. The combat Marines soon heard that the Army had been driven back and had lost the territory they had fought hard for. The Army blamed the Marines for having claimed the island "secure" when actually it still was crowded with enemy. The Marines blamed the Army for losing the ground to "a few little Japs." They called the army 'doughs' incompetent fighters.

In my opinion, the combat Marines and the Army infantrymen were equally tough, each being trained well for a certain duty. With the high standards the Marines set up for enlistments and the hard-disciplined boot training program they experienced,the Marines have very good reason for calling their lot the "toughest".

When the Marines set up high standards for recruits, it was surprising to see so many Mexican-American boys in the olive-drab gyrene uniforms. Actually there were a lot of our young men who qualified in the physical, mental and height aspects of the requirements and it is impossible to guess just about what percentage of our boys served in that branch.

In Southern California, one would see the camps at Pendelton, El Toro, Elliott and Santa Barbara filled to capacity and full of activity in and around the area during World War II. Well sprinkled among them were Mexican-Americans. They weren't any undersized individuals either. Though it is an accepted fact that our people generally are of short and medium stature, most of these rugged individuals in the Marines were tall, strong, solid-built, and every inch a Marine.

Take for example the Leathernecks that landed with the First and Second Marine Divisions, who faced the enemy in the very first encounters between United States and Japanese combat forces in the wild jungles of Guadalcanal in August of

1942. Among them were Joe Prado, a six-footer from Downey, California; "Big Rudy" and Frank "Largo" Galeana, 6'3" and 6'5" tall brothers from Los Angeles with the 1st Marines. Previously mentioned was Emilio Luna, a 200 pounder from Norwalk, California, who stands at 5'11" and enlisted prior to Pearl Harbor; and Pancho De La Cruz, 250 lbs., a former prize fighter. Cruz ran out of opposition in the service, and easily won the Pacific Heavyweight Championship while with the Marines.

TARAWA

After Guadalcanal, the Marines in the Second Division covered themselves with glory in the bloody battle of Tarawa, where so many were lost in what to this day is still a debatable action.

Tarawa was the most costly of all enemy territory won by any of our combat troops in World War II, as far as casualties suffered are concerned. Said Marine General Julian Smith: "The one thing that won this battle was the supreme courage of the Marines . . . who kept coming ashore in spite of the enemy's heavy machine gun fire." Many writers have attempted to describe clearly the horrors of Tarawa, but Marines who were there insist the real story can never be adequately told. Combat films and actual shots of the ghastly battle of Tarawa gave the folks back home a brutal shock of what our fighting men were going through in the Pacific.

On November 20th, 1943, after heavy naval and aerial bombardment, the first two waves of the 2nd and 8th Marines riding amphibian tractors ran into the coral barrier reef which encircled the L-shaped atoll. During the first few hours of the landing, most of the tractors were hit and could not be used. Succeeding waves had to disembark from Higgins boats and wade ashore in face of murderous fire from the entrenched Japanese.

They were alarmed to find themselves facing a living hell

when their landing barges were held up by the high coral reefs forcing them to wade ashore with their heavy equipment on their backs. The water around them was soon crimson with Marine blood . . . Those who did make it ashore took temporary respite behind a long wall of coconut logs near the shore. The frying heat added to the discomfort of the holocaust. Interlocking machine gun fire and mortar barrages kept them cringing to the small shelter of the sea wall. Only after their able leaders reorganized the units, or formed new ones of the men that were left, were they able to go over the wall into the hail of heavy fire.

All day, all night, and still by next afternoon, the issue was in doubt. The Japanese defenders were well barricaded in the well-built pillboxes that had taken them 15 months to prepare.

It was here that Cpl. Jacobo Cruz, Los Angeles, with the 6th Marines, earned the Silver Star the first day of the landing and his first time in action. When the machine-gunner assistant in Cruz' squad fell from a hail of bullets, the squad leader asked for volunteers to pull the ammo carriers back to safety. Cruz, who was in a well protected shell hole volunteered, and was fatally wounded in his effort to save his comrade.

SAIPAN

After a brief rest, the 2nd Marine Division was again in campaigns at the Marshalls, Kwajalein, Truk, and New Guinea Islands. The 2nd then moved on to Saipan, an island of the Marianas chain.

On June 15th, 1944, the 2nd Marines once again waded ashore in Saipan, another island where the Japanese were waiting for them. Together with the 4th Marines and the 27th Infantry (Army) Division, they stormed ashore in "Am-tracs" to again face the short, stubborn enemy, who did not believe in defeat and could only attain glory by victory or by death.

Two well-known professional fighters from Los Angeles

participated in the landing of Saipan. They were Charlie "Chuckie" Garcia (KIA), a lightweight from the Eastside, who had compiled an undefeated record of twelve victories in the ring. The other, Cpl. Ramon Fuentes, the rugged welterweight, who like Pancho De La Cruz, also won the South Pacific Championship in his weight. A machine-gunner with the 10th Battalion of the 2nd Marines, Fuentes' occupation in civilian life was that of a grave digger. Fuentes and his *compadre,* Art Gaitan, also of Los Angeles, sent many an enemy soldier to his grave with their blistering heavy machine gun fire.

GABALDON CAPTURES OVER 1000

Guy Louis Gabaldon of Bellflower, California, went ashore in the third wave with Pfc. Ariel Hernandez, Mercedes, Texas, with the 2nd Division and bagged thirteen Japanese on the first day. Gabaldon, who grew up in Los Angeles' Eastside, had moved in with Japanese-American friends in his early teens and learned the Japanese language. He was left alone when his "foster parents" were taken away to an internment camp in the early days of the war. Having just turned 17, and just tall enough to meet the requirements, Gabaldon decided to enlist in the Marine Corps.

After the landing in Saipan, Guy was pulled back to Regiment because he could speak Japanese and he was assigned to Intelligence, but Gabaldon was fond and proud of his BAR. He found it awfully dull at Regiment, and the next morning he sneaked off into the jungle by himself. He came back with five prisoners.

His achievement made him a minor hero; and his superiors ignored the fact that he had disobeyed orders by leaving and throwing his rifle and helmet away to replace them with a lighter carbine and a more comfortable Seabee cap.

Japanese soldiers didn't surrender easily, and Guy was pretty proud. So, he slipped off the following morning and returned with 10 more. His knowledge of idiomatic East Los Angeles Japanese was paying off. "Usually," he said, "I'd flush them out. But sometimes I'd just walk through the jungles and call out, promising 'em things."

From that day, Guy became a one-man Marine Corps and a legend. His daily collections of prisoners ran as high as 30, and his buddies would make bets every morning on how many he'd bring back.

After a month of lone forays, he hit a bigger jackpot.

He sneaked up on six Japanese soldiers in an open field and got the drop on them. While their hands were over their heads, he talked to them. He told them they were going to be treated well and given water and food, and medical care. "I'm keeping three of you here," he said. "The other three can leave and bring some friends back." But if they didn't come back, he warned, he'd blast the hell out of the three left behind.

They came back with half a dozen more prisoners but Guy wasn't satisfied. Again he sent half of the group out. They came back with more, and still, more were sent out.

In seven hours, Pfc. Gabaldon was surrounded by 800 prisoners.

Two patrolling Marines spotted the operation through field glasses and went to the scene. Guy dispatched them for more aid and trucks, and his day's work was done.

A couple of weeks later, Guy was shot in the arm and hand on similiar missions, and his fighting career ended. As recognition, he received the Silver Star "for the capture of over 1000 enemy."[1]

The 2nd Marines along with the 3rd, 4th, and 1st Divisions kept the pressure on the desperate-fighting Japanese as they continued their island-hopping campaign in the South, Southwest, and Central Pacific and into the Far East.

---

[1]Paul V. Coates, Mirror-News, Los Angeles, April 8, 1957.

Marine fighters next appeared in the Far East island of Iwo Jima. They landed on the five-mile long by two-mile wide strip on February 19, 1945. Among the men who fought on Iwo were Tony Acosta, formerly of Clarksdale, Arizona, now living in Los Angeles, and Joe Arenas who was born in Cedar Rapids, Iowa, and now lives in San Francisco where he starred in professional football for the San Francisco 49ers. Acosta served with the artillery of the 5th Marine Division while Arenas was wounded in action with the 4th Marines.

The Japanese put up fanatical resistance at the strategic island where Americans would find themselves only 750 miles from Tokyo. United States Marine losses were 4,189 officers and men killed, 15,306 wounded, in 26 days of heavy fighting at Iwo Jima.

OKINAWA

Okinawa was the final great battle of the glorious Marines and it was by no means any less bitter than other island battles. Once again our men distinguished themselves. Among the leaders of Marine forces was Major General Pedro Del Valle who commanded the First Marines, and Lieutenant Dennis Chavez, Jr., of Albuquerque, New Mexico, son of the bantam-sized, reknowned Senator of New Mexico. He had commanded the 22nd since the battle of the 6th, at Guam.

The 6th Marine Division landed on Okinawa along with the 1st and 2nd, which was made up—for the most part—of combat veterans from Marine Raider battalions. The 22nd Marines had faced the enemy many times before at such renowned places as the Battle of the Tenaru at Guadalcanal; Tarawa's Betio Beach, Saipan's Tapotchau; Peleliu's Bloody Nose Ridge; and Iwo's Mt. Suribachi.

On Easter Sunday, April 1st, 1945, Marines of the 6th Division made the landing on Okinawa. Among the first to come to grips with the stubborn Japanese defenders were Gilberto Valeriano, Pico, California, Co. L 4th Marines, Fernando Gonzales, also of Co. L and Joe Olivas, Co. G, a former football star at Roosevelt High, both from Los Angeles. Out of the California trio, Valeriano was the only lucky one to return home after receiving wounds in action. The other two Mexican-American Marines sacrificed their lives in Okinawa.

Olivas was killed when an enemy shell made a direct hit on his dug-in position. The heroic action performed by Fernando Gonzales in Okinawa exemplifies the type of valiant men we had in the Marine Corps.

The following action which earned the Bronze Star for Gonzales was witnessed by Valeriano and was carried in local newspaper columns:

> One example of heroism never officially recognized is that of a "Mexican" Marine who did the fighting for an entire company for more than three hours during an ambush on Okinawa in May, 1945. Pfc. Fernando E. Gonzales of Los Angeles was pinned to the ground in a small ravine together with his company by the crossfire from camouflaged caves on surrounding ridges. Gonzales moved up the ridge and established a position behind a small knoll. During the next three hours he sprayed the Jap-held area with a steady stream of fire while Marines in the ravine snaked their way out of the ambush and withdrew the wounded. Later, Gonzales left his gun to aid a wounded Marine and was killed while dragging the man to safety.[2]

---

[2]From the editorial page of the Los Angeles Daily News, November 2, 1945, commenting on the worthy citizens of Mexican extraction of Los Angeles, in rebuttal to a reader's views.

XIII

IN THE NAVY

The Navy was another branch that had not lured very many of us before World War II. Perhaps it was due to the standards set or because as in WW I, almost everytime one of our own who was drafted or volunteered, was automatically sent to the Army. In World War II, there were just as many volunteers for the Navy as there were for the Army. Only the fact that Navy quotas were rather small and were soon filled, turned many an aspiring would-be-sailor into a dog-face infantryman in the Army.

Our young men who served in the Navy also fought in all war areas of the world. The first man to lose his life in World War II from the community of San Gabriel, California, was Reyner Aguirre[1] who died on the S.S. Arizona in the surprise attack on the U.S. fleet at Pearl Harbor. Aguirre was born in San Gabriel, July 31, 1912. He was a graduate of Alhambra High School. He volunteered for the Navy on June 6, 1941.

Quartermaster Edward Vecerra (address unknown) is another listed among the many killed or wounded. Vecerra was on the "West Virginia" (the wallowing Virgin), and was among the wounded on that historic day of December 7, 1941.

Among many heroic accounts released by the Navy is that of Frankie Abasta, 18-year-old naval gunner from Los Angeles on the W.W. "Warrior". Frankie Abasta lost his life and was awarded the Silver Star posthumously. His citation read:

---

[1]American Legion Post No. 748, San Gabriel, California, has been named in honor of Reyner Aguirre.

His ship was torpedoed by a Japanese submarine in South Pacific waters on July 1, 1942. Despite the fact that the ship began settling by the stern immediately after the explosion, Abasta remained at the side of his commanding officer after the rest of the crew had abandoned the vessel, and from a precarious position on the sloping deck, he continued to man a three-inch gun with utter disregard for his own personal safety.

Not until his commanding officer had left did Abasta think of himself, but already the ship had completely upended. As he tried to put on a life jacket he missed his footing, slipped, fell, and disappeared into the sea. Abasta's heroism kept the sub from shelling the ship and fleeing lifeboats, enabling the others to escape the sinking vessel.[1]

Tony Aldapa, Hermosillo, Sonora, Mexico, was in naval action off Casablanca when the first United States troops invaded North Africa, November, 1942.

Electrician's Mate 2/c Oscar Almanza, popular youngster from East Los Angeles, lost his life November 30, 1942, when his ship, the "Pensacola" along with four other American destroyers, ran into seven enemy ships, engaging them in a savage naval battle off Savo Island. Almanza was down in the boiler room when the "Pensacola" was struck by a torpedo. Badly crippled, the "Pensacola" was tugged and beached.

"Smiley" Rosales, San Marcos, Texas, drove an LST full of assault troops in the landing effected by the United States Army in Kiska, Aleutian Islands, in May, 1943.

Seaman 2/c Alex "El Indio" Moisa and Corpsman 3/c Vince Rodriguez, Los Angeles, who later became brother-in-laws, fought off attacks by the Japanese "Divine Wind" or

---

[1]Griffith, Beatrice, *American Me,* Houghton Mifflin Co., Boston, 1948, p. 262.

Kamikaze, so-called suicide planes in the Lingayen Gulf and Okinawa.

An outstanding Navy man who was claimed by both the Marines and the Navy, was a 22-year-old youngster who came from the small city of Ysleta, Texas. He gave his life for his country in the Marine Peleliu Island campaign. This was Pharmacist's Mate 3/c Carlos V. Porras, Jr.

CHARLES VICTOR PORRAS

Awarded the Navy Cross (posthumously)

September 22, 1944, Peleliu, Palau Islands. While with an assault platoon of Company L, Third Battalion, 1st Marine Division, during action against enemy Japanese forces at Peleliu. When one Marine was killed and two others seriously wounded while attempting to evacuate casualties in a reconnaissance patrol, Pharmacist's Mate, Third Class, Charles Victor Porras, unhesitantly proceeded far in front of his own lines to go to the aid of his helpless comrade. Courageously advancing alone under a withering barrage from Japanese machine guns, he succeeded in treating and carrying back, unaided, four of the wounded men before he himself was fatally struck down. By his unswerving devotion to duty and great personal valor, Porras was an example and inspiration to all his comrades and his unselfish action throughout was in keeping with the highest tradition of the U.S. Navy. He gallantly gave his life for his country.[2]

In June, 1942, Charles Victor Porras, Jr., was picked as the "Most Likely to Succeed", by his classmates when he graduated from Ysleta High School. The red-haired youngster starred in football in high school, and El Paso School of Mines (Texas

[2]Citation and award of Navy Cross, posthumously awarded by Ralph A. Birch, Acting Secretary of the Navy to Mr. & Mrs. Victor Porras, Los Angeles.

PM 3/c CHARLES VICTOR PORRAS, JR.
El Paso, Texas
Navy Cross
South Pacific World War II

Western) where he attended one semester before enlisting in the Navy in December, 1942. Porras was the only son of Marcela Ruiz and Victor Porras, formerly of El Paso, and now living in Los Angeles. The elder Porras was a Commander of the El Paso Spanish-American War Veterans W.W. I Organization.

After boot training in San Diego, Porras first saw action as a Corpsman with the 1st Marines in June, 1943, at Rendova. Then at Cape Gloucester in September with the 1st Amphibious Marines, and at Bougainville in December of the same year.

Porras showed exceptional heroism and loyal devotion to his country in the thick of battle on a hard-fought for tiny island in the Pacific when he courageously advanced, alone and unarmed, under heavy Japanese machine gun fire to treat and carry back the wounded before he was fatally shot himself.

"Red" was equally loved by the Marines of Company L and all officers. First hand accounts of Porras' last days in combat are described in the heart-touching letter written to his parents by the officer in charge of the Battalion Aid Station where Porras worked untiringly to bring aid and comfort to the wounded and dying Marines on Peleliu. The letter, addressed to his parents is undoubtedly one of the most soul-stirring reports of the last moments in the life of one of our courageous fighting men. It reads in part:

> ". . . I first got to know your son when I joined the battalion. During the seven months that followed we worked together—we played and we talked—I censored some of his letters home. He impressed me as having an intense interest in all that he did, he had ability to learn readily and his motive attitude set him apart as an individual. I knew him as "Red" or "Porras".
>
> Red was offered the chance to leave the company and work in the sickbay. He was a good corpsman, we wanted him there and it was safer than combat. He chose to stay

in the company—there he had closer contact with the men he was treating, he liked the more rugged life they led, and he was liked by the Marines who wanted him to stay.

I knew him as a good corpsman who was interested in the work, who learned from my lectures, who asked questions, and who had a sense of duty in doing his best for any Marine in his company. The men and officers recognized him as an excellent corpsman but also a good Marine. Lt. Cochran once told me, "Why, Red is a better Marine than a Corpsman. He knows how to dismantle and fire a machinegun better than many of my men." When on maneuvers Red would share the load of a tired Marine—his load, as a corpsman, being lighter.

War is a futile, wasteful and costly business—in materiél and men. It was impressed on my mind with each casualty I saw, with each of my men that was wounded. I was never more fully aware of it than the afternoon of the ninth day on Peleliu when I was told "they got Red this morning."

I had seen him the afternoon of the first day. He had been working for about 5 hours in the thick of battle—he was tired, hungry, thirsty, and his dungarees were torn—he was unhurt. His medical supplies had run out and he was back at the beach for a new supply, he immediately went back to his job of treating men.

Again on the fourth day I talked with him while his company was in reserve. Casualties had been heavy but Bloody Nose Ridge had to be taken. He had been close to death but was unchanged in his typical optimistic and cheerful attitude.

During the next four days we heard of the fighting for the ridge. My aid station was at its base and we had firsthand accounts from the casualties he had treated that Red was doing an exceptionally outstanding job. His sense of duty to a wounded Marine was above and beyond any thought of himself. I was told later that Red, who happened to be weapon-less except for an entrenching tool, jumped into a hole to avoid a sniper. A Jap was in the hole and Red had to kill him with the shovel to save his life.

Your son lost his life in the execution of the most devoted duty known to man. He was saving the life of another man. Twice before that morning he had gone *beyond* the front lines into rugged dangerous terrain to bring back wounded men who were doomed to sure death otherwise. The third time he was unsuccessful. Further advance was impossible due to severe opposition and thus our Marines were unable to rescue his body.

At noon the battalion was replaced by elements of the 81st Army Division. After eight and one-half days in the lines, we had sustained about 2/3 casualties—we were tired, weak, ineffective. The battle had been won and the fresh troops cleaned up the rest of the ridge. I have never been informed if your son's body was recovered by them.

True, your son's body is dead, but his soul lives on. His actions are forever imprinted on the minds of every living man of L Company—they remember with reverent pride. The men whose lives he saved remember him with a soul-filling thankfulness experienced only by those who have been faced with death. I will forever remember him as a man, full and mature, one who showed no fear; one who was selfless in his thoughts and actions; one who put the abolition of pain and the saving of lives far above his own.

Your son, Red, lives as an inspiration to all who knew him.

You have the citation awarded him, the Navy Cross. His commanding officer felt, as did all of us, that such deeds should not go unnoticed. It is no reward—no recompense. It is a gesture, a symbol of the people of the United States to express their gratefulness for what he did for their sons.

. . . Most Sincerely, Joseph E. Christophenson, Rochester, New York."

XIV

THE AIR FORCE

This story was intended to glorify the combat infantrymen and other ground troops who saw action at the front. But since we have taken into account the deeds of Mexican-American servicemen, the story would not be complete if we did not mention the men who served in the Air Force. One such standout was Lt. Colonel Jose Holguin, who undoubtedly is one of the greatest air aces among Americans of Mexican descent. He has earned his share of awards, and today he continues his career in the Air Force where he has won additional honors.

JOSE L. HOLGUIN

Awarded the Distinguished Flying Cross and Oak Leaf Cluster

June 11, 1943. Rank: 1st Lieutenant. For extraordinary achievement while participating in 200 hours of operational flight in the South Pacific area during while hostile contact was probable. This operation included long range bombing, missions against enemy airdrome installations, and attacks on naval vessels and shipping.[1] Throughout this he showed outstanding ability, courage, and devotion to duty. His citation for the Oak Leaf Cluster reads:

Captain Jose L. Holguin, A-0728388, United States Air Force. Distinguished himself by extraordinary achievement while participating in aerial flights on June 26, 1943. Capt. Holguin was navigator of a B-17 type air-

[1]Promoted to Captain.

craft on a mission to Vanakania Airdrome, Rabaul, New Britian.

Although the aircraft had sustained severe damage, Capt. Holguin, in spite of his own wounds, aided wounded crew members and assisted the pilot in controlling the aircraft after the co-pilot had been severely wounded. When the controls became ineffective, he assisted other crew members to bail out. The exceptional courage and exemplary devotion to duty displayed by Capt. Holguin reflects great credit to himself and the U.S. Air Force.[2]

Additional awards earned by Holguin include:

Purple Heart and Oak Leaf Cluster

For wounds received in action in the Pacific area on March 3, 1943.

The Air Medal

For meritorious achievement in an aerial flight over hostile convoys near Wewak, New Guinea, on April 10, 1943.

After flying through heavy thunderstorm and difficult icing conditions the target area was reached and a 7,000-ton enemy cargo vessel was sighted, a low-level bombing attack was effected from an altitude of 150 feet. Two 1000 pound bombs were dropped and near misses were scored on the vessel, the explosion turned the boat 30° to its original position. In the face of heavy anti-aircraft fire, a second bombing run was made on Wewak and hits were scored on important installations. The courage, ability and devotion to duty shown by Lt. Holguin in conduct of the mission is worthy of commendation.

—Awarded January 11, 1945.

[2]Awarded at Washington, D.C., 21 April, 1949. Colonel Jody, Air Adjutant General, signed W. Stuart Syminton, Secretary U.S. Air Force.

LT. COL. JOSE L. HOLGUIN
Los Angeles, California
Being decorated with Air Force Commendation Medal by
GENERAL CURTIS E. LE MAY, Commanding General,
Strategic Air Command, Offutt Air Force Base, October 15, 1955
Wartime decorations include;
Silver Star, Distinguished Flying Cross, Air Medal, and Purple Heart
Southwest Pacific World War II

Silver Star

For gallantry in action over Hansa Harbor, New Guinea in April 14, 1944.

Jose Holguin is recognized as one of the sharpest bombing brains in the world. A native of Santa Ana, California, born in 1921, he attended Belmont High School in Los Angeles. He was a member of the Scholastic Honor Society and participated in track and basketball at this school. He married Celia Rebecca Martinez of Garden Grove, California. The Holguins now have five children: Rebecca, Curtis, Claudia, Carlos, and Bret.

Holguin entered the service ten days after the Pearl Harbor attack. He received his wings at Mather Field, Sacramento, California, in 1942. His record over the Southwest Pacific is 40 combat missions as a B-17 Navigator.

The highlight of Holguin's war experiences came when his plane was shot down May 15, 1943, by Japanese fighters in a night raid over Rabaul. Wounded, and his co-pilot killed outright, he was thrown out when his plane fell into a spin and a wing came off. His parachute popped open and he fell out just as his plane exploded. He was thrown clear an instant before his plane hit the ground. After landing on terra firma, he crawled to the B-17 and was able to account for most of the crew's bodies that were with him in the crash.

With his back badly injured, his jaw broken in two places, and a bullet hole in his leg, Holguin managed to crawl to a stream which led to a large river. With the aid of his Mae West, he floated down the river, battling the swirling waters for a considerable time. He searched for food in the thick underbrush by the river's edge and in the jungleland. His food consisted of frogs and berries, and a bird he shot with his .45. He traveled in and out of the river for almost a month hoping to get to the coast where he might find friendly natives and get away from the Japanese.

He was rescued in a half-starved condition. Too weak to walk, he was carried piggy-back by natives into their village where he was fed and housed. He was well treated, but being intimidated by the Japanese, one of the natives, an informer, turned Holguin in. He was taken to Rabaul where he was threatened with death unless he gave them information they wanted. A ferocious-looking guard with a huge sword menaced him and went through all the motions of beheading him up to the point of actually taking a whack at Holguin's neck. Jose was so sick he didn't much care if they killed him or not. They finally gave up the threats and put him in solitary confinement with one meal a day which consisted of rice and fish soup.

The situation of the Japanese worsened in the latter days of the war and the treatment Holguin and his fellow prisoners received at the hands of their captors became even more harsh. Many of the prisoners were shot, others died of dysentery, beri-beri and malaria. Holguin and four others were used for guinea pigs in Japanese malaria tests. They were injected with malaria germs and held under observation. Three of the prisoners died in a short time, Holguin and the other prisoner barely survived.

Holguin stayed at the Rabaul prison for two years until war ended. Out of a total of 64 prisoners only six of them survived. After the second atomic bomb the prisoners at Rabaul were liberated by an Australian Naval Squadron. Holguin remembers the scene well . . . It was night and the whole area was lighted by floodlights. Thousands of men cheered as the liberated prisoners went by in transports. It was the closest Holguin came to crying since he was a kid.

XV

END OF WORLD WAR II

May 8, 1945—VE Day. Germany effected an unconditional surrender to end the fighting on the European front. V-J Day came on August 14, of the same year, after we dropped the atom bomb on Hiroshima and Nagasaki, putting an end to all hostilities between the Allies and the Axis in World War II.

Both occasions were marked by joy-filled demonstrations all over the world. Servicemen and civilians, overjoyed at the sudden realization that there would be no more shooting and that they would soon be going home, celebrated in wild fashion in all parts of the globe.

THE WAR WOUNDED

In US Army hospitals and abroad, crowded with war wounded patients, things were different on VE and VJ Day. There, thousands of ex-combat soldiers faced the prospect of a long stay in the service. There would not be much going home for them. The war wounded did not feel much like celebrating. The war had been over for them long before, but the scars and memories would linger long afterward. Most of them were undergoing medical treatment and care before being declared eligible for a medical discharge.

THE TRIP BACK

For the soldier who had been felled on the battlefield with battle injuries, the return trip home was an interesting experience and quite different from our first trip overseas to the war front. Our return trip from the front began back at the outdoor battallion aid station close to the front after having received first aid treatment from the front line medic. Our first bandages were removed and new dressings were applied. More sulfa and penicillin were given and a shot of morphine to ease our pain. We were then taken by ambulance to a US Army evacuation hospital, some 20 or 30 miles to the rear of the frontlines. This was a large old brick building that had been used by the German Army located in Strasbourg. We were then given a bed with clean sheets and we enjoyed a few comforts, such as hot and cold running water, heat in our room, and an attendant in care of the patients in our room.

Casualties from other combat areas arrived at that hospital at all hours. All the wounded men coming in from the battlefields appeared to be in the same dazed condition. They portrayed an identical pathetic sight. The same dirty mud-caked clothes clung to their weary bodies, the same heavy growth of beard, a wild look of agony and desperation in their eyes. They represented a picture of defeat and a low morale. These battle casualties suffered many types of wounds. Some had face wounds, others fractured skulls, there were many stomachs and backs filled with shrapnel. Sights of GI's with arms and legs blown off, eyes blinded by fire or concussion, and bodies severely burned with peeling skin but very much alive were not uncommon. Some of them still in shock made no outcry . . . others moaned low and hoarse . . . some cried like babies; but most of them bore their pain very manly. They cursed aloud and plenty, as if to ease their pain or for personal relief of their troubled minds.

Less serious but just as well-attended were many "combat-fatigue" or "crack-up" cases, frozen feet and 'trench foot', and also many wounded enemy soldier prisoners of war.

Experienced army surgeons—and we had many top-flight

members of the medical profession in the service—performed skilled surgery on the most critical cases. We owe much to these capable medics and their assistants, who, along with modern equipment and apparatus, managed to save many lives that were on the brink of death.

In World War One, many battle casualties with similar injuries died because medical practice had not reached the advanced stages of today. In addition, communications and transportation of the modern era were not in use then.

From the Evac hospital, all patients were moved to a United States Army Base hospital in Besancon, situated further away from the shooting. The rumble of the big guns became very faint now, and not as often as heard at the front.

At the larger hospitals, where more medical facilities were available, advanced surgery was performed on the needful cases. The amount of surgery required had much to do with the decision whether to have patients shipped back to the Zone of Interior in the US or England, or to be returned to the front after convalescence. Everyone of the wounded ex-combatants tried their best to convince the staff doctors that his case merited the trip back to the States. There was no way of telling what decision the officers in command would make. They refused to comment on your case.

After many days of 'sweating out' the doctors' verdict, one cannot describe how happy we were when we learned that we were to be "ZI'd," which meant that we would be taken out of the war zone. Each patient that was going back was given a tag with his name, rank, serial number, destination and number of case. We were then taken by ambulance to the railroad station and boarded on a US hospital train.

Some of the patients had recovered sufficiently and were able to get around. Those that could not walk or stand were made "wheel chair Commandos." The most helpless were the litter patients, those who could not or were not allowed to get out of bed. The litter patients were given a special attendant and the best of care. They were given back-rubs twice a day and were spoon-fed if unable to move their arms, seriously injured or blind.

The hospital train we rode in was manned by a complete staff of hospital personnel of the Medical Corps. We had ward boys, nurses, a chaplain, cooks and kitchen helpers, medical officers of all ranks, topped by a Medic Colonel who was in charge. The train took us into Marseilles where an ambulance crew met us and transferred the patients to another US Army hospital at the French port. The hospital at Marseilles was a much larger hospital with a larger number of patients and further away from the front. In addition to the frontline casualties, we had the regular run of patients as found in any other US hospital. American patients who were ill or had been injured in accidents somewhere in France other than the front. There also were many female patients, even a maternity ward for expectant mothers—WAC's, nurses, or officers' wives who had married in France. We also had quite a number of wounded Germans and Italians, prisoners of war who were being treated for battlewounds. Those that recovered were put to work at the hospital.

Marseilles was a port of embarcation in reverse. From here, we were to be sent back to the Zone of Interior, an army term for United States. Some of the war casualties were flown back to the States, others were sent to US Army hospitals in England. The majority of returnees were sent by ship.

On February 3, 1945, one month exactly after being wounded in action, we left the port of Marseilles on the hospital ship, "Blanche F. Sigman." We bade goodbye to France, glad to leave the ETO alive and very anxious to be back in good old United States.

The "Blanche F. Sigman," a converted ocean liner was loaded to full capacity with battle casualties. Life on the large hospital ship was very comfortable. The food was good in contrast to the unsavory dehydrated stuff we had on the "SS West Point," the troop ship we had gone across in to Europe. We had good attention, our medical treatment was continued without interruption, and we had daily entertainment of movies and show skits. Stacks of reading material was provided by the Red Cross and the ship's radio kept up with the latest news from the war front and from home. Still, everyone complained of the slow pace we were traveling. We were all over-anxious to get back home. We sailed by the Rock of Gibraltar, along the Spanish coastline into the Atlantic by Portugal, the Azores and along the east coast of the United States. The trip back took over two weeks, while the trip over to the war front had only taken eight days.

The "Blanche F. Sigman" landed in the old southern port of Charleston, South Carolina, by-passing the regular port where people go out to greet the ships that come in. We went past the regular port and disembarked in the Army's private pier where no outsiders were permitted to watch the arrival and the unloading of the many wounded and sick patients. The Army had taken special precautions so that the American people would not get demoralized by seeing for themselves the tragic results of the war. All Army personnel, especially patients, were strictly prohibited from giving anyone any information about our injuries or to talk about the war we had been through.

Our next hospital was the Stark General, in Charleston, an Army receiving hospital, catering to war evacuees. From there we were to be transferred to another general hospital where we would receive specialized treatment for our particular type of wound. Many GI's were angered because they were being transferred to a hospital far away from their hometown, but later realized that they were being sent to a hospital that would best serve their injuries.

I was grouped with other patients with similar injuries and we were sent to the De Witt General Hospital, situated about eight miles north of Auburn, in the mining country of Northern California. This suited me fine, at last I was back in my home state.

I soon learned that we were in for a long stay at De Witt. I was to be given a complete comprehensive study of my injuries, I was to be given primary treatment, to be operated on, and then a long period of convalescence.

Being together for quite some time, we soon were well-acquainted and got along very well with the nurses and officers of our ward. Every ward in the hospital was full. Patients were being discharged every day, but new ones kept coming in, keeping the hospital at full capacity. Unable to get around, I could not visit the other wards. I was very interested in finding out how many *Chicanos* there were in the other wards. Somehow, it had not been the same as in the days when the majority of us were *hermanos de raza.* In the old days of basic training and during the early days overseas we had a good "grapevine" system that enabled us to keep up with the latest doings of the gang we were with and also the latest happenings with our folks back home. It had been quite a while since I had talked to one of the gang. Once in a while I would catch a glimpse of one passing by the hall. I yearned for a little Spanish conversation.

I did not have to wait too long. One day I was taken by surprise to find four familiar-type patients standing at my bedside. *"Orale, . . . Ese, . . ."* the same old greetings. Although I did not know their names, they seemed quite familiar to me. Their warm smiles, flashing dark eyes, hair neatly combed, and their hospital reds (pants) worn *pachuco* style! I had never met them before, but I could tell all their characteristics, their likes and dislikes, everything—all I had to do was to ask myself. They introduced themselves—Pete Zaracho, Paul Yanez, Bob Talamantes from Los Angeles, and Al Velasco from Chicago. They were paying a visit to the other wounded *Chicanos* in the different wards. I learned from them that the place was full of Mexican-Americans, and most of them were from Los Angeles.

It was a pleasant surprise to find a lot of the *palomilla* in De Witt. There were many happy reunions with buddies I had known at Camp Roberts and at the shipping-out centers of Fort Meade and Myles Standish. I also met a few fellow-patients I had known before in the pre-war years at such places as San Antonio, Pueblo, Jerome (Arizona), Santa Barbara, and of course from Los Angeles. Among the patients there from Los Angeles I met "Memo" Terrazas,[1] who was slowly recovering from a brain injury, partially paralyzed, and loss of speech. I also met Frank Carrillo,[2] and Florencio Rodriguez,[3] both veterans of the North African campaign; Vincent Gonzales, Ernie Ochoa, Larry Vasquez, George Yorba, of Los Angeles, and many more whose names I do not recall. There must have been over one thousand Mexican-Americans in that hospital.

It did not take us long to find acquaintances once we were able to get around. We would meet, going to and fro through the different wards in the hallways. Patients with shattered legs began to hobble around on crutches, those with bashed-in skulls ventured out to show their new crop of hair sprouting from their tight head skin which covered a metal plate, others with their chests or stomachs well-taped, or arms in armslings and many free-wheeling "chair Commandos." It was amazing how fast most of them recovered from their war injuries.

---

[1]See page 78.
[2] and [3] see page 32.

During the days we spent recovering our health, we had some very interesting get-togethers, talking about our experiences in the war. There were many tall tales about the places the men had been and the things they had seen. The wounded men would talk of many things, but never about their own exploits. It was impossible to tell if you were talking to a non-Com or what rating anybody held, since we all wore the same hospital garb. Most of them were reluctant to admit they had earned any decorations or promotions. Only when they wore a uniform could you tell the rank they held by their stripes and the patch of their outfit, but no ribbons or decorations. The decorated men did not feel like showing off their ribbons to the other wounded combat soldiers.

It was very easy to spot phonies there. They were about the only ones who would brag of how rough it had been where they were. When they dressed to go out, they covered their uniforms with all kinds of ribbons and battle stars. In those days you could not get a war-wounded GI to wear his campaign ribbons, battle stars, or other decorations, even though he had earned them the hard way. The only decoration they would wear was the Infantryman Combat Badge. The Mexican-American veteran was very proud of his Infantry Combat Badge.

These *Chicanos* were different from the Mexican-Americans that we had known before we left the States and went overseas. Although still full of fun and deviltry as ever, they now were well-seasoned and experienced American soldiers. No longer were we chided and shunted by other GI's and Army officers. Where we had been held in contempt by others who disliked us because of our constant Spanish chatter or our lax in military discipline, we were now admired, respected, and approved by all those around us including most of our commanding officers.

An example of this was Staff Sergeant Johnny Gomez[1]. Johnny Gomez came from a small town in South Texas. He had been raised in a section where the majority of the Anglo citizens were hostile towards all Mexicans, foreign or native-born. He had been subjected to the worst type of prejudice. In his youth and late teens he had been called all kinds of insulting names in connection with his Mexican ancestry. He felt that he had never been given an even break. It had always been an up-hill struggle in schooling, housing, and job opportunities.

Fighting the enemy overseas, Johnny was another of Uncle Sam's many rugged combat infantrymen. In Italy, Johnny really proved his mettle when he singlehandedly stood off a squad of hostile German assault troops with his BAR, killing five of them, wounding or capturing five others before getting banged up himself. He came out with very bad leg and arm wounds. The feat had been widely publicized by his division publicists, there had even been recommendations for a medal. Yes, he definitely had become a war "hero."

He became a "right guy" with the rest of his outfit and the CO let him know how he stood with him when he elevated him to the rank of Staff Sergeant. Back in his hometown, the local papers played up the story. He became known as "our Johnny." He was a big hero to all the folks back home.

Now Johnny was getting married at the hospital chapel. On the surface, it looked like just another hospital romance, so common after the war in Army and Naval hospitals where wounded veterans came in contact with many WAC's, nurses, and civilian female employees, and where many "boy meet girl" romances began . . . but this one was different. Johnny Gomez was not just another of our average American young men who had been to war, he was a Mexican-American who

---

[1]Fictitious name.

came from the other side of the tracks, and his bride was Edith Johnson[2], a 2nd Lieutenant US Army Nurse.

When Edith Johnson first met Johnny, he was only one of the many wounded men among hundreds she had attended at De Witt General Hospital. She hardly noticed him, she told me, except that she remembers he was one of the most obstinate patients she had ever attended. After a short time he began to change, he was cheerful and very friendly. When he kept staring and continuously commented on her charms, she took it in stride, thinking it was only that he was "making recovery progress." This was the usual sign the very ill patient showed when he was well on the road to recovery. After a while, Nurse Lt. Johnson became interested in Johnny Gomez. She learned all about his background, his family, and his views on life.

When he realized things were getting serious, Johnny began to feel uneasy . . . even a little afraid. He worried what would happen if they should marry, and if he would take her back to his hometown. He remembered the deep-rooted ideas the people back there had and their racial prejudices. He was sure they would both suffer humiliations. He told her about this and about what he feared would happen if they were to marry. He tried to discourage her, but none of it altered her feeling towards him. She saw him only as another of this nation's gallant men who now owned a full share of America.

---

[2]Fictitious name.

XVI

KOREA

After the end of World War II, and while we were beginning to get a firm hold on civilian life again, things began to break out in Korea. United States and Russia could not get together on the settlement of the Far East peninsula.

Korea had been bi-sected through an agreement reached at Potsdam in 1945 between the two countries. It was decided that the 38th parallel would be the dividing line between the occupation forces; Russia to the north and the United States to the south. This agreement was purely on a temporary basis to facilitate the surrender of the Japanese troops in that country. Soviet troops who occupied Korea north of the 38th parallel, effectively sealed off North Korea from South Korea, creating a political vacuum in that country.

An agreement was reached at the Moscow conference of December, 1945, whereby the US and USSR commands in Korea were to form a joint commission which, in consultation with Korean democratic parties, was to make recommendations to the four powers relative to the organization of a provisional Korean democratic government. Needless to say these talks proved fruitless. All efforts on the part of the US to secure an agreement from the USSR on the unification of Korea failed. The US then laid the matter before the United Nations Organization. It wasn't long after the entrance of the UN into the dispute, that a shooting war developed.

It was on June 29, 1950, that President Truman made his fateful decision, authorizing General Douglas MacArthur to use supporting ground units in Korea, USAF to conduct missions on specific military targets in North Korea, and ordered an immediate Naval blockade of the entire Korean coast. Reserves were called back into uniform and teenaged youths were drafted, quickly trained and sent to the combat zone. Once more our youth went off to the wars.

The "Police action" (term applied by the UN) was just as ghastly and horrible as all other modern wars. Veteran combat men who fought in World War II agreed that Korea was the same old miserable campaign against foul weather, dreadful guns, and a hard fighting enemy. Only this time there were none of the superiority in numbers of supporting troops and weapons we enjoyed in World War II.

As was demonstrated in World War II, the quality and fibre of our fighting men was of the finest calibre and their bravery equaled and matched that of other great heroes this country has produced. Once more we had many Lopez', Garcia's, Rodriguez' and others among the valiant combat troops to add their share to the fine chapter in the history of American fighting men. The following Mexican-American soldiers and marines saw action in the Korean incident and were Awarded the Congressional Medal of Honor:

PFC. EUGENE A. OBREGON[1]

Awarded the Congressional Medal of Honor (*Posthumously*)

Seoul, Korea, September 26, 1950. While serving as an ammunition carrier of a machine gun squad in a Marine rifle company which was temporarily pinned down by hostile fire, Private First Class Obregon observed a fellow Marine fall wounded in the line of fire. Armed only with a pistol, he unhesitatingly dashed from his covered position to the side of the casualty. Firing his pistol with one hand as he ran he grasped his comrade by the arm

[1]The Eugene Obregon American Legion Post 804 in East Los Angeles, has been named in his honor.

with his other hand and despite the great peril to himself, dragged him to the side of the road. Still under enemy fire, he was bandaging the man's wounds when hostile troops of approximately platoon strength began advancing toward his position. Quickly seizing the wounded Marine's carbine, he placed his own body as a shield in front of him and lay there firing accurately and effectively into the hostile group until he himself was fatally wounded by enemy machine-gun fire.

By his courageous fighting spirit, fortitude and loyal devotion to duty, Private First Class Obregon enabled his fellow Marines to rescue the wounded man and aided essentially in repelling the attack, thereby sustaining and enhancing the highest traditions of the United States Naval Service. He gallantly gave his life for his country.[2]

The wounded comrade saved by Eugene Obregon, was Private First Class Bert Johnson, 19, of Grand Prairie, Texas. He was hospitalized, recovered and returned to duty in the United States at Camp Lejeune, N.C.

Eugene Obregon was born November 12, 1930, at Los Angeles, Calif. He attended public schools in that city before enlisting in the Marine Corps on June 7, 1948, at the age of 17.

Following recruit training at San Diego, Calif., he was assigned to the Barstow Supply Depot. He was serving as a fireman there at the outbreak of war in Korea, and was transferred to the First Provisional Marine Brigade for combat duty. He was in action by August 8, 1950, along the Naktong River, and participated in the Inchon landing. Then, on September 26, during the assault on the city of Seoul, came the act in which he gave his life.

In addition to the Medal of Honor, Private First Class

[2]Citation, Congressional Medal of Honor, awarded posthumously by the Secretary of the Navy Dan Kimball to Mr. and Mrs. Peter R. Obregon (parents of Eugene) at Los Angeles, Calif, on August 30, 1952.

MARINE PRIVATE FIRST CLASS EUGENE A. OBREGON
Los Angeles, California
Congressional Medal of Honor
Korean Conflict

Obregon also was posthumously awarded the Purple Heart Medal, Presidential Unit Citation, and Korean Service Medal with three Bronze Stars.

SGT. JOSEPH C. RODRIGUEZ

Awarded the Congressional Medal of Honor

Munye-ri, Korea, May 21, 1951. Sergeant Joseph C. Rodriguez, (then Private First Class) Infantry United States Army, Company F, 17th Infantry Regiment, distinguished himself by conspicuous gallantry and intrepidity at the risk of his life above and beyond the call of duty in action against an armed enemy of the United States.

Sergeant Rodriguez, an assistant squad leader of the 2nd Platoon, was participating in an attack against a fanatical hostile force occupying well-fortified positions on rugged commanding terrain, when his squad's advance was halted within approximately 60 yards by a withering barrage of automatic weapons and small arms fire from five emplacements directly to the front and right and left flanks, together with grenades which the enemy rolled down the hill toward the advancing troops. Fully aware of the odds against him, Sergeant Rodriguez leaped to his feet, dashed 60 yards up the fire-swept slope, and, after lobbing grenades into the first foxhole with deadly accuracy, ran around the left flank, silenced an automatic weapon with two grenades and continued his whirlwind assault to the top of the peak, wiping out two more foxholes and then, reaching the right flank, he tossed grenades into the remaining emplacement, destroying the gun and annihilating its crew. Sergeant Rodriguez' intrepid actions exacted a toll of 15 enemy dead, and,as a result of his incredible display of valor, the defense of the opposition was broken, the enemy routed, and the strategic strongpoint secured.

His unflinching courage under fire and inspirational devotion to duty reflect highest credit on himself and uphold the honored traditions of the military service.[2]

Joe "Chuck" Rodriguez was born on November 14, 1928, at San Bernardino, Calif. His father, Joseph N. Rodriguez, resides there at this time. After induction on October 24, 1950, Sergeant Rodriguez received training at Camp Carson, Colo., before being sent to the Far East Command. He holds the Purple Heart for wounds received on May 29, shortly after the valorous actions which won him the Medal of Honor. He has also been awarded the Combat Infantryman Badge.

An eyewitness account of the heroic actions of the young Infantryman is furnished by a member of his platoon, Sergeant John J. Phelan, Jr., of Tannersville, Green County, New York:

"On May 21, 1951, Company F was committed in the vicinity of Munye-ri, with the mission of securing the high ground north of the village. After obtaining a toe-hold on the ridge the Third Platoon pushed on to take a small peak dominating the ridge line. The enemy withheld its fire until our forces were within 100 yards of the objective. Then they opened up with intense automatic weapons and mortar fire. The Third Platoon failed to dislodge the enemy after three assaults. The Second Platoon, in which I led the first squad, pushed through the Third Platoon. The Platoon Sergeant found that the enemy fire was so heavy that he was forced to use the first, third and weapons squad as a base of fire, and maneuver with only one squad, the second. Since I commanded one of the squads laying down the base of fire, I had an excellent view of the whole action. The second squad

---

[2]Citation and Medal of Honor award, U.S. Army, Washington, D.C., December 10, 1951.

STAFF SERGEANT JOSEPH C. RODRIGUEZ
San Bernardino, California
Congressional Medal of Honor
Korean Conflict

moved toward the peak under the cover of our fire. About 60 yards short of the objective the squad came under such heavy enemy fire that they were unable to move. I then noticed that Private First Class Joseph Rodriguez was making his way up from the rear of the squad, meanwhile picking up hand grenades from his squad members. After obtaining the grenades Rodriguez left all cover and dashed 60 yards up the slope, yelling and throwing grenades with no regard for the murderous fire aimed at him. He dropped several grenades in the first hole and then ran around the left flank where he silenced an automatic weapon with two more grenades. He then dashed across the top of the peak, dropping hand grenades in two enemy holes as he passed. Reaching the right flank, he assaulted the remaining enemy automatic weapons and killed all of its crew. As the enemy fire subsided the squad then moved up the hill as Rodriguez was throwing his few remaining grenades at the fleeing enemy. There is no doubt that this courageous action on the part of PFC Rodriguez was responsible for the accomplishment of the Company's mission. His unselfish willingness to disregard his own safety undoubtedly saved the lives of many of his comrades who lay exposed to the enemy fire."

CPL. RODOLFO P. HERNANDEZ

Awarded the Congressional Medal of Honor

Wontong-ni, Korea, May 31, 1951. Corporal Rodolfo P. Hernandez, Infantry, United States Army, a member of Company G, 187th Airborne Regimental Combat Team, distinguished himself by conspicuous gallantry and intrepidity above and beyond the call of duty in action against the enemy near Wongtong-ni, Korea, on May 31, 1951. His platoon, in defense positions on Hill 420 came under ruthless attack by a numerically superior and fanatical hostile force, accompanied by heavy artillery,

> mortar and machine gun fire which inflicted numerous casualties on the platoon. His comrades were forced to withdraw due to lack of ammunition but Corporal Hernandez although wounded in an exchange of grenades, continued to deliver deadly fire into the ranks of the onrushing assailants until a ruptured cartridge rendered his rifle inoperative. Immediately leaving his position, Corporal Hernandez rushed the enemy armed only with rifle and bayonet. Fearlessly engaging the foe, he killed six of the enemy before falling uncounscious from grenade, bayonet and bullet wounds but his heroic action momentarily halted the enemy advance and enabled his unit to counterattack and retake the lost ground. The indomitable fighting spirit, outstanding courage and tenacious devotion to duty clearly demonstrated by Corporal Hernandez reflect the highest credit upon himself, the Infantry and the United States Army.[3]

Rodolfo Hernandez was born in Colton, attended school in Fowler and now lives in Fresno, California, with his wife and his mother, Mrs. Guadalupe Hernandez. He enlisted in the Army in March, 1949, went to jump school at Ft. Benning and was assigned to the 187 Airborne. He sailed to Korea from Fort Campbell, Kentucky.

A witness to Cpl. Hernandez' valiant acts was Pfc. Carl M. Handrick, Swandale, West Virginia who offered this version:

"At about 2 a.m., the enemy assaulted the positions of the third platoon where Hernandez and I were together in a foxhole on Hill 420. Both of us opened up on them with machine gun and rifle fire, in a fierce grenade battle that followed both of us were wounded."

The men around them started to withdraw as the small

---

[3]Citation and Medal of Honor award, U.S. Army, Washington, D.C.

PRESIDENT JOHN F. KENNEDY congratulates Congressional Medal of Honor Hero of Korean Conflict **CORPORAL RODOLFO P. HERNANDEZ** of Fresno, California, at White House reception.

arms fire became heavier. Hernandez continued to fire his rifle until his weapon became useless because of a ruptured cartridge.

"Without saying anything, the brave little Mexican jumped out of the hole and charged toward the enemy and began throwing hand grenades. He ran about ten yards towards the enemy and then disappeared into the darkness." Handrick continues, "I saw the result of his fight with the enemy when we found him at daybreak the next morning. He was about 25 yards in front of our position lying head to head with a dead enemy soldier. There was another one about five yards behind him, and more to his front. They had been bayoneted by Hernandez."

PFC. EDWARD GOMEZ

Awarded the Congressional Medal of Honor (*Posthumously*)

Kajon-ni, Korea, Sept. 14, 1951. Boldly advancing with his squad in support of a group of riflemen assaulting a series of strongly fortified and bitterly defended hostile positions on Hill 749, Private First Class Edward Gomez consistently exposed himself to the withering barrage to keep his machine gun supplied with ammunition during the drive forward to seize the objective. As his squad deployed to meet an imminent counterattack, he voluntarily moved down an abandoned trench to search for a new location for the gun and, when a hostile grenade landed between him, he grasped the activated charge in his hand. Determined to save his comrades, he unhesitatingly chose to sacrifice himself and, diving into the ditch with the deadly missile, absorbed the shattering violence of the explosion in his own body. By his stouthearted courage, incomparable valor and decisive spirit of self-sacrifice, Private First Class Gomez inspired the others to heroic efforts in subsequently repelling the outnumbering foe, and his valiant conduct throughout sustained and enhanced the finest traditions of the United States Naval Service. For conspicuous gallantry and intrepidity at the risk of his life above and beyond the call of duty while serving as an ammunition bearer in Company E. Second Battalion, First Marines, First Marine Division (Reinforced) in action against enemy aggressor forces in Korea. He gallantly gave his life for his country.[4]

Private First Class Edward Gomez was born August 10, 1932, in Omaha, Nebraska. He attended Omaha High School before enlisting in the Marine Corps Reserve Aug. 11, 1949, at the age of 17. After recruit training at San Diego, he trained at Camp Pendleton, Calif., and went to Korea with the Seventh Replacement draft. In addition to the Medal of Honor, Pfc. Gomez was awarded a Gold Star in lieu of a second Purple Heart Medal, the Korean Service Medal with Bronze Star, and the United Nations Service Medal. His parents are Mr. and Mrs. Modesto Gomez of Omaha.

CPL. BENITO MARTINEZ

Awarded the Congressional Medal of Honor (*Posthumously*)

Satae-ri, Korea, September 6, 1952. Corporal Benito Martinez, Infantry, United States Army, a machine gunner with Company A, 27th Infantry Regiment, 25th Infantry Division, distinguished himself by conspicuous gallantry and outstanding courage above and beyond the call of duty in action against the enemy. While manning a listening post forward of the main line of resistance, his position was attacked by a hostile force of reinforced company strength. In the bitter fighting which ensued,

---

[4]Citation and Medal of Honor Award, (Posthumously) U.S.M.C. Washington, D.C.

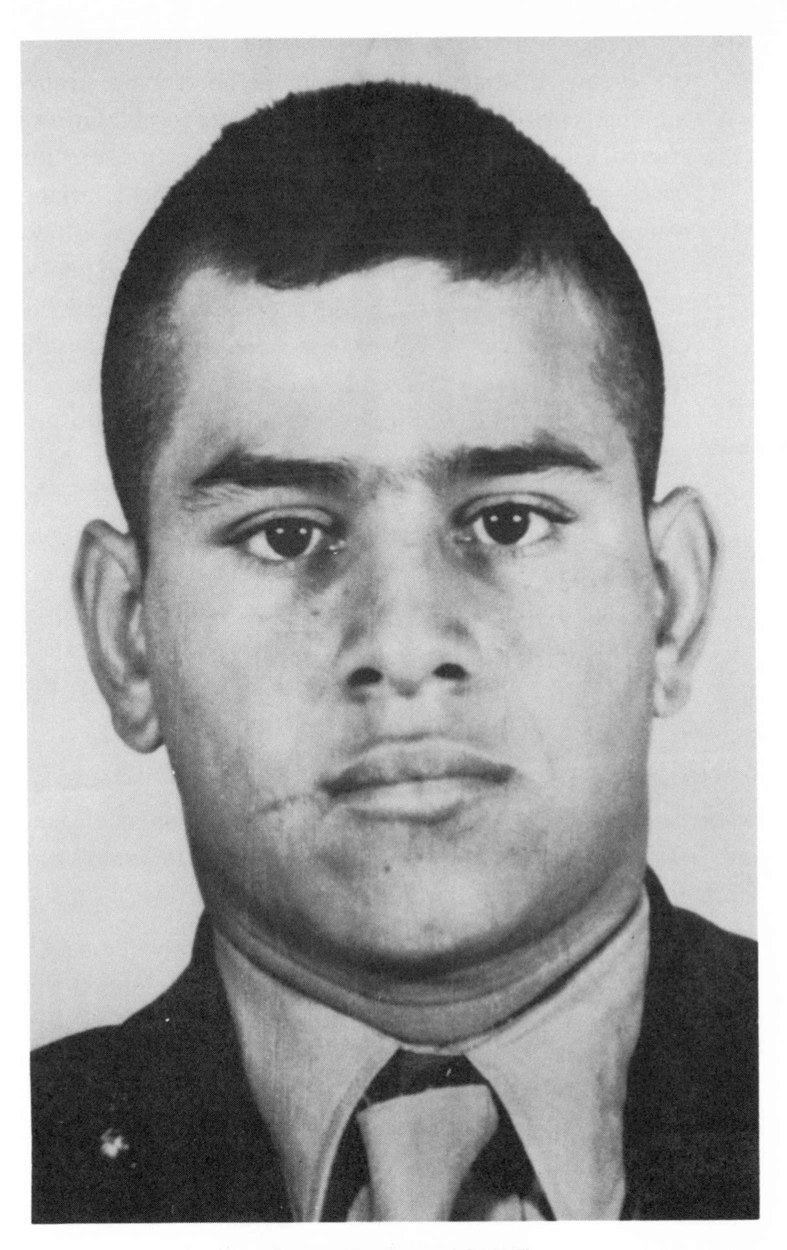

PFC. EDWARD GOMEZ
Omaha, Nebraska
Congressional Medal of Honor
Korean Conflict

> the enemy infiltrated the defense perimeter and, realizing that encirclement was imminent, Corporal Martinez elected to remain at his post in an attempt to stem the onslaught. In a daring defense he raked the attacking troops with crippling fire, inflicting numerous casualties. Although contacted by sound-power phone several times, he insisted that no attempt be made to rescue him because of the danger involved. Soon thereafter, the hostile forces rushed the emplacement, forcing him to make a limited withdrawal with only an automatic rifle and pistol to defend himself. After a courageous six hour stand and shortly before dawn, he called in for the last time, stating that the enemy was converging on his position. His magnificent stand enabled friendly elements to reorganize, attack and regain the key terrain. Corporal Martinez' incredible valor and supreme sacrifice reflect lasting glory upon himself and are in keeping with the honored traditions of the military service.[5]

The story of the 21-year-old Infantryman from Texas, who singlehandedly defended a vital front-line position while under heavy enemy attack, gives further proof of the valor and courage of the Mexican-American soldier.

Corporal Benito Martinez, son of Mr. and Mrs. Francisco Martinez, was born at Fort Hancock, Texas. He entered the army on August 16, 1951, and was assigned to the Far East Command in March, 1952. A machine gunner with Company A, 27th Infantry Regiment, 25th Division, he savagely defended his position during a six-hour struggle with a bitter enemy despite being greatly outnumbered, while stationed at a listening post at the "Sandbag Castle", near Satae-ri, Korea. An eyewitness account of Cpl. Martinez' heroic act is furnished

---

[5]Citation and Medal of Honor Award, (posthumously) U.S. Army, Washington, D.C., Sept. 15, 1953.

Mrs. Francisco M. Martinez is presented the Congressional Medal of Honor awarded posthumously to her son, **CPL. BENITO MARTINEZ,** Ft. Hancock, Texas, for gallant action in Korea, by Secretary of the Army, Robert T. Stevens. Looking on are General Matthew B. Ridgway, Chief of Staff, U.S. Army (center), and 1st Lt. Freeman V. Horner, Congressional Medal of Honor winner, who escorted Mrs. Martinez. The presentation was made in the Pentagon Building.

by Harrison J. Hall, who was in Martinez' company at the time of the action.

"At approximately 12:45 a.m. on September 6th, 1952, I was in the alert bunker at the entrance to "Sandbag Castle" and I had telephone contact with Cpl. Benito Martinez in his listening post. I talked to him off and on until approximately 6 A.M., he would call me and tell me everything that was going on at the listening post.

"He called and told me that he was going to be surrounded on all sides, that he wasn't sure how long he could hold the enemy back, but that he would do everything he could to stop them from taking the "Castle". I asked him if there was anyway that we could get him aid and he said that he didn't even want us to try, because it would be too dangerous for the men to make such an attempt against such large enemy forces.

"At approximately 3:30 A.M., Martinez called me again and stated that he had just killed three North Koreans with his machine gun. In about thirty minutes he called me again and said that the North Koreans had rushed him and that he had to pull back about ten yards and that he had to leave his machine gun, so all he had now was an automatic rifle and a .45 caliber pistol.

"Cpl. Martinez called only once more after that, about 5:55 A.M. and told me that the North Koreans were digging through the sides with picks and bayonets. Then he told me to hold on for a minute and he left the phone.

"I could hear a lot of firing going on over the sound power phone, and after shots died down, Martinez didn't come back to the phone.

"Corporal Martinez was not afraid while I was talking to him on the phone. And even though he knew he would probably die, he was determined to stay on his position and fight off the enemy himself rather than escape or have us send out a patrol to try to open up a hole so that he could withdraw to our lines."

The next day, Martinez' body was found near his listening post. He had an empty pistol ammunition clip in his left and a .45 caliber pistol in his right hand. Three dead North Koreans were lying across his body. They had died from his pistol fire.

Because of Corporal Martinez' daring one-man stand, friendly rear positions were protected from being overrun and his comrades were given time to reorganize and effect a counter-attack.

SGT. AMBROSIO GUILLEN[1]

Awarded the Congressional Medal of Honor (*Posthumously*)

> Sanguch-on, Korea, July 25, 1953. Sergeant Ambrosio Guillen was cited for his heroic leadership of a platoon of Marines near Sanguch-on, Korea. That day his unit had been defending an outpost well forward of the main line of resistance. That night it was pinned down by mortar and artillery fire. Under cover of both the darkness and the barrage, two enemy battalions attacked. With no thought for his own safety, Sergeant Guillen deliberately exposed himself to withering fire while directing the defense of the outpost and supervising the treatment and subsequent evacuation of the wounded. Inspired by his leadership, the platoon rallied quickly to meet and repulse the enemy in fierce hand-to-hand combat. Sergeant Guillen himself was mortally wounded, but he refused medical aid and continued to direct his men until the enemy was routed in confusion. A few hours later he died of his wounds.[6]

---

[1]Picture not available.

[6]Citation and Medal of Honor Award, (posthumously) U.S.M.C. Washington, D.C. Presented to his parents Mr. and Mrs. Pedro H. Guillen.

The personal heroism of Sergeant Ambrosio Guillen, only two days before the cease-fire in Korea, was responsible for turning an overwhelming enemy attack into a disorderly retreat.

Staff Sergeant Ambrosio Guillen was born December 7, 1929, at La Junta, Colorado. He enlisted in the Marine Corps at the age of 18. After 'boot' training at San Diego, he was assigned to the 6th Marine Regiment, 1st Marine Division. Later he was chosen for Sea School, and served, after graduation, aboard the USS Curtis. Following his tour of sea duty, he was appointed a drill instructor at the Marine Corps Recruit Depot, San Diego.

As a drill instructor, Sergeant Guillen trained two honor platoons and was given a Letter of Appreciation by his Commanding General. In that letter Major General John T. Walker observed that "your success in training these two platoons has demonstrated your outstanding ability as a leader." That ability was proved beyond a doubt in combat soon after Sergeant Guillen arrived in Korea. After the truce, the heroic Sergeant's body was escorted to the United States by his brother, Pfc. Ramon B. Guillen, who had been serving in the Far East with the Army. Sergeant Guillen was buried in El Paso on October 20, 1953, at Fort Bliss National cemetery.

XVII

PRIVATE CITIZENS, FIRST-CLASS

It felt very good to have come back from the wars. Things were happening to us that had never happened before. This was a new America for us . . . we felt like shouting . . . *Hey! We did it! The Allies won the war and the Americans played a prominent part in it. Americans! . . that meant us!* As returning veterans, we were being welcomed enthusiastically everywhere. We were openly admired, loved and respected. It was a wonderful feeling, we were overwhelmed.

Most returning American war veterans found very few changes in their hometowns. Overjoyed with excitement incident to being home again, they gave no thought nor noticed many changes in the American way of life. Furthermore, most of them did not want it to be any different from that of the day they had left. This was home . . . they preferred it this way—this was the way the remembered it in their dreams during the long days overseas.

For the returning Mexican-American veteran, things *were* different and furthermore he did not want to find things the way he had left them. Not that he had not dreamed of coming home to his loved ones, but there were a few things he did not care for when he got back.

For too long we had been like outsiders. It had never made very much difference to us and we hardly noticed it until we got back from overseas. How could we have played such a prominent part as Americans over there and now have to go back living as outsiders as before? We began to ask ourselves, how come? How long had we been missing out on benefits derived as an American citizen? Oldtimers had told us and we had read in books how the early settlers had invaded our towns and had shoved us into the 'other side of the tracks'. But we ourselves had never made much attempt to move out of there. The towns had grown up, population had increased, State, County, City and community government had been set up and we had been left out of it. We never had any voice. Here now was the opportunity to do something about it.

Soon now, we left the other side of the tracks and began to move into town. We moved to better neighborhoods and, thanks to the GI Bill, we continued our education. We were able to buy new homes. We began to go into business for ourselves, obtain better positions of employment and some even managed to get chosen, appointed or elected to public office.

We acquired new ways in everyday doings. New thoughts and dreams entered our minds. We embarked on many unheard-of—for us—projects and developed many ideas and new perspectives. In the old days, our lives were governed mostly by patterns set by our elders. We had accepted without question edicts, taboos, restrictions, traditions and customs that our ancestors had brought over from the old country. Many such were long since outdated in Mexico proper. After having been to many other parts of the world, meeting other people from different parts of the country, we cast aside these old beliefs and we began anew in America.

Many were the things we could enjoy now, that had not been easy to acquire before. One was Priority. Never had we been given preference over anyone in the purchase of goods, automobiles, new homes, homesteading, leases or rentals and employment in civil service. Now, as veterans, we had priority over non-veterans in all these shortages and it was something new to us.

Loans and Credit. Limited credit was about all we could get before. Prior to the war Bank Loans were hard to get.

Nowdays we are just as eligible as any other citizen and bankers no longer consider racial background as a yardstick on ability to pay. If you are a veteran, you are eligible for a loan.

Our purchasing power increased greatly. With better jobs, Government allotments and compensation pay, we could well afford luxuries we never before could buy, such as good clothes, expensive furniture and late-model autos. Many alert businessmen and store owners began to scheme ways to snare our dollars. They hired Spanish-speaking clerks and salesmen, and solicited our trade through well-conducted advertising campaigns in Spanish newspapers and Spanish radio programs.

We entered the business field. The grand old American system of free enterprise had never meant much for us. Not because anyone would keep us from going into business for ourselves, but mostly because there would not be very many customers for us. Now we have added grocery markets, service stations, *tortillerias,* insurance and real estate offices, accounting, hardware, and drug stores in addition to the Mexican restaurant, the small *cantina* and corner grocery store we had in the old days. Then there are the many service fields we entered which were not too common before WW II; television and radio repair, auto mechanics, upholstery, painting, plumbing, trucking, carpentry and electrical work, dry cleaning, barbering, cabinet-making and printing—all were included. Many veterans who were employed in these trades before going into the service are now owners of small business establishments, or are employers with several employees in the same trade.

We also have now many veterans who have taken advantage of the educational opportunities offered by our government, engaged in professional occupations. Today, many of our people have entered the medical, legal and educational professions, and others have earned high degrees in all kinds of specialized fields. Many men and women have achieved high success in the entertainment and sports fields. The art, music and theatre circles, bi-lingual radio broadcasting programs, advertising and sports—other than boxing—have been invaded by our veterans and their contemporaries all over the Southwest where Spanish-speaking Americans abound.

We developed intense pride in America. Our standard of living has improved 100 percent. As veterans, we have become serious-thinking Americans. We have enlarged our circle of friends to include not only Mexican-Americans like ourselves, but Americans of many other nationalities.

In organization we have also made great strides. After World War II a wave of social development unfolded. The Mexican-American became more aware of the growing need for self-improvement. He has become better informed on the changing complexities of the State and Nation. Responsibility and participation has developed a greater Race and ethnic-consciousness. All post-war organizations that have emerged propose improvement, envolvement and unification of the Mexican-American. Among the standouts are, (CSO) Community Services Organization, The American GI Forum, a veterans family organization with a program geared to improving the status of the Mexican American in the United States: and in politics, it is (MAPA) Mexican-American Political Association, also known as (PASO), Political Association of Spanish-speaking Organizations.

World War II and the Korean Conflict were without a doubt the prime factors in having our economical, educational and social status raised far above that which we had prior to World War II. It definitely made a great change in the lives of all Mexican-Americans in the United States of America.

—END—

INDEX

INDEX

INDEX

INDEX

INDEX

INDEX

INDEX

INDEX

INDEX

INDEX